D1624661

Advance Praise for *Total Performance Scorecard:*

"There is often a disconnect between organizational goal-setting and the way individuals establish individual objectives and are reviewed. *Total Performance Scorecard* fills the gap with a complete system that unites individual and organizational performance scorecards, linking continuous improvement efforts with individual learning and development programs. If you are looking for a comprehensive toolkit for improving results in your company, this is the book to buy."
—**Philip Anderson,** Professor of Entrepreneurship, INSEAD Alumni Fund
Chair in Entrepreneurship, Director, 3i Venturelab

"Total Performance Scorecard is a desperately needed direction that management of organizations should adopt. It stresses the importance and need of developing an organizational structure and philosophy that combines the goals and aspirations of the individual with those of the company. It is a melding process which results in a corporate culture that is both individually and organizationally driven. The concepts embodied in this management concept provide solutions to preserving and utilizing individual rights and capabilities while adjusting the organizational structure and philosophy to this new environment."
—**Edward H. Barker,** Professor at University of LaVerne, CA

"Hubert Rampersad takes the balanced scorecard and other management ideas and puts them in a framework of personal integrity. By unifying organizational change strategies with individual ethics he has written an outstanding synthesis which is addressed to the corporate challenges of managing in the 21st century."
—**Paul Bracken,** Professor of Management, Yale School of Management

"Dr. Rampersad's book is just as timely an exhortation to American business as was *In Search of Excellence.* In this case, the survival of corporations depends on possessing an integrity that can both fuel their drive for performance and keep it in check. Such integrity cannot be legislated by government or management. Fortunately, Dr. Rampersad's processes bring organizations face-to-face with their own moral fiber (and many other important issues). He couldn't have come along at a better time."
—**George Cline,** MBA, President, VitalConcern, Tampa, FL

"Dr. Rampersad's latest book makes a most useful contribution to the never-ending challenge of aligning individual motivations and behaviors with enterprise performance aspirations."
—**Jon R. Katzenbach,** co-author of the international bestseller
The Wisdom of Teams and editor of *The Work of Teams,*
a Harvard Business Review compendium

Total Performance Scorecard

Total Performance Scorecard

Redefining Management to Achieve Performance with Integrity

Dr. Hubert K. Rampersad

With a Foreword by
**Dorothy A. Leonard, The William J. Abernathy Professor of
Business Administration, Harvard Business School, Boston**

An Imprint of Elsevier Science
Amsterdam   Boston   Heidelberg   London   New York   Oxford
Paris   San Diego   San Francisco   Singapore   Sydney   Tokyo

Butterworth–Heinemann is an imprint of Elsevier Science.

Library of Congress Cataloging-in-Publication Data

Rampersad, Hubert K.
    Total performance scorecard : redefining management to achieve performance with integrity / Hubert K. Rampersad.
        p.   cm.
    Includes bibliographical references and index.
    ISBN 0-7506-7714-7 (alk. paper)
    1. Total quality management.   2. Performance—Measurement.
3. Employee motivation.   4. Organizational learning.   I. Title.

    HD62.15.R3598 2003
    658.4′013—dc21

                                            2002043879

British Library Cataloguing-in-Publication Data
A catalogue record for this book is available from the British Library.

The publisher offers special discounts on bulk orders of this book.
For information, please contact:

Manager of Special Sales
Elsevier Science
200 Wheeler Road
Burlington, MA 01803
Tel: 781-313-4700
Fax: 781-313-4882

For information on all Butterworth–Heinemann publications available, contact our World Wide Web home page at: http://www.bh.com

10 9 8 7 6 5 4 3 2 1

Printed in the United States of America

To my wife Rita and my sons Rodney and Warren

Doing the right things right is determined by enjoyment, passion, self-knowledge, learning, and compliance with the highest ethical and moral standards.

Hubert K. Rampersad

Contents

1

2

The TPS Concept 9. The Balanced Scorecard 18. The TPS Cycle 33.

3

Formulating the Personal Balanced Scorecard 40. Formulating the Organizational Balanced Scorecard 61.

4

Communicating the Balanced Scorecard 99. Linking the Balanced Scorecard 102.

5

6

7

8

9

10

11

Foreword

Ask any manager what the primary assets of her organization are and the answer is usually "people." We are far removed from the days when an employee checked his brains at the door at the same time he removed his overcoat. We recognize that the tacit (unarticulated) dimensions of knowledge in a person's head may be as vital to achieving the organization's goals as are the explicit, codified forms of knowledge that have been built up over time.[i]

In fact, who is *not* a "knowledge-worker" in the developed world? Farmers possess the most sophisticated knowledge of seeds and seasons. Steel workers run highly computerized machinery. Custodial staff can make fine distinctions in types of stains and cleaning materials. The know-how possessed by anyone who has been doing certain tasks for long enough to build up a repertoire of experiences can be extremely valuable to the organization for whom he works.

On the other hand, ask any manager how she spends most of her time, even in very technically oriented organizations, and the answer is usually "handling people problems." This term covers everything from highly egotistical, self-centered behavior by "prima donnas" who can't work in teams, to alcoholism or other personal problems that lower productivity, to ingenious modes of resistance to change and unwillingness to share knowledge.

Managers have always faced the dual challenge of exploiting individual knowledge and skills for the benefit of the organization while demonstrating appreciation for those employee contributions so as to motivate continued productivity. However, in recent decades, the need both for employee generosity in sharing individual intelligence and for managerial sophistication in rewarding employee effort has intensified.

Today's organizations are generally running very, very lean and in the throes of great environmental change. Therefore, they need innovation and employees who cannot only bend with change but thrive on it. In particular, perhaps more than ever before, organizations today desire two abilities in their employees: (1) rapid learning, and

---

[i] See Dorothy Leonard. *Wellsprings of Knowledge: Building and Sustaining the Sources of Innovation*. Boston: Harvard Business School Press, 1995, 1998.

(2) creativity. Organizational leaders cannot expect to inspire those skills merely by demanding them. Rather, leaders need to develop considerable insight into how and why people learn and into what stimulates creativity. Let us consider each in turn.

First, learning. Business organizations no longer represent lifelong commitments for most employees. Rather, today's knowledge workers are free agents, typically carving out two or more careers in life and with the expectation that they will work in multiple organizations during their work life. Employees, therefore, are preoccupied with gaining skills from employment and increasing their own value in their chosen field, not just in their organization. Fortunately for organizational leaders, humans do have a strong need for community; we are social animals and in general like to learn with and from others. Therefore, managers can link individual identity to corporate brand, individual aspirations to business goals, and individual learning objectives to needed organizational capabilities. But such linkages have to be individually forged, and with the full understanding that when you hire someone today, you hire the whole person—personal aspirations included. This is the good news and the bad news. It is good because a person whose personal learning goals are aligned with those of the organization are likely to be fully engaged and highly productive. It is bad because people are not always clear about their own objectives and even if they are, managers are not always able to align employees' personal goals with organizational needs. Ambiguity leads to frustration.

Moreover, managers often mistakenly equate learning with formal training sessions. But we do not gain know-how through reading manuals, observing PowerPoint slide presentations, or attending training lectures. From such sessions, we can certainly obtain useful mental frameworks and armatures (know-what) to which we attach knowledge. However, we learn deep skills from practice and experience—and gaining experience takes time. Job rotation helps, as does assignment to cross-functional project teams, but the best managers also regard themselves as coaches and teachers. Coaches use a variety of approaches, from one-way directives to joint problem solving, but the more that the learner is guided through experience, the more lasting is the knowledge.[ii] Organizations whose leaders regard the provision of guided experience as essential, and development of people as

---

[ii] See Dorothy Leonard and Walter Swap. "The Value of 'Been There, Done That.'" In F. Hesselbein, M. Goldsmith, I. Somerville (eds.), *Leading for Innovation and Organizing for Results.* San Francisco: Jossey-Bass, 2001, pp. 165–176.

one of the primary responsibilities of *all* managers—one for which they are held accountable in job evaluations—have a competitive advantage.

It is also in the power of leaders to inspire more creativity in the groups they lead.[iii] As noted earlier, an employee's identity in today's world is unlikely to be tied long term to an organization; therefore, managers have to create loyalty and commitment not through patronizing (the organization will take care of you) but through providing an interesting and exciting place to work. Creativity cannot be managed or controlled, but it can certainly be nurtured or killed. In the search for meaning to their lives, people find great satisfaction in having created something—a product, a service, an innovation that leads to improved conditions for someone. Too often we do not make the link between what an individual is doing on a daily basis and some larger purpose. Most people do not spring out of bed in the morning, eager to make 10% more for the stockholders of their company. That is too abstract a goal, directed toward unknown individuals (and financial gain for someone else is an unlikely aspiration)! Even personal financial gain may not be enough of a motive. Research shows that individuals are motivated best by a combination of intrinsic motives (I enjoy doing this for some personal reason) and extrinsic ones (doing this gains me more recognition or more financial security). Therefore, leaders who can provide both intrinsic and extrinsic motives for their employees are more likely to retain them and their valuable knowledge.

Unfortunately, there are serious barriers to both learning through experience and to creativity today. A primary one is time constraints. Information can be delivered at huge speed (the old analogy to drinking from the firehose) and people can be thrown into a situation to "sink or swim," but know-how takes time to develop. Time pressures, recent research in multiple organizations shows, inhibit creativity.[iv] Another constraint is managerial lack of understanding of basic human behavior. We need leaders who have enough life experience to understand, for example, what motivates people, the best forms of interpersonal communication, and the human inclination to interpret intellectual or positional disagreements as interpersonal attacks. Managers who have a sophisticated understanding of human

---

[iii] See Dorothy Leonard and Walter Swap. *When Sparks Fly: Igniting Creativity in Groups.* Boston: Harvard Business School Press, 1999.

[iv] See Theresa Amabile, Constance N. Hadley, and Steven J. Kramer. "Creativity Under the Gun." Special Issue on The Innovative Enterprise: Turning Ideas into Profits. *Harvard Business Review* 80, no. 8 (August 2002):52–61.

psychology and who know how to use it in the workplace are more likely to have an innovative employee base.

In this book, Hubert Rampersad has amassed and synthesized a huge amount of material written on these and related topics. The book serves as a practical guide, in that there are numerous exercises and business illustrations. However, it is also an extensive reference guide to many other works on management if the reader wishes to delve more deeply into any of the singular bodies of knowledge that the author has brought together into the Total Performance Scorecard.

Dorothy A. Leonard
The William J. Abernathy Professor of Business Administration,
Harvard Business School, Boston

Preface

There is a kind of re-education needed to connect business management with normal life. There has always been an enormous gap between the way people treat colleagues at work and the way they treat friends and family. With regard to the latter, we do not see friendship, tolerance, etc. as sentimental and "soft" when we deal with friends and family, but rather as a lubricant for the relationship. Could we not extend this to the business community as well? The gap between these two views is currently decreasing; perhaps here rests the solution for tomorrow's problems.

Roger Evans and Peter Russell

Real learning gets to the heart of what it means to be human. Through learning we recreate ourselves. Through learning we become able to do something we never were able to do. Through learning we reperceive the world and our relationship to it. Through learning we extend our capacity to create, to be part of the generative process of life. There is within each of us a deep hunger for this type of learning.

Peter M. Senge

For many years it was assumed that organizational improvement and change depended on internal and external analyses, the description of business processes, the preparation of measurement programs, the review of measured results, and the diagnosis of organizational culture. If organizations successfully formulated and implemented the right goals and strategies resulting from these procedures, then improvement and change would be a done deal. Over time, however, it became evident that this approach was no longer satisfactory. Due to the influence of modern market developments and the development of new management theories during the past few years, the process of organizational change evolved from one of quality improvement into one of improvement and change management. These days, people have begun to realize that organizational improvement involves more than the aforementioned; it is not an analytical process, but a creative learning process based on a strategic vision as well as new values and norms. In this book I introduce a new holistic concept of improvement and change management called Total Performance Scorecard (TPS). In the TPS concept, improvement, development, and learning are treated as ethical and cyclical processes whereby the development of personal and organizational competence and inner involvement reinforce each other.

This concept refers to a way of life within organizations, whereby the power of Balanced Scorecard, Total Quality Management, Performance Management, and Competence Management have been expanded and deepened with new management insights. TPS encompasses a philosophy and a set of rules that form the basis both for continuous process improvement and the personal improvement of individual employees.

Although this concept deals with organizational change, it starts first with individual and collective behavioral changes that are brought about through learning. It is an *"inside out"* approach that uses the essence of individual identity as a starting point.

This cyclic learning process encompasses an uninterrupted quest for self-knowledge. It is a journey of discovery on the road to improvement and change, as well as a mobilization of creativity and inventiveness. Through TPS you will get to know yourself and the environment in which you are functioning better, and you will be able to improve yourself on an ongoing basis. In turn, the organization will achieve more insight into its own structure, surroundings, and future possibilities. TPS will also create a broad basis for the effective guidance of improvements within the entire organization. This book shows you the way to achieve these goals.

Total Performance Scorecard refers to the maximum personal development of all corporate associates and the optimal use of their capabilities for the realization of the highest organizational performance. TPS is based on a personal vision of one's own future and a shared vision of the organization's future. This approach differs substantially from traditional management concepts. An important difference is that TPS is an inspiring and integrated management concept that regards personal ambition as the starting point. Traditional improvement and change management concepts are insufficiently committed to learning and rarely take the specific personal ambitions of employees into account. In consequence there are many superficial improvements, marked by temporary and cosmetic changes, which are coupled with failing projects that lack sufficient buy-in by personnel and, in some cases, even have an adverse effect.

The TPS concept starts with learning and formulating the personal ambition of individuals, then balancing this with the personal behavior and the shared ambition of the organization. This benefits the durability of improvement and change actions that are subsequently implemented. After all, real organizational improvement and change are only achieved if people change and improve inwardly. Furthermore, such personal involvement stimulates individual and team learning, creativity, and self-guidance. Indeed, if personal ambition is the starting point, people will cooperate with more commitment, loyalty, and devotion, which in turn inspires motivation, enjoyment, passion, inspiration, and enthusiasm.

This approach fits very well within learning organizations, which learn continuously because knowledge quickly becomes obsolete. Learning organizations consist of people whose personal ambitions are in line with the organizational mission and vision and, as a result, have a positive approach towards improvement and change. These organizations consist of people who learn individually and as a team. In teams composed of a balance of learning styles, employees continuously learn from their own mistakes, share knowledge with one another, trust one another, and communicate openly with each other. Learning organizations also have leaders who coach, help, inspire, motivate, and stimulate, as well as business processes that are reviewed continuously based on performance measures and feedback.

In the TPS concept, all of these aspects complement each other, and together they form trusted guidelines for the expansion of the organizational learning capacity. This book makes explicit the mutual connections between *improving*, *developing*, and *learning*, and provides an integral insight into the essential elements of organizational improvement and change. It will help you implement the improvement, development, and learning cycle in all facets of your work. This book picks up where the respected management gurus Stephen Covey, Robert Kaplan, and David Norton left off. In this book, the TPS theory alternates with case studies, examples, and exercises; these are based on my experience over the last twenty years as a management consultant in the field of organizational behavior and development.

Due to the general practicality of some new models, methods, and tools contained in this book, it is suitable as a guide for managers and employees in the business community and in government. It is useful for all those who want to improve, develop, and change themselves successfully, as well as their work, and their organization. It is also useful for advisors involved in organizational change and improvement projects, and for business management students at universities. The modular construction and clear arrangement of this book give the reader an opportunity to work systematically through several phases in each of the introduced management models.

This book is a synergistic product of the minds and efforts of many business writers and thinkers, from whom I have benefited. I am grateful for their inspiration. They deserve much of the credit here. I also wish to acknowledge Lucinda Hollenberg's and Trevie Feurich's assistance in the preparation of this book. I am also grateful to George Cline, Harbour Fraser Hodder, Jodie Allen, Karen Maloney, and Katie Hennessy for their editorial suggestions and assistance.

Thanks are also due to professor Dorothy A. Leonard at Harvard Business School and professor Cornelis A. de Kluyver, dean of the Peter F. Drucker Graduate School of Management, who both have given constructive feedback and encouragement.

Finally, I would like to express my thanks to my wife Rita and my two sons Rodney and Warren, for putting up with my obsession to complete this book.

I hope that this book will assist you during your search for self-knowledge and the continuous improvement and development of your self, your job, and your learning organization. I welcome your feedback about the contents of this book at www.Total-Performance-Scorecard.com or Hubert.Rampersad@Total-Performance-Scorecard.com.

Hubert K. Rampersad
Quality Management Consulting, Rotterdam, The Netherlands

Introduction

> The most important, and indeed the truly unique, contribution of management in the 20th century was the fifty-fold increase in the productivity of the manual worker in manufacturing. The most important contrubution management needs to make in the 21st century is similarly to increase the productivity of knowledge work and the knowledge worker.
>
> *Peter F. Drucker*

> The wealth of nations is increasingly based on the creation and exploitation of knowledge. The best possible advantage must be taken of this new form of progress available to community firms since it is an area in which the community enjoys a substantial lead.
>
> *ICIMS News*

Current global developments require a keen, pleasant, and ethical way of working within organizations. In turn, organizations should be characterized by vision, self-guidance, learning, and a balanced relationship between the personal ambition of individuals and the shared organizational ambition.

In my work as a management consultant, I have noticed that many companies have not yet comprehended the importance of these aspects. In most cases, improvement and development projects are handled with the traditional methods previously mentioned, and the results are usually temporary and cosmetic. Subsequently, many opportunities for the achievement of durable competitive advantage are missed. I developed this book, the learning objectives of which are mentioned in the boxed text, to meet the need for a more inspiring approach to organizational development and learning.

Learning Objectives

After reading this book you will

- know how to increase your self-knowledge and personal effectiveness, which will enable you to fine-tune your behavior to the needs of your environment and deliver innovative job performance;
- better understand your own thinking, which will enable you to discover your unconscious motivation, handle internal conflicts, generate positive energy, think creatively, and be more proactive;
- know how to create the conditions needed for a sustainable learning organization, based on the holistic TPS concept, and the practical tools introduced here;
- know how to create inner peace by balancing your personal ambition and your personal conduct, and thereby improve yourself, your work, and your organization;
- know how to stimulate commitment, loyalty, and dedication in your organization through the integrated Personal Balanced Scorecard concept, as well as how to create conditions for an organizational climate marked by self-guidance, creativity, enjoyment, passion, single-mindedness, enthusiasm, and ethical behavior;
- know how to decrease the gap between your normal life and your way of life within your organization;
- know how to improve and control your business processes continuously in order to achieve competitive advantages;
- know how to stimulate maximum personal growth in your employees, and how to develop and employ their talents optimally;
- know how to establish a more effective job appraisal system within your organization, and how to link it to both the shared organizational ambition and the personal ambition of individual employees;
- know how to imbue the shared organizational ambition with ethics;
- be able to realize durable organizational change based on high ethical standards;
- know how to communicate the corporate scorecard effectively to your employees and colleagues, and how to translate it to departmental scorecards, team scorecards, and individual performance plans;
- know how to develop your interpersonal communication skills and apply them to all aspects of your work;
- know how to improve the customer orientation of your organization;
- know how to create a working environment where there is individual as well as team learning, and where people can develop their talents continuously; and
- know how to deal with resistance to change, taking into consideration the particular organizational culture.

Chapter 2 describes the essence of and the basic ideas behind the philosophy of the Total Performance Scorecard. The TPS-cycle has been developed, which is related to this management concept. In this holistic cycle, I have related the essential elements and patterns of organizational change and development to each other in order to improve our understanding of these processes. Successful organizational change and development can only be realized if the three fundamental powers in this cycle—improving, developing, and learning—become increasingly balanced. The TPS-cycle is meant to be helpful for the successful implementation of your Personal and Organizational Scorecard. Chapter 3 is devoted to the formulation of the Personal and Organizational Balanced Scorecard as illustrated by a fictitious case related to the airline company Business Jet. This case will be returned to throughout the book. The Personal Balanced Scorecard focuses on the personal improvement of individual employees and is aimed at their well-being and success. The focus of the Organizational Balanced Scorecard is on the continuous improvement of the business processes. How to link shared organizational ambition with ethics will also be discussed in Chapter 3, through an examination of the Enron debacle. In order to employ the Organizational Balanced Scorecard effectively, it is necessary to communicate it decisively to all employees and to translate it into departmental scorecards, team scorecards, and the performance plans of individual employees. When this is done the entire organization is made conscious of the importance of strategic thinking, continuous improvement, development, and learning. This process is the center of the discussion in Chapter 4.

The next phase in the TPS cycle involves *improvement*, in which the focus is on the implementation of both personal and organizational improvement actions. The Deming cycle is used for both types of improvement actions to (1) improve the business processes based on the Organizational Balanced Scorecard, and (2) encourage personal improvement in individual employees based on the Personal Balanced Scorecard. This phase is discussed in Chapter 5.

The *development* phase will be discussed in Chapter 6. It entails the cyclic process of result planning, coaching, appraisal, and the job-oriented competence development of individual employees aimed at effective job fulfillment. The competence profile, which consists of the individual performance plan and a set of job-related competences, comprises the input of this process. The result planning, coaching, and performance appraisal discussions with individual employees and the application of the related 360°-feedback system will also be covered. This process is illustrated with the description of the Business Jet case in Appendixes A and B.

Reviewing and learning is the final phase in the TPS cycle. In this phase what went right or wrong during the previous steps is checked, and the execution or the formulation of the scorecards and the individual performance plans can be adjusted. The review of the scorecards is related to individual and collective learning and is based on Kolb's learning cycle. As a result of this learning process the organization will better know itself and its business environment, which positively influences the learning ability of the entire organization. To support this result, a knowledge management quick scan has been developed. All aspects of the reviewing and learning phase are discussed in Chapter 7.

Almost everything within the scope of Total Performance Scorecard is done as a team, therefore special attention is given to teamwork in Chapter 8. Here we take a closer look at team composition and roles, team learning and development, interpersonal communication, the

Figure 1.1

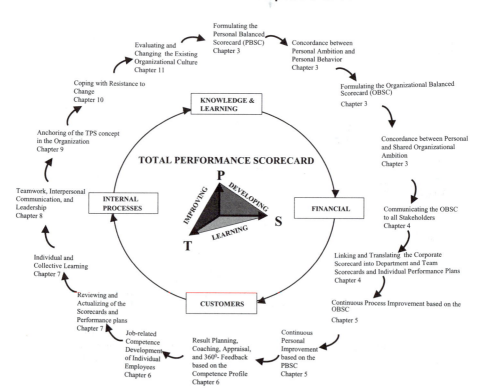

Correlation between Chapters 3 to 11

coaching of team members, leadership styles, effective meetings, and team review.

Chapter 9 explains the organization of the improvement process and the anchoring of the TPS concept within the organization through the formation of improvement teams and circles.

Attention is also given to the important issues of how to deal with resistance to change (Chapter 10) and how to accommodate prevailing organizational cultures (Chapter 11). Figure 1.1 shows the correlation between Chapters 3 to 11.

The Foundations of Total Performance Scorecard

Total Performance Scorecard

2

The Lord works from the inside out. The world works from the outside in. The world would take people out of the slums. Christ takes the slums out of people, and then they take themselves out of the slums. The world would mold men by changing their environment. Christ changes men, who then change their environment. The world would shape human behavior, but Christ can change human nature.

Ezra Taft Benson

Knowing others is wisdom, knowing yourself is enlightenment.

Lao Tzu

The Total Performance Scorecard concept is an *"inside out"* approach, one that has as its point of departure personal identity. This chapter provides an introductory description of this concept.

The TPS Concept

You cannot teach a man anything; you can only help him discover it in himself.

Galileo Galilei

Total Performance Scorecard (TPS) encompasses an amalgamation and expansion of the concepts of Balanced Scorecard, Total

Quality Management, Performance Management, and Competence Management (Rampersad, 2002). TPS is defined as a systematic process of continuous, gradual, and routine improvement, development, and learning that is focused on a sustainable increase of personal and organizational performances. Improving, developing, and learning are the three fundamental powers in this holistic management concept. They are closely interrelated and must be kept in balance.

> TPS = PROCESS OF CONTINUOUS [<IMPROVEMENT> +
> <DEVELOPMENT> + <LEARNING>]

Total Performance Scorecard entails the whole complex of personal and organizational mission and vision, key roles, core values, critical success factors, objectives, performance measures, targets and improvement actions, as well as the resulting process of continuous improvement, development, and learning. This holistic concept consists of the following five elements (see Figure 2.1):

1. **The Personal Balanced Scorecard (PBSC)** encompasses the personal mission, vision, key roles, critical success factors, objectives, performance measures, targets, and improvement actions. It includes the continuous improvement of your personal skills and behavior, focusing on your personal well-being and success in society. Here personal mission, vision, and key roles are called personal ambition. Self-management, self-development, and self-coaching stand central to the PBSC and focuses on the managers as well as the employees within the entire organization.

2. **The Organizational Balanced Scorecard (OBSC)** encompasses the organizational mission, vision, core values, critical success factors, objectives, performance measures, targets, and improvement actions (Kaplan and Norton, 1996, 2000). Here, organizational mission, vision, and core values are called shared organizational ambition. This concept includes the continuous improvement and control of business processes and the development of strategies that focus on achieving competitive advantages for the company. This corporate scorecard is communicated and translated into business unit scorecards, team scorecards, and performance plans for individual employees. The emphasis here is on strategy development and implementation.

3. **Total Quality Management (TQM)** is a disciplined way of life within the entire organization whereby continuous improvement is central. Defining problems, determining root causes, taking

actions, checking the effectiveness of these actions, and reviewing business processes are accomplished in a routine, systematic, and consistent way (Imai, 1986; Rampersad, 2001A). TQM emphasizes the mobilization of the entire organization in order to satisfy the needs of the customer continuously. It is a philosophy as well as a set of guidelines that forms an ever-improving organization on the basis of the effective Deming cycle (Deming, 1985). The Deming cycle consists of the following phases: **Plan** (develop an improvement plan); **Do** (execute this improvent plan on a limited scale); **Check** (review the results of the improvement actions; and **Act** (implement the proven improvements). This learning cycle, also called PDCA learning, is used in the TPS concept for continuous and gradual personal and process improvement. The emphasis here is on PDCA learning and process management.

4. **Performance and Competence Management** encompasses the process of the continuous development of human potential within the organization. Performance Management and Competence Management are discussed in combination here because they have common goals—namely, continuously delivering top performances with a motivated and developed community. They are both focused on the maximum development of employees and make optimal use of their potential in order to achieve the goals of the organization. Performance and competence management involves the development of job-related competences; a collection of information, capabilities, experience, skills, attitudes, standards, values, views, and principles (knowledge) that is focused on the expert fulfillment of your job. The development cycle is central here, which consists of the following phases: *result planning, coaching, appraisal,* and *job-oriented competence development.*

5. **Kolb's Learning Cycle.** This process of *instinctive learning*, or learning by experience, is seen in all four management concepts mentioned. Together with the process of *conscious learning*, or learning by education, these learning forms result in individual and collective behavioral changes. These two learning processes, as well as *individual learning, PDCA learning,* and *collective learning*, are important principles in the TPS concept. They are used to create the conditions for effective organizational change. Kolb's learning cycle contains the following four phases (Kolb, 1984):

- gaining hands-on experience;
- observing this experience, reflecting upon it, and then assessing the experience;

- drawing conclusions from this experience, and converting gained impressions into rules of experience, concepts, hypotheses, models, and theories in order to be able to draw conclusions from similar experiences; and
- testing these ideas in experiments, which again will result in new behavior and experiences.

After planning the steps above, this cycle starts again from the beginning.

Figure 2.1 illustrates the correlation between the different elements of the Total Performance Scorecard. This philosophy includes a synthesis of closely related management concepts that together form a harmonious whole.

There are overlaps between the Personal Balanced Scorecard, the Organizational Balanced Scorecard, Total Quality Management, and Performance and Competence Management, as may be seen in Figure 2.2. The shaded area in the center of the figure illustrates the similarities between these management concepts. Improving, developing, and learning represent much of this common area.

In the Total Performance Scorecard the PBSC focuses on your personal life, well-being, and behavior. The OBSC, on the other hand, is a strategic management concept used for the development and implementation of the organizational strategy, as well as the systematic management of the organization based on its mission, vision, core values, critical success factors, objectives, performance measures, targets, and improvement actions. The Balanced Scorecard was developed in the early 1990s by Robert Kaplan and David Norton (1996, 2000); it offers a means to maintain balance between financial and nonfinancial measures and to connect strategic and operational standards.

The cyclical process of continuous improvement in TPS is concerned with the gradual improvement of business processes and the personal skills and behavior of individual employees based on PCDA learning. By contrast, the cyclical process of continuous development deals with the phases of *result planning, coaching, appraisal,* and *job-related competence development* of individual employees so that they can routinely improve their daily work. The cyclical process of continuous learning is related to Kolb's learning cycle in which four skills are central: to *do, reflect, think,* and *decide.* These three cyclical processes of advancing insight are continuously followed and form a stable foundation for learning organizations. In the integrated TPS concept, the key elements of improving, developing, and learning are defined as follows:

Figure 2.1

The TPS Concept

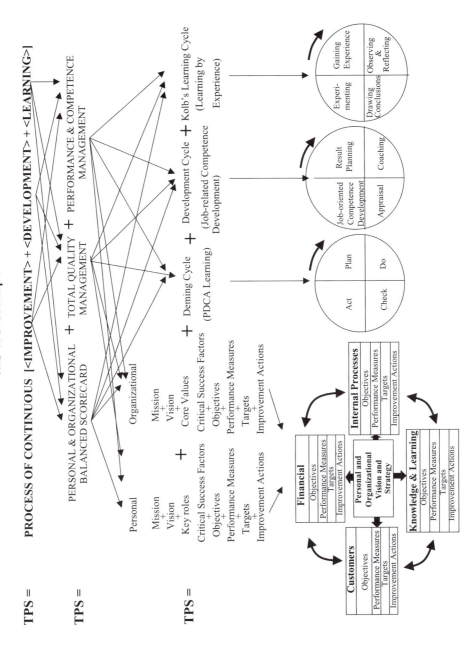

TPS = **PROCESS OF CONTINUOUS [<IMPROVEMENT> + <DEVELOPMENT> + <LEARNING>]**

TPS = PERSONAL & ORGANIZATIONAL + TOTAL QUALITY + PERFORMANCE & COMPETENCE
          BALANCED SCORECARD   MANAGEMENT   MANAGEMENT

TPS =

Personal   Organizational
Mission   +   Mission
   +   +
Vision   Vision
   +   +
Key roles   Core Values
   +
Critical Success Factors   Critical Success Factors
   +   +
Objectives   Objectives
   +   +
Performance Measures   Performance Measures
   +   +
Targets   Targets
   +   +
Improvement Actions   Improvement Actions

+ Deming Cycle   + Development Cycle   + Kolb's Learning Cycle
   (PDCA Learning)   (Job-related Competence   (Learning by
                         Development)   Experience)

Financial
Objectives
Performance Measures
Targets
Improvement Actions

Internal Processes
Objectives
Performance Measures
Targets
Improvement Actions

Personal and Organizational Vision and Strategy

Knowledge & Learning
Objectives
Performance Measures
Targets
Improvement Actions

Customers
Objectives
Performance Measures
Targets
Improvement Actions

Act | Plan
Check | Do

Job-oriented Competence Development | Result Planning
Appraisal | Coaching

Experimenting | Gaining Experience
Drawing Conclusions | Observing & Reflecting

Figure 2.2

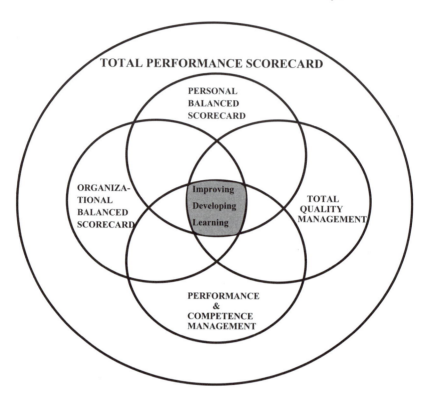

The Interrelated Parts of the TPS Concept

> **Improving:** This process encompasses the improvement of individuals and business processes based on PDCA learning. The focus here is on the improvement of personal skills and behavior of individuals related to their functioning in the society as well as process improvement (controllability of business processes).
>
> **Developing:** This process entails gradual individual development and education through the absorption of knowledge. It focuses on performance improvements that are directly related to the daily activities of individuals within the organization (job-related competence development of individual employees).
>
> **Learning:** This process entails internalizing and actualizing knowledge in order to change behavior. Learning is a personal transformation that depends on self-knowledge and that, in turn, results in collective behavioral change.

Total Performance Scorecard is a continuous voyage of discovery involving improvement, development, and learning. TPS differs in essential ways from traditional improvement, change management, and strategy development concepts (e.g., Chang and Morgan, 2000; Harrington, 1995; Kaplan and Norton, 1996, 2000; and Oakland, 1995), which insufficiently consider the important first step of formulating the personal ambition of individuals and balancing this with the personal behavior and the organizational shared ambition, needed to achieve enduring organizational and strategy development. When traditional concepts are used, the improvements are in many instances cosmetic and sometimes even have an adverse effect. Real change and organizational improvement are achieved only if people change and improve inwardly.

Such personal involvement is an integral part of Total Performance Scorecard. The aim is maximum commitment and devotion on the part of all involved as well as the encouragement of individual learning, team learning, and creativity. The thesis here is that if the personal ambition of an employee is engaged, then he or she will work and think according to the shared ambition of the organization. This approach also inspires motivation, creativity, enjoyment, passion, commitment, inspiration, and enthusiasm. Through these TPS principles, a more durable learning organization may be created. Table 2.1 illustrates the six principles on which the TPS philosophy is founded and that form a stable basis of such organizations.

Implementing the Total Performance Scorecard means managing and making decisions based on facts and figures and in relation to the organizational vision. This concept only works when it is based on a strategy development process in which the personal and organizational mission and vision, critical success factors, objectives, performance measures, learning processes, and planning complement each other. Together they contribute to the realization of continuous improvement within the entire organization and the development of human potential.

The following section focuses on the strategy development process based on the Balanced Scorecard concept, and the section after that introduces the TPS cycle. This cycle is meant to be helpful for the successful implementation of the Personal and Organizational Scorecard. The various phases of the TPS-cycle are further explained in Chapters 3 to 6.

Table 2.1

The Six TPS Principles

Focus on Customer Satisfaction

- Customer orientation is an essential part of the Personal and Organizational Balanced Scorecard.
- Customer-oriented behavior is one of the competences by which employees are judged.
- Employees and customers are mutual partners.
- We are acquainted with and understand our customers.
- Customer needs are integrated into our daily activities.
- More is done for the customer than the customer expects.
- Satisfied customers are our number one priority.
- Changes in customer needs are systematically collected and improved upon.
- Preventing complaints rather than reacting to complaints is our goal.

Passion and Enjoyment

- The organizational environment is characterized by passion, enjoyment, motivation, commitment, inspiration, and enthusiasm.
- Fear and distrust have been chased out.
- The voluntary and active involvement of everyone is a priority.
- Teamwork, open communication, and mutual trust are valued.
- Investment in people (training) is emphasized.
- Employees are empowered.
- Entrepreneurship and leadership is encouraged in all business units.

Consistent Personal and Organizational Objectives

- Managers and employees have formulated their own Personal Balanced Scorecards and use them as a compass for personal improvement, development, and learning.
- A shared and inspirational organizational ambition is developed and propagated decisively at all levels of the organization.
- Critical success factors, objectives, and performance measures are formulated and communicated to all associates.
- Managers' behavior about the formulated Balanced Scorecards is consistent.
- Guidance is provided for performance improvement.
- Top management is committed to change and improvement.
- Managers act as coaches, are action-oriented, and encourage a fundamental learning attitude.

Ethical and Fact-Based Behavior

- The shared organizational ambition is guided by ethics.
- The organization cares about ethics and corporate social responsibilities.
- The behavior of people is based on high moral standards.
- Performance measures are linked to targets.
- Work is done based on facts and performance indicators.
- The causes and consequences of problems are analyzed based on the principle that "measuring is knowing."
- Data is purposefully gathered and correctly interpreted.
- Measurements are based on figures and targets.
- The assessment of individual associates is based on concrete competences and results, which, in turn, are related to

- performance measures and targets.
- The organizational culture is characterized by simplicity, self-confidence, teamwork, and personal involvement.

Focus on Durable Improvement, Development, and Learning
- Formulation of the PBSC results in the personal improvement of individuals and is aimed at their personal well-being and success in the society.
- Formulation of the OBSC results in improvement and control of the business processes and is aimed at achieving competitive advantage for the organization.
- Formulation of the competence profiles and performance plans of individual employees results in job-related competence development and is focused on effective job fulfillment.
- Employees improve themselves and their work and help others improve themselves and the organization.
- Emphasis is on continuous improvement based on Deming's PDCA learning cycle.
- Emphasis on the continuous development of human potential based on the development cycle and 360°-feedback.
- Emphasis is on continuous learning that is based on self-knowledge.
- Emphasis is on prevention instead of correction.
- Improvements are based on a cross-functional approach and are continuously documented.
- A working climate exists where routine improvement, development, and learning are a way of life.

- People are open to change, improvement, and renovation.
- Making mistakes is permitted, for we learn constantly from our mistakes.
- Feedback is given regarding the improvement actions accomplished by employees.

Process Orientation
- Processes are guided based on performance measures.
- Internal customers are also satisfied.
- The effectiveness of business processes is measured.
- Suppliers are seen as long-term partners.
- Process variation reduction takes place continuously.
- Errors are regarded as an opportunity for improvement.
- Improvement, development, and learning are seen as continuous and gradual processes.
- Knowledge is constantly implemented and incorporated in new products, services, and processes.
- Improvement teams are created in which different learning styles are represented.

The Balanced Scorecard

> For any organization to compete successfully in today's market, it must focus on building not only from the outside but from the inside as well.
>
> *David Ulrich and Dale Lake*

The Balanced Scorecard is divided into the Personal and the Organizational Balanced Scorecard. This section starts with a description of the well-known Organizational Balanced Scorecard, which forms the basis for the Personal Balanced Scorecard.

The Organizational Balanced Scorecard

The Organizational Balanced Scorecard (OBSC) is a top-down management instrument that is used for making an organization's strategic vision operational at all organizational levels (Kaplan and Norton, 1996, 2000). It is based on the critical success factors, objectives, performance measures, targets, and improvement actions discussed thus far. The OBSC is a participatory approach that provides a framework for the systematic development of the organizational vision. It makes this vision measurable and translates it systematically into actions. The elements of the OBSC are divided along various perspectives. These perspectives are crucial categories of business results. There are various result areas that are central to the OBSC (corporate scorecard) as well as to the business unit scorecard, the team scorecard, and the individual performance plan. Depending on the organizational typology, different essential areas may be identified that are unique to the organization and from which results need to be obtained, such as *finances, customers, internal processes, knowledge and learning, service quality, market share*, and so on. The perspectives most used are the following four (Kaplan and Norton, 1996):

1. *Financial:* financial soundness. How do shareholders see the company? What does it mean for our shareholders?
2. *Customers (external):* customer satisfaction. How do customers see the company? What does it mean for our customers?
3. *Internal processes (internal):* process control. How can we control the primary business processes in order to create value for customers? In which processes do we have to excel to continuously satisfy our customers?
4. *Knowledge and learning:* skills and attitudes of the employees and the organizational learning ability. How can the company remain

successful in the future? How should we learn and communicate to improve ourselves and through this realize our vision? This important perspective is explained in detail in the boxed text.

The four selected perspectives cover financial success, market leadership, customer loyalty, capital development, control of business processes, and, in part, the consequences for the community.

Knowledge

The TPS concept consists of three key elements: improving, developing, and learning. Knowledge is the cross-section of these three elements (see Figure 2.3).

Knowledge is a function of information, culture, and skills (Rampersad, 2002):

<Knowledge> = f (<Information>, <Culture>, <Skills>)

Figure 2.3

Knowledge Serves as the Binding Tie in the TPS Concept

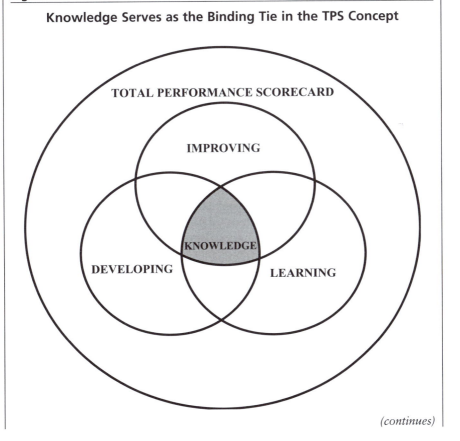

(continues)

The function <f> specifies the relationship between knowledge on the one side and information, culture, and skills on the other. In this context *information* comprises the meaning given to data obtained according to certain conventions; it is also known as *explicit knowledge* (Nonaka and Takeuchi, 1995). On the one hand, *culture* is the aggregate of standards, values, views, principles, and attitudes of people that underscore their behavior and functioning. On the other hand, *skills* are related to their capability, ability, and personal experience; it relates to what people can do, know, and understand. The knowledge components of culture and skills represent *implicit knowledge*, which depends on the individual people and is stored in their minds. This concept is difficult to describe, since it is based on experience, is practical in nature, and finds its source, among other things, in intuitions. Explicit knowledge, on the other hand, is not dependent on the individual. It is theoretical in nature and is specified as procedures, theories, equations, manuals, drawings, and other resources. This knowledge is mainly stored in management information and technical systems, and organizational routines.

The central question here is: how can knowledge be transformed into new behavior? In other words, how can people learn effectively so that they can function better? If knowledge is going to lead to competent action, then learning should receive special attention, and the organizational culture should encourage and support it.

Learning

Knowledge ages rapidly and is liable to wear. For this reason, everyone needs to learn constantly. *Learning is a continuous personal transformation*. It is a cyclic and cumulative process of actualizing your knowledge (adding new information to your knowledge repertory) in order to change your behavior so that you can function more effectively. Learning creates a permanent change in knowledge and behavior due to repeated experiences. In view of the increasing shift from *lifetime employment* to *lifetime employability*, people must make sure that their knowledge is up-to-date. An organization is indeed more successful if its employees learn more quickly and can implement knowledge faster than the workers of the competition (Geus, 1997). An organization that does not learn continuously and is not able to list, develop, share, mobilize, cultivate, put into practice, review, and spread knowledge will not be able to compete effectively. The ability of an organization to improve existing skills and acquire new ones is its most valuable competitive advantage (Hamel and Prahalad, 1994). It is imperative, therefore, to know what knowledge is essential, where it is available in the organization, which associate possesses the needed skill, how this knowledge can be adequately utilized, how it can be shared, how it provides added value, and how it can be maintained.

The knowledge infrastructure within an organization must be arranged in such a way that effective teamwork, creativity, positive thinking, self-confidence, and a good learning environment are stimulated by, for example, computers, Internet and intranet use, a knowledge bank, a library, continuous training, an auditorium, brainstorm sessions, review meetings, and so on. The ability of an organization to learn from experience depends on the willingness of its employees to think about problems and the opportunity for them to identify and solve common problems together; the willingness of management to intervene preventively; and the existence of a working atmosphere where every employee feels responsible for the company's performance.

In practice, organizations are especially able to become learning organizations if their employees have a sense of direction with a collective ambition (mission and vision) and work with all their might to realize this ambition. When such a mission exists, employees feel a strong common bond, which motivates them to learn together. Under these inspiring circumstances, they are also willing to share their knowledge with their colleagues and match their personal objectives with those of the organization. In this way, a *learning organization* emerges in which learning is a collective process based on both personal and collective ambition.

According to Peter Senge (1990) learning organizations are organizations where people expand their capacity to create the results they truly desire, where new and expansive patterns of thinking are nurtured, where collective aspiration is set free, and where people are continually learning to see the whole together.

Learning organizations have the ability to facilitate all facets of the learning process and thus continuously transform themselves. Such organizations consist of teams with balanced learning styles and of employees who have a personal ambition that correspond to those of the organization, thus they have a positive attitude toward improving, changing, and learning. Learning organizations are also composed of people who constantly learn from their own mistakes, share knowledge, and communicate openly with each other. These organizations have leaders who coach, help, inspire, motivate, stimulate, and intuitively make decisions, and they have processes that are constantly reviewed based on performance measures and feedback (see also Leonard, 1998). Managing the knowledge stream within the organization is essential for such review, as well as for changing the way we think and deal with each other.

According to Peter Senge (1990) learning organizations deal with *mental models* (the images, assumptions, and stories we carry with us), *personal mastery* (the ability to achieve results and control the principles on which these results are based), *systems thinking* (the aggregate of methods, instruments, and principles directed at the observation of the interconnection of forces that are considered part of a large process), *a shared vision* (the collective ideas that form an organization's guides and beacons), and

(continues)

Figure 2.4

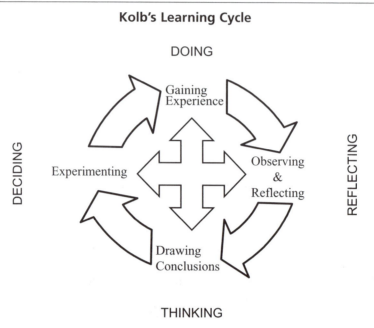

Kolb's Learning Cycle

DOING

DECIDING

REFLECTING

THINKING

team learning (teams that learn, think, and act from a synergetic perspective and are coordinated through a feeling of unity). This implies that people must give up their traditional way of thinking, develop their own skills and be open to change, understand how the whole organization functions, and collectively formulate the shared organizational ambition in order to fulfill this ambitious dream as a team.

These basic elements of learning organizations are also based on people's experiences. In practice, the tempo in which the abilities of an organization increase are to a great degree determined by the efficiency with which its members learn from experience. In order to obtain an optimum learning effect, people should have a certain educational level as well as the opportunity to acquire experience, because people with experience learn faster. This learning process is based on Kolb's learning cycle (see Figure 2.4). The starting point in this learning cycle is empirical learning, and the phases are *gaining experience, observing and reflecting, drawing conclusions,* and *experimenting.* These four phases relate to the following skills: *doing, reflecting, thinking,* and *deciding* (Kolb, 1984).

Learning organizations consist of teams with a balance of these learning styles, in which every team member knows his or her favorite learning style. Such self-knowledge allows each person to learn individually and thus undergo a behavioral change. The resultant change in collective learning is then associated with a change in organizational behavior—in other words, organizational change. These two learning

Figure 2.5

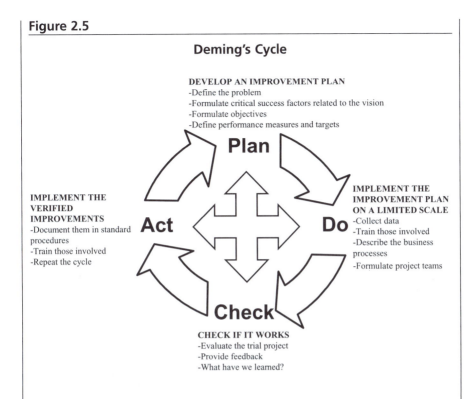

Deming's Cycle

DEVELOP AN IMPROVEMENT PLAN
-Define the problem
-Formulate critical success factors related to the vision
-Formulate objectives
-Define performance measures and targets

Plan

IMPLEMENT THE VERIFIED IMPROVEMENTS
-Document them in standard procedures
-Train those involved
-Repeat the cycle

Act

IMPLEMENT THE IMPROVEMENT PLAN ON A LIMITED SCALE
-Collect data
-Train those involved
-Describe the business processes
-Formulate project teams

Do

Check

CHECK IF IT WORKS
-Evaluate the trial project
-Provide feedback
-What have we learned?

processes of individual and collective learning will be discussed in depth in Chapter 7. As explained in the previous section, the Deming circle (see Figure 2.5) is also a learning cycle. Kolb's and Deming's learning cycles are continuously undergoing in the TPS concept, and together they form an excellent basis for creating a sustainable learning organization and increasing its learning capacity. Therefore, it is important to accept that every employee is able to learn and to ensure that he or she is motivated to do so, and to emphasize that learning is not a passive but an active and continuous process in which associates need guidance.

The elements of the Personal and Organizational Balanced Scorecards are presented in Figure 2.6. The elements of the OBSC will be examined first, followed by those of the PBSC.

Organizational Mission

The organizational mission contains an organization's identity and indicates its reason for existing (see Figure 2.7): Why, to what extent, and for whom does it exist? What is the ultimate objective and

Figure 2.6

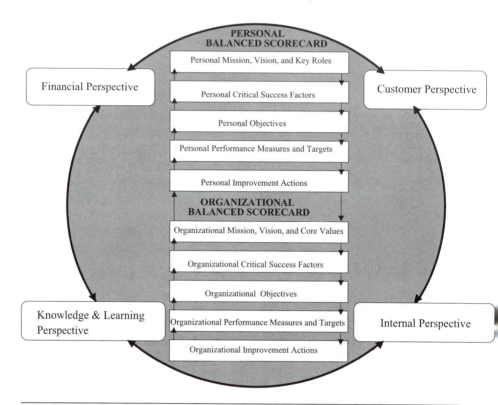

The Elements of the Personal and Organizational Balanced Scorecards

Source: Rampersad, 2002.

primary function of the organization? Which basic need does it provide, and who are its most important stakeholders? An effectively formulated mission creates a sense of unity in the behavior of employees, strengthens their like-mindedness, and improves both communication and the atmosphere within the organization.

Organizational Vision

The organizational vision contains the most ambitious dream of the organization. It provides a shared vision of a desired and feasible future situation, as well as the route needed to reach it. It indicates what the organization wants to achieve, what is essential for its success, and which critical success factors make it unique. Standards, values, and principles are also part of the organizational vision (see Figure 2.7). The vision, in contrast to the mission, is tied to a timeline. An effectively formulated vision guides personal ambitions and creativity,

Figure 2.7

Questions Pertaining to the OBSC Elements

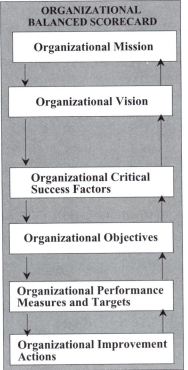

ORGANIZATIONAL BALANCED SCORECARD

- Organizational Mission
- Organizational Vision
- Organizational Critical Success Factors
- Organizational Objectives
- Organizational Performance Measures and Targets
- Organizational Improvement Actions

WHY DO WE EXIST?
Why does our organization exist? Who are we? What do we do? Where are we? What is our identity? What is the purpose of our existence? What is our primary function? What is our ultimate main objective? For whom do we exist? Who are our most important stakeholders? What fundamental need do we fulfill?

WHERE ARE WE GOING TOGETHER?
What is the most ambitious dream of our organization? How do we envision the future?
What are our long-term ambitions? What do we want to achieve? Where do we go from here?
How do we see a desirable and achievable shared future situation, and what are the change routes needed to reach it? What changes lie ahead in the business landscape? What do we stand for? What connects us? Who do we want to be? What is important in our attitude? What do we believe in (our core values)?

WHICH FACTORS MAKE US UNIQUE?
What is the most important factor of our organizational success? Which organizational factors are essential for our organizational viability? What are our core competences?

WHAT RESULTS DO WE WANT?
Which short-term measurable results must we achieve?

HOW CAN WE MEASURE THE RESULTS?
What makes the organizational vision and objectives measurable? Which values must be obtained?
What are the targets?

HOW DO WE WANT TO ACHIEVE THE RESULTS?
How can we realize the objectives? Which improvement actions are we going to implement?
How do we create a platform for the developed strategies? How will we communicate this to the people? How do we see that we learn continuously?

Source: Rampersad, 2002.

establishes a climate that is fertile for drastic changes, strengthens the organization's belief in the future, and therefore releases energy in people. Together the organizational mission and vision express the soul of the organization. They form its collective organizational ambition and have an important impact on the relationship between the employees and the organization. A successfully formulated organizational ambition shows people how their activities contribute to the larger whole. When they are working together towards strategic objectives, it often leads to higher performances. Because of this, they feel pride in making a useful contribution towards something worthwhile. The organizational mission and vision direct an organization and function both as its compass and its road map. They also make employees proud of their organization, letting them focus on relevant activities and in turn create value for customers, thus eliminating unproductive activities. In an organization without a mission and vision, employees are exposed to ad hoc decisions and short-term chances.

Organizational Critical Success Factors

A critical success factor is one in which the organization must excel in order to survive, or, one that is of overriding importance to organizational success. Such strategic issues determine the competitive advantage of an organization. They are factors in which the organization wants to differ from others and make itself unique in the market, and as such are related to its core competences. Critical success factors are also related to the four mentioned BSC perspectives and thus form an integrated part of the organizational vision. These perspectives along with the critical success factors are the main concepts in the Scorecard.

Core Values

The organizational vision is also based on a set of shared values that are used to strengthen the like-mindedness, commitment, and devotion of employees and to influence their behavior positively. These core values determine how one must act in order to realize the vision. They function as the guiding principles that supports people's behavior at work. Core values articulate the way we treat each other and how we see customers, employees, shareholders, suppliers, and the community. If the principles, norms, and values of the employees match those of the organization, then their efforts and involvement are often optimal. Therefore, the core values are also strongly related to the personal mission, vision, and key roles of the individual employees. After all, with an organizational mission and vision based on shared values, the personal objectives of individual employees will correspond closely to those of the organization. The core values must be ethical in order to pass the test of moral scrutiny. Everyone within the organization should act in accordance with these principles and moral standards.

Organizational Objectives

Organizational objectives are the measurable results that must be reached. They describe the expected results that should be achieved within a short-term interval of time in order to realize the long-term vision. These objectives are derived directly from the critical success factors and create realistic milestones. Quantifying objectives, however, is avoided in the BSC; it will take place at a later phase via performance measures and targets. Each critical success factor has one or more objectives that are related to one of the four BSC perspectives. These strategic objectives form part of a cause-and-effect chain, resulting in the final organizational objective.

Organizational Performance Measures

A performance measure is an indicator related to the critical success factor and the strategic objective and is used to judge the functioning of a specific process. These indicators are the standards by which the progress of the strategic objectives is measured. They are essential when putting strategic plans into action. When they are interconnected such that managers can deduce a certain course of action from them, they provide management with timely signals for organizational guidance, based on the measurement of (process) changes and the comparison of the measured results to the standards. Therefore, performance measures make the organizational vision and objectives measurable.

Organizational Targets

A target is the quantitative objective of a performance measure. It is a value that an organization aspires towards, and the realization of which can be measured by means of a performance measure. In other words, targets indicate values to be obtained.

Organizational Improvement Actions

Improvement actions are strategies undertaken to realize the organizational mission, vision, and objectives. The actions, which provide the largest contribution to the critical success factors, are chosen for implementation.

OBSC = organizational mission + vision + core values + critical success factors + objectives + performance measures + targets + improvement actions

---

The scorecard elements are discussed in more detail in the Chapter 3, where they are illustrated through a case study.

The Personal Balanced Scorecard

In the Total Performance Scorecard concept, individual, job-related, and organizational competence development are the focal points. The Personal Balanced Scorecard (PBSC) relates to the individual, and the Organizational Balanced Scorecard (OBSC) relates to job-related and organizational competence development. The PBSC functions as a personal improvement and self-coaching instrument for individuals, and focuses on their personal well-being and success in the society (also at home, in the club, etc.). Of particular importance here are the personal lives, skills, and social behavior of individuals. For several reasons, the formulation of the PBSC is the initial and most important step in the process of improvement, development, and learning. First of all, it enables you to distance yourself from your own mindsets—the mental framework of assumptions and beliefs that color your experience of the world and to listen effectively to your inner voice. It also allows you to improve your behavior and create your own future. After all, as we become more conscious of ourselves, our inner processes, and our motives, we become more creative. When we scrutinize ourselves we improve our learning ability by means of increased self-knowledge and a better self-image. *Self-knowledge means self-awareness.* Formulating your personal ambition involves a search for your identity. And understanding your identity is the key to action.

The second reason that the PBSC approach is so important is that finding the proper balance between your personal ambition and your behavior results in inner peace, the expenditure of less energy, and the ability to be guided by your inner voice—all of which develops personal charisma. People with this perspective on life matter to one another and create a stable basis for their own credibility. When you achieve this inner authority, you also have a positive effect on the feelings of loyalty, motivation, and dedication of those around you. According to Kouzes and Posner (1999) the credibility of leaders depends on the following:

- Trustworthy leaders practice what they preach.
- They keep their word.
- Their actions match their words.
- They suit the action to the word.
- They keep their promises.
- They do what they said they would do.

The third reason for the PBSC is that if there is an effective balance between the interests of individual employees and those of the organization, employees will work with greater commitment toward the development and implementation of the OBSC. The formulation of the PBSC also involves enjoyment, passion, and enthusiasm. The development of the collective and personal ambition takes place simultaneously. When we answer the question of what we want for the organization and where we want to go together, we also ask what we want for ourselves and which win-win situation accommodates both interests. Behind our behavior are the inner needs that arise from our own personal experiences and mindsets. These needs and those of the organization must be aligned for the sake of higher productivity. Moreover, having a clear personal objective gives meaning and direction to one's life. By formulating a Personal Balanced Scorecard and reflecting on it, you will get to know yourself better as well as gain more control over your own life.

The fourth reason for using the PBSC as first step in the strategy development process is this: it is the right thing to do. Don't waste any more time with strategy development and organizational improvement and change according to traditional, cosmetic approaches. This is especially true if you are dealing with a learning organization, where working with the Personal Balanced Scorecard is an essential condition for sustainable improvement and change. The PBSC allows you to reformulate your own ambitions, objectives, principles, standards, and values, then makes these available to you and to others you care about for the benefit of the ideas you support.

According to Peter Senge (1990), when an organization uses the personal ambitions of its employees as a starting point, it becomes an instrument of self-realization instead of simply a machine to which they are enslaved. He points out that managers usually assume that encouraging employees to develop and express their personal ambition will only lead to organizational anarchy and confusion. Experience shows, however, that these assumptions are totally unfounded and that most employees are more than willing to align their personal ambition to that of their organization. Stephen Covey (1993) also argues for an *"inside out"* approach. He explains that the core of your identity must be your starting point. In order to improve your relations with others, you must begin with yourself (see also Ulrich and Lake, 1990). This means that you must succeed in your personal life before you can achieve something in the world, and that you must be loyal to yourself before you make promises to others.

Six Functions of the Personal Balanced Scorecard

1) To give you the opportunity to distance yourself from your mindsets and listen effectively to your inner voice, which will allow you to know yourself better, improve your behavior, and act ethically. With the PBSC you can better identify your strengths, gifts, and personal objectives, on the basis of which you can create your future and discover your destiny. A better self-image and greater self-knowledge then results in greater learning ability. The PBSC is also a tool for

(continues)

self-management, self-coaching, self-development, and personal time management.

2) To find a balance between your personal ambition and your behavior, which will form the basis for creating inner peace and strengthening your credibility with others.

3) To find a balance between your personal ambition and the shared organizational ambition, which will stimulate self-guidance, motivation, creativity, enjoyment, passion, devotion, inspiration, enthusiasm, and ethical action.

4) To create a framework for your own future and personal improvement, focus on maximum individual development, personal well-being, and success in society (also in private life).

5) To function as input for the competence development of individual employees.

6) To decrease the gap between your normal life and your way of life within your organization.

The same four perspectives of the OBSC (financial, customers, internal processes, and knowledge and learning) form the starting point for the PBSC (see Figure 2.8). In this context, however, they have a different meaning. Here the perspectives include the personal results (result areas) that are of essential importance to your self-development, personal well-being, and success, namely:

1. *Financial:* financial stability. To what degree are you able to fulfill your financial needs?

2. *Customers (external):* relations with your spouse, children, friends, employer, colleagues, and others. How do they see you?

3. *Internal processes (internal):* your physical health and mental state. How can you control these in order to create value for yourself and others?

4. *Knowledge and learning:* your skills and learning ability. How do you learn, and how can you remain successful in the future?

Personal Mission

Your personal mission statement encompasses your philosophy of life and your overall life objectives, indicating who you are, why you are on this earth, your purpose in living, and what your deepest aspirations are. This formulation is based on your quest for personal identity (self-knowledge).

Personal Vision

Your personal vision statement describes where you want to go, the values and principles that guide you, what you stand for, what you

Figure 2.8

Questions Dealing with the PBSC Elements

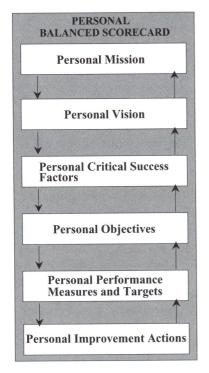

PERSONAL BALANCED SCORECARD

Personal Mission

Personal Vision

Personal Critical Success Factors

Personal Objectives

Personal Performance Measures and Targets

Personal Improvement Actions

WHO AM I?
What is my philosophy of life? Why am I on this earth?
What are my overall life objectives?
For what reason do I live? What are my deepest aspirations?

WHERE AM I GOING?
Which values and principles lead me to this path?
What do I want to realize? What do I stand for? What do I believe in?
What are my ideals? Which key roles do I want to fulfill?

WHICH FACTORS MAKE ME UNIQUE?
What is decisive for my personal success?
Which factors in my personal mission, vision, and key roles are essential to
the realization of my personal objectives?
What are my most important competences?

WHICH PERSONAL RESULTS DO I WANT TO ACHIEVE?
Which measurable short-term personal results do I want to achieve?

HOW CAN I MEASURE MY PERSONAL RESULTS?
What makes my personal objectives measurable?
Which values do I have to obtain?
What are my targets?

HOW DO I WANT TO ACHIEVE THE RESULTS?
How can I realize my personal objectives?
Which improvement actions do I need to achieve them?
How do I see to it that I learn continuously?

Source: Rampersad, 2002.

want to help realize in your life, what you want to achieve, the ideal characteristics you want to possess, and what are your ideal job situation, living environment, state of health, and so on. The formulation of your personal mission and vision is meant to improve your learning ability and thus enable you to improve your behavior. This individual behavioral change results in organizational learning, which in turn results in a collective pattern of change called organizational change.

According to the holy Hindu scriptures known as the Vedas, personal vision is related to knowledge (Leifer, 1997). A visionary is a person who sees or knows what others do not see. The Buddhist concept of vision defines wisdom. Wisdom signifies that one clearly sees the nature of existence and the human situation in that existence. The opposite of wisdom is ignorance. The Sanskrit word for ignorance is *avidya*, which means blindness. The Tibetan word for ignorance is *ma-rig-pa*, meaning unintelligence. According to Eastern philosophy visionary people are wise (knowledgeable) and people without a personal vision are blind and ignorant (unintelligent). Such ignorance also applies to people with wrong personal visions that result in preposterous and useless deeds that create misery for themselves and others. From these insights I have extrapolated the following: *organizations without a vision—or with a wrong one—are blind and unintelligent, which creates a lot of suffering for their stakeholders.*

Key Roles

Your key roles relate to the way you wish to fulfill the various essential roles in your life and thus realize your personal mission and vision. What type of relations would you like to have with your colleagues, friends, family, neighbors, and others? The formulation of your key roles will also result in greater self-knowledge and a better self-image, which in turn improves your learning ability as well. According to Stephen Covey (1993), your personal ambition (mission, vision, and key roles) is a personal constitution on which your life and behavior is based. This in turn forms the basis for determining your decisions about what you want to achieve and do. Your key roles should be formulated in such a way that you will be stimulated to reflect on your life and all your endeavors.

Personal Critical Success Factors

The central questions here are: Which factors make me unique? What determines my personal success? Which factors in my mission, vision, and key roles are essential for the realization of my personal objectives? What are my most important competences? The personal critical success factors are derived from the personal mission, vision, and key roles. They are also related to the four BSC perspectives (financial, external, internal, and knowledge and learning).

Personal Objectives

The central question here is: Which measurable short-term personal results do I want to achieve? Your personal objectives describe a personal result that you want to achieve in order to realize your personal vision. They are derived from your personal critical success factors and also result from an analysis of your strengths and weaknesses. They serve as achievable milestones. Quantifying personal objectives is avoided in the PBSC; this will take place at a later stage by means of personal performance measures and targets. Each personal critical success factor has one or more objectives that are related to one of the four scorecard perspectives.

Personal Performance Measures

This section of the PBSC deals with the following questions: How can I measure my personal results? What makes my personal objectives measurable? A personal performance measure is a measuring point with which you can assess your own functioning in relation to your personal critical success factors and objectives. These indicators are criteria that measure—for each scorecard perspective and each personal critical success factor—your personal objectives. Personal performance measures make your personal vision and objectives measurable.

Personal Targets

A personal target is a quantitative objective of a personal performance measure. It is a value that is pursued then assessed through a personal performance measure. Targets indicate values that should be obtained.

Personal Improvement Actions

Personal improvement actions are strategies used to realize your personal mission, vision, and objectives. They are utilized to improve your personal competences and behavior, thus to improve your performances. *How* is central here: How do I want to achieve my personal results? How can I realize my personal objectives? How can I improve my behavior? How can I ensure that I learn continuously, individually as well as collectively? How can I get to know myself better?

PBSC = personal mission + vision + key roles + critical success factors
+ objectives + performance measures + targets
+ improvement actions

In the following chapter all the PBSC elements are discussed and explained in detail by means of a case study. But first I will introduce the TPS cycle, which is meant to be helpful for the implementation of the scorecards.

The TPS Cycle

The key to success is simplicity; of the people, the organizational structure, the business processes, the products, and the language used by managers.

Hubert Rampersad

In my quest for simplicity I have thus far discussed the essential elements and patterns of organizational change and development in order to improve our understanding of this concept. This has resulted in a holistic model in which the interplay between the three powers of *improving, developing,* and *learning* is central. Together they form a power field that I call the Total Performance Scorecard cycle. This integrated cyclic model will be helpful for successfully implementing your Personal and Organizational Balanced Scorecards. It consists of the following five phases (see Figure 2.9):

1. **Formulating.** This phase involves the formulation of the Personal and Organizational Balanced Scorecards. This personal and organizational strategy-forming process kicks off with a two-day informal workshop in which the corporate team actively takes part. The first day starts with the formulation of the personal scorecard by individual participants, and the second day is spent on formulating the corporate scorecard.
2. **Communicating and linking.** Here all stakeholders share in the new business strategy by effectively communicating and translating the corporate scorecard to all scorecards of the underlying business units and teams, and finally linking the team scorecard to the individual performance plan of the employees. One should take care to actively involve everyone in the organization in this top-down and bottom-up learning process.
3. **Improving.** This indicates the process of continuously improving yourself and your work. It concerns the implementation of individual and organizational improvement actions that are focused on personal success and organizational competitive advantage, respectively. The focus here is on how to correct mistakes, improve existing things, do things right the first time, and obtain new skills and capabilities through step-by-step improvement. Organizational improvement actions are related to:
   a. *Improving.* This process deals with *doing existing things better, cheaper, and faster,* such as streamlining business processes through the elimination of bureaucracy and rework, work simplification, reduction of throughput times, change of working methods and procedures, automation, and so on. The focus here is on *efficiency,* or *doing things right.*
   b. *Renewing.* This process deals with *doing existing things differently,* such as process innovation, new process design, organizational restructuring, realization of cultural change, and so on. The accent here is on *effectiveness,* or *doing the right things.*
   When implementing the organizational improvement process, the following three phases are identified (Rampersad, 2001A):

1. *Process selection:* selection and definition of the critical business processes related to the improvement actions.
2. *Process evaluation:* description, review, and documentation of the selected processes.
3. *Process improvement:* continuous improvement of the described and reviewed processes using the Deming cycle. Personal improvement actions also result from this PDCA learning.
4. **Developing.** This process entails the continuous development of the job-related competences of individual employees based on the development cycle. Here the emphasis is on the job-related development and growth of individual employees, through their absorption of knowledge as well as the optimal use of their abilities. In this way they can fulfill their jobs more effectively. The development cycle is continuously repeated and consists of the following phases: *result planning* (drafting the competence profile and making related appointments regarding the results to be obtained); *coaching* (helping to gain the agreed upon results, providing individual guidance, and giving feedback); *appraisal* (judging the functioning, checking if and how all appointments are met and results are obtained, giving 360°-feedback, and reviewing the results); and *job-oriented competence development* (competence development of the employee through courses, on-the-job training, etc.).
5. **Reviewing and learning.** This process encompasses the collection of feedback information, the review of the scorecards, the actualization of these scorecards based on changing conditions, the documentation of the lessons learned, and the identification of improvement opportunities and follow-up activities. Here, evaluation deals with checking which things went well and which went wrong during the previous phases. It also concerns the testing of the realized level of the formulated objectives. Depending on these evaluation results the implementation or the formulation of the scorecards may be adjusted. Thus, reviewing deals with learning from gained experiences, based on Kolb's learning cycle. It refers to internalizing acquired knowledge and actualizing it through experience in order to change both the individual and collective behavior of employees and thus enable the organization to perform better. To achieve this, there needs to be individual as well as collective learning, for which the essential conditions should be created. Collective learning results in collective behavioral change (organizational change).

As we can see from Figure 2.9 the TPS cycle consists of a number of large and small wheels. These all need to be interrelated and turning in

Figure 2.9

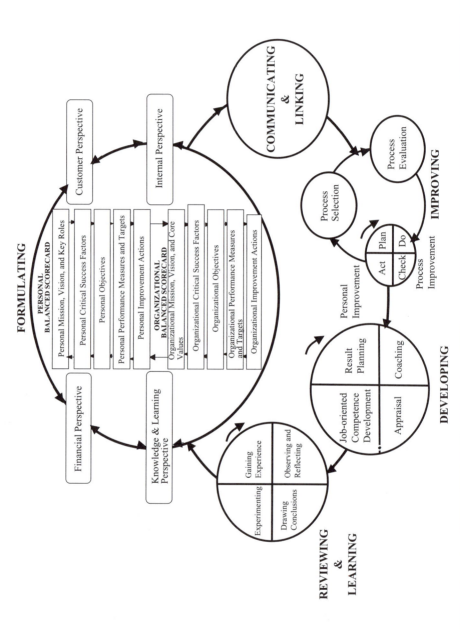

The TPS Cycle

Source: Rampersad, 2002

Figure 2.10

TPS Activities

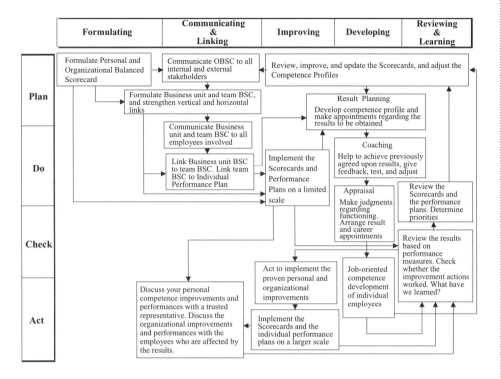

the right direction in order to get the wheel of the larger Total Performance Scorecard moving successfully. The model gives us insight into both the way this wheel can be mobilized and the coherence between its different aspects. After the last phase is complete the cycle is again followed in order to align the scorecards to the surroundings on a continuous basis. Thus your organization will come to know itself and its surroundings and so improve itself.

Naturally, the same also applies to you. For example, by reviewing your PBSC quarterly with a trusted friend and learning from previously obtained experiences, you will know both yourself and your surroundings better, which will allow you to improve yourself. Strategy formation, improvement, development of human potential, and learning are thus a perpetual process. Continuously progressing through the TPS cycle will result in the continuous improvement of business results through the years. Successful organizational change and development is only possible if the balance between the three fundamental powers in this model (improving, developing, and learning) has been increased. Figure 2.10 illustrates the integration of the Deming cycle in

Figure 2.11

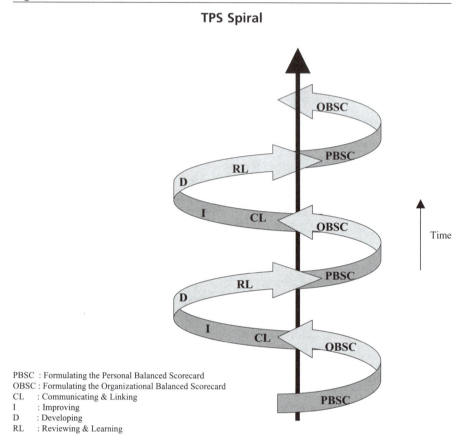

TPS Spiral

PBSC : Formulating the Personal Balanced Scorecard
OBSC : Formulating the Organizational Balanced Scorecard
CL   : Communicating & Linking
I   : Improving
D   : Developing
RL   : Reviewing & Learning

the TPS cycle. It shows that the TPS cycle is a continuous, iterative process that spirals through time as in linked phases of formulating, communicating and linking, improving, developing, and reviewing and learning (see Figure 2.11). In the following chapters, each of these phases will be discussed in depth.

In this chapter I discussed the Total Performance Scorecard concept globally and provided insight into the correlation between its different elements. I also introduced the Total Performance Scorecard Cycles, which can be used to successfully implement this management concept. In the next chapter, I will give a detailed explanation of the first step in this cycle: the formulation of the Balanced Scorecard.

Formulating the Balanced Scorecard

3

The companies that survive longest are the one's that work out what they uniquely can give to the world—not just growth or money but their excellence, their respect for others, or their ability to make people happy. Some call those things a soul.

Charles Handy

Believe in yourself! Have faith in your abilities! Without a humble but reasonable confidence in your own powers you cannot be successful or happy.

Norman Vincent Peale

In this chapter, I focus on the formulation of the Personal and Organizational Balanced Scorecards. This strategy-forming process differs from the traditional yearly planning ritual, in which top management develops an organizational strategy and then forces employees to accept it. In the TPS concept, in contrast to current practice, this process starts with the Personal Balanced Scorecard. The formulation of the Personal and Organizational Balanced Scorecards begins at the highest organizational level, after which the Organizational Balanced Scorecard is translated into the scorecards of the business units and teams. Finally, the team scorecard is linked to the individual performance plans of the employees themselves. Therefore, this learning process begins with top management and is then passed down through the organization layer by layer. I will explain how this is done later by means of a case study.

It is advisable to start the strategy-forming process with a two day informal workshop—preferably far away from the organization in a luxurious hotel in a natural setting. Invite the board of directors and all the top managers to be present and actively participate in the BSC formulation process. The first day begins by having individual participants formulate their own personal mission, vision, and key roles. Give them the opportunity to develop their personal ambition and then to discuss it with each other. Advise everyone to think about how their personal ambition may be aligned with their own behavior. In addition, let them check how their personal ambition can be incorporated with the shared organizational ambition that will be formulated later. This will be explained later.

The first day of the workshop emphasizes the formulation of the PBSC, which then functions as the input for the formulation of the OBSC on the second day of the workshop. Balancing personal and shared ambitions should also be discussed at this point in the workshop. It is also advisable to execute this strategy forming process not only at the strategic level, but also at the tactical and operational levels. Figure 3.1 illustrates the different steps in this first phase of the TPS cycle, which I will explain in more detail over the course of this chapter.

Formulating the Personal Balanced Scorecard

> The Kingdom of God is within you.
>
> *Jesus Christ*

The Personal Balanced Scorecard is comprised of the personal mission, vision, key roles, critical success factors, objectives, performance measures, targets, and improvement actions. I outlined these PBSC elements in the previous chapter and will now elaborate on them in detail.

Formulating Personal Ambition

Formulating the PBSC is the starting point of the TPS concept, which uses self-knowledge and self-image to create an effective balance between personal ambition and behavior on the one hand, and personal and shared ambition on the other. The purpose of beginning with self-knowledge is to develop inner peace and stability, composure,

Figure 3.1

The First Phase of the TPS Cycle

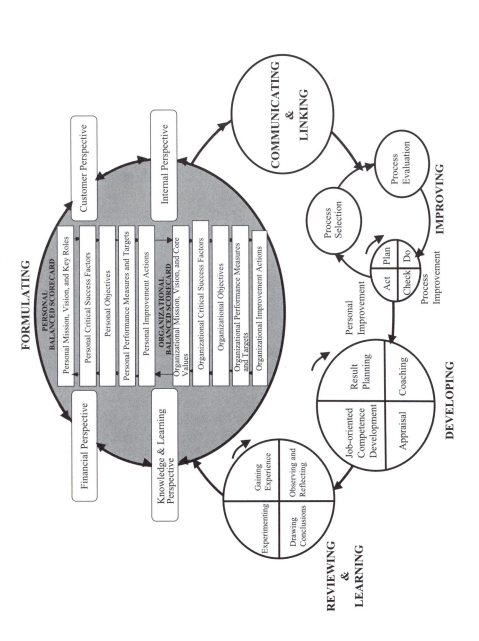

harmony, self-guidance, motivation, commitment (absolute will), loyalty, devotion, and positive thinking. When these qualities are cultured in individuals, a foundation is built for a continuously improving learning organization. The first three components in your PBSC (personal mission, vision, and key roles) are meant to allow you to express your personal ambition as well as to gain more insight into yourself, in terms of both the strong and weak points of your personal behavior. They are meant to give you insight into your own self-image, which influences your attitude towards others and your emotional intelligence. They are meant to allow you to know more about yourself. *After all, we do not know what we don't know. Even worse: We do not even know that we don't know this.* By focusing inwardly and thinking about our actions through self-examination, we learn more and more about ourselves and can therefore function better.

"Who am I?" is an identity question (Leifer, 1997). It initiates a legitimate self-examination of your *personal identity* (the unique position you want to be in) and a voyage of discovery for self-knowledge. This journey is akin to the great discoveries of men such as Galileo Galilei (1564–1642), who found through astronomy that the earth was not the center of God's universe, but simply a small detail among billions of constellations in the vast universe; Isaac Newton (1643–1727), who discovered gravity and formulated the basic laws of mechanics; Charles Darwin, (1809–1882) who argued that we were not created by God on the seventh day but evolved from animals over the course of millions of years; Sigmund Freud (1856–1939), who theorized that we do not know our own minds but are blind towards ourselves and driven by subconscious drives; and Albert Einstein (1879–1955), who developed the theory of relativity. Inspired by these discoveries now try to discover who you truly are. Try to discover the powers Freud mentioned by listening intently to your inner voice. Abraham Maslow said the following about this:

> There exists a personal I that which I sometimes call "listening to your intuitions." This means: letting your own I emerge. Most of us do not listen to ourselves but to the interrupting voice of others.

When you observe your own thoughts from a meditative position, you can let your own "I" emerge and distance yourself from your mindsets. You will learn to look at your own life with new eyes and observe what is happening inside of you. By means of this you will know where you stand in life. Formulating your personal ambition can also serve as a crowbar to be used to pry off your rusty mindsets, which block your creativity. You will be better equipped to create your own future and discover your destination. *After all, only if you know yourself will you be able to discover your talents and develop your personal goals, then put them to the service of yourself and others.* It is, therefore, important to listen to your inner voice, the one that is trying to tell you what is best for you and how you can control your inner processes. An important rule here is: listen effectively to yourself, trust your inner voice, and obey it. You'll then act from conviction. Selvarajan Yesudian (1991, p. 41), the Indian yoga guru, says the following about this:

> Let us make it our habit to constantly focus our attention inwardly and dwell within ourselves. Then we build our house on sturdy ground and not on quicksand. Looking from the safe height of our heart we can observe our own development, our growth, and the expansion of our awareness without losing our inner peace. This way, we'll be able to understand and accept every situation we experience and every phase of development we go through.

Formulating your personal ambition is primarily done by transcribing your inner voice, based on your contemplation on a couple of probing questions (which will be discussed later in this chapter). Although this voice is present in all of us, it cannot always be heard because: (1) most of us are not capable of hearing this voice because we are too focused on the outside world; and (2) the inner voice is drowned out by the noise around us. According to Evans and Russell (1991, p. 127), to hear your inner voice you must tune into the same wavelength in which your spirit communicates with yourself. In order to accomplish this they recommend the following:

> Take half an hour off, look for a quiet place where you will not be disturbed, sit down, close your eyes, relax as much as you can, and open yourself to all the pictures that present themselves. Imagine that you are in a garden and that a wise person is approaching you; after introductions, you ask him or her questions about things you need advice about. Listen intently to what he or she has to say. The answers can be surprising. They are what we are supposed to say to ourselves, but could only hear after our inner voice obtained a symbolic form. By using metaphors a more lively and creative impression of you will be evoked.

The PBSC is certainly not a fashionable trend. It is a personal note about yourself and is meant to inspire you to act with determination and energy and to stimulate your inner involvement. By writing down

Table 3.1

Primary Questions That Are Central to Your Personal Mission and Vision	
Personal Mission	**Personal Vision**
• Who am I? • What is my philosophy of life? • Why am I on this earth? • What are my overall life objectives? • What do I live for? • What are my deepest aspirations? • Why do I do what I do? • What are my unique talents? • Where do I stand now? • What are my core beliefs?	• Where am I going? • Which values and principles guide my way? • What do I want to help realize? • What do I want to achieve? • What are my long-term intentions? • What is my ideal? • What do I stand for? • What do I believe in? • Which contribution to society do I strive to make? • How do I want to distinguish myself in society? • How do I see myself? (What is my self-image and my sense of self-worth?)

your personal mission, vision, key roles, and objectives, you are putting yourself in front of a mirror; on the basis of this acquired clarity, you will have more creative ideas, improve your ability to learn, and become more successful. Therefore, everyone in the organization should be encouraged to formulate his or her own PBSC in order to develop self-knowledge. A better self-image and greater self-knowledge lead, after all, to greater learning ability. To that end we have to ask ourselves and be open to three primary questions: *Who am I? For what purpose am I here on earth? And where am I going?*

These questions involve our personal ambition. When the personal mission and vision are expressed, they should be formulated positively and in the present tense, as if everything is happening now. In Table 3.1 you will find the basic questions to answer. Your personal mission statement includes your life philosophy and your primary life objective. It indicates what you are living for and what your deepest aspirations are. It functions as an ethical compass that gives direction to your life. To put your personal mission into words, you will also have to determine what you enjoy doing and what satisfies you. Your personal vision statement describes where you want to go, which values and principles guide your way, what you want to help realize in your life, which ideal characteristics you would like to have, which qualities you would like to have if you could be exactly who you wanted to be, and what your ideal is with respect to your profession, environment, health, and other issues. Your personal mission and vision is a concrete translation of your inner longings. Therefore, your inner voice and your deeper convictions about how your life should be play an important role here.

Your key roles regard the way you wish to fulfill different roles in your life, in order to realize your personal mission and vision. For example, what type of relationship would you like to have with your friends, family, neighbors, and others? According to Stephen Covey (1993), these three elements (personal mission, vision, and key roles) form a "constitution" on which your own life and behavior are based and by which you review decisions regarding what you want to achieve and do. They involve your inner needs and motives as well as your self-consciousness, power of imagination, and conscience. Through your conscience you come into contact with your principles, which in turn are made effective through your personal talents. On this basis, you will be able to give direction to your life. The pesonal mission, vision, and key roles, which I call personal ambition, should be formulated in such a way that you are inspired to reflect upon your life and everything you undertake. According to Covey, you will gain insight into your personal mission, vision, and key roles when you answer the following two questions: What do you want to have engraved on your tombstone? Which memories would you like to leave behind after you pass away? In other words, what would you like people to say about you after your death, and what difference do you want to make with your presence here on earth?

Personal mission and vision statements are most effective when they comply with the following criteria:

- The mission is short, clear, simple, and formulated in the present tense; it is concrete and can be used as a guideline. It can also be visualized by means of a drawing.

- The mission and vision are unique for each person and are recognizable to others.

- The mission and vision are specific to each person and also include ethical starting points, with an emphasis on skills, principles, values, and standards, such as integrity, reliability, trust, helpfulness, credibility, frankness, teamwork, and other values. Integrity, which entails the discipline to live according to your inner truth, is a concept that often appears in personal mission statements.

- The mission and vision are formulated positively and captivatingly and are durable.
- The vision is ambitious and inspiring; it gives direction to personal initiatives and creativity, and combines personal power and energy.
- The vision is directive; it takes care of inner guidance and determines today's actions in order to reach an optimum future.
- The vision indicates how a person wants to distinguish himself or herself in society.
- The vision is also based on self-image, self-knowledge, self-acceptance, and self-development; it requires a positive image of ourselves and of others. The biggest hindrance to success in creating our vision and mission is our own thinking. Ordinarily we do not really think about ourself and we are blocked by our mindset.

Answering the mentioned simple but profoundly personal questions can help you formulate your personal mission, vision, key roles, and objectives. These questions are connected to your inner voice and enable you to discover the truth about yourself and your life—that is, your identity. The following breathing exercises can help you turn your attention inward. In fact, breathing and the ability to think have the same origin in human beings. Thought control follows breathing control and vice versa (Yesudian, 1991). For this reason I am here introducing a breathing exercise that will help as you formulate your Personal Balanced Scorecard (Rampersad, 2002).

Breathing Exercise

Sit on the ground or in a chair with your back in an upright position and your shoulders relaxed. Let your hands relax on your knees and close your eyes. Inhale slowly, deeply and relaxed, then hold your breath for a moment and feel how, with every slow exhalation, vitality flows from your lungs through your whole body. You will feel yourself becoming light and totally relaxed. With each inhalation and exhalation ask yourself one of the questions below and listen closely to the answers of your inner voice. Remember these answers and write them down immediately after this meditation exercise. Because of the large number of questions, it is advisable to make a selection of the most important questions listed below and to do this exercise in a couple of stages of 15 to 20 minutes each. By doing this regularly, you will not only gain more self-knowledge but also more energy, which will enable you to achieve a lot of things by yourself. For this breathing exercise you can use the following questions:

- Who am I? What is my identity?

- What is my self-image? How do I see myself?

- What kind of person am I? What do I stand for? What do I believe in?

- Which values and principles are closest to my heart, are sacred to me, and are rooted most deeply in my life? For example: honesty, helping others, self-development, expertise, money, enjoyment, affection, working together pleasantly, getting respect, status, etc.

- Which of these values clash with each other and with my strong sides?

- How do I create meaning in my life and see to it that everything is not about earning money?

- To what extent is material wealth important to me?

- Where do I stand and where do I want to go?

- How and what do I want to be? What do I hope to become? In the broadest sense, what do I want to achieve with my life? What do I live for?

- What prevents me from being who I want to be and what I want to be?

- How do I want to know myself and be known to others?

- If I die, what legacy would I like to leave behind, and what would I like to have meant to others?

- What difference will it have made that I existed?

- What do others say about me? What do I think about others?

- What are my ambitions and deepest aspirations about the community in which I want to live? What do I want to help realize?

- What do I most want to learn? What do I very much like to do? What do I think is very important? What do I find nice and attractive? What makes me happy or sad? What am I willing to sacrifice to realize my objectives? What do I really want?

- What do I want to invest in life and what do I want to gain from it?

- How would I prefer my daily life to be?

- What gives me satisfaction?

- In which kind of environment do I prefer to be?

- How is my health?

- To what extent are spiritual values important to me? What do I think of religion?
- How do I connect with my life companion, friends, family, colleagues, and others?
- Why did I go to work for my present employer?
- How am I at work?
- Why do I do what I do? What is the importance of what I do?
- What am I good at and what not? In what did I fail? What are my biggest failures?
- What have I done up till now, and what have I achieved?
- What is difficult for me to give up in my private, social, and business life?
- Which social questions intrigue me? Which social contributions would I like to make?
- What do I want to be in my organization? What am I trying to achieve? What is keeping me back?
- Which contribution am I trying to make to the realization of the organizational mission and vision?
- What are the most important motivators in my job?
- To which job do I aspire? What are my wishes? What do I strive for?
- What is happening to my profession, material possessions, family, life companion, friends, and others?
- Why am I active in a certain club?
- Will the things mentioned above still be important to me ten years from now?

All these questions are related to being and becoming. This exercise allows you to think deeply about yourself and makes you aware of yourself and your core beliefs. By listening closely and intently to your inner voice, which systematically answers the above questions for you, you will be able to discover and change your obstructive beliefs. By doing this, you will gain more insight into the workings of your mind and the influence this has on your personal behavior, thinking, and learning ability. Through this you can also accomplish the following:

- Increase your personal effectiveness and deliver mind-expanding performances.

- Discover your subconscious motives and through this get more out of yourself and coach yourself effectively.
- Understand your thoughts better and thus better control your inner conflicts (between feelings and reason) and come in contact with your inner truth.
- Deal with your environment with greater inner peace, harmony, self-confidence, and involvement.
- Create positive energy and utilize this effectively for the sake of yourself and others.
- Make optimum use of your personal abilities and capabilities, and eliminate annoying behavior.
- Think and act more proactively, deal with your attitude in a more conscious way, and create a positive atmosphere.
- Deal better with emotions, stress, and burn-out.
- Divide your attention more satisfactorily between work, hobbies, and family.
- Improve your personal learning style.

In addition to all this, you will gain more insight into your personal ambitions.

To illustrate the aforementioned, an example of a personal mission statement is given here (Fijlstra and Wullings, 1998):

Personal Mission of a Manager: *Reviving the organization and the lives of the people I love.*

The boxed text shows the personal vision statement of Henry Ford (1863–1947), who was the first to introduce the assembly line, in 1914, and to mass-produce cars (Lewis, 1907, p. 494). The price of cars then dropped, which made them accessible to the general public. Until 1920 Ford had the largest and fastest factory in the world.

Personal Vision of Henry Ford

"I will build a motor car for the great multitude . . . constructed of the best materials, by the best men to be hired, after the simplest designs that modern engineering can devise . . . so low in price that no man making a good salary will be unable to own one—and enjoy with his family the blessing of hours of pleasure in God's great open spaces."

Another nice example of a personal vision is that of Joanne Kathleen Rowling: *I want to become a writer.* She has become the most successful author in history due to the success of the Harry Potter books. She had always wanted to be a writer and started writing at the age of six. Divorced, unemployed, and living on unemployment benefits, she wrote her first Harry Potter book while trying to keep warm in Edinburgh coffee shops with her baby sleeping beside her. At the moment she is the first author who has become a billionaire from the sale of her books.

Balancing Personal Ambition and Personal Behavior

The first step on the way to sustainable personal improvement is to give attention to your personal ambition. Aligning your ambition with your behavior is necessary for developing inner peace and personal charisma, as well as for improving your credibility with others (Rampersad, 2003). When you do this you avoid conflict with your conscience and act in an ethical manner. Indeed, whereas we judge ourselves by our invisible behavioral patterns, others judge us by our visible behavioral patterns—what we do and say. This balancing process is about the interaction between, on the one hand, your aspirations, intentions, purpose, principles, ethical standards, and values— in other words, your personal ambition—and, on the other hand, how others interpret you. There is always potential difference, which is often difficult to accept, between how you see yourself and who you want to be, and how others see and judge you.

To become the person you have envisioned in your personal ambition, you also have to know how others see you and what they think of you. When you know this, your self-knowledge increases and you are able to improve the effectiveness of your actions. Therefore, this process of developing self-knowledge involves the establishment of a balance between your personal ambition (which envisions a higher level of consciousness) and your personal behavior (which refers to your present behavior), see Figure 3.2. As we have discussed, your personal ambition is also shaped by your mindsets. Behind these mindsets are hidden your motives and inner needs, which are expressed in your personal behavior. Thus, behind our behavior are hidden motives. Our most important motive is *to be happy*; in order to achieve this the most important conditions are good health and a balanced mind. Our behavior is therefore determined more by our inner needs than by external surroundings. In order to achieve real personal improvement and change it is necessary first to find a balance between behavior and inner motives. The central questions in this contemplative process are: How do my ideals, ambitions, intentions,

Figure 3.2

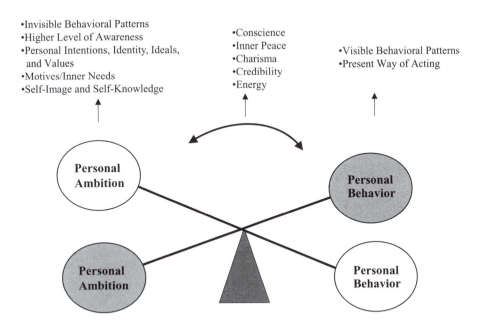

Balancing Personal Ambition and Personal Behavior

needs, and deepest desires fit my present actions? Does my personal ambition reflect my desire to act ethically? Are there contradictions in my personal ambition? In what way does my behavior influence my views, and vice versa? Do I act in accordance with high ethical standards?

> Personal (<Mission>, <Vision>, <Key Roles>) ≈ Personal Behavior
> Personal Ambition ≈ Personal Behavior

When people find harmony between their personal ambition and their personal behavior, they will not come into conflict with their own *conscience* and will be able to work efficiently in a goal-oriented way for continuous improvement, development, and learning. According to Selvazajan Yesudian (1991, p. 47), our conscience is the inner voice that talks to us with firm conviction to help us distinguish between right and wrong, between fact and fiction. It is a voice that whispers to us what we can do best and guides us in our daily activities. It is a voice that we can trust and on which we can build our existence. It is the only reliable compass to follow if there is a conflict between the mind that reasons and the heart that decides.

Figure 3.3

The Personal Ambition of Frank Jansen

Personal Mission
To live with integrity and mean something to others.

Personal Vision
I want to fulfill my mission in the following way.
- Be honest with others
- Work with others harmoniously, help each other, inspire others, and share knowledge
- Do things that make a difference in the lives of others
- Take initiative, learn from mistakes, and continuously improve and develop myself
- Strive for physical, mental, and financial health
- Have respect and appreciation for others, as well as be appreciated by my family, friends, employer, and associates
- Deliver high-quality work so that my employer is continuously satisfied

Key Roles
In order to achieve my mission, the following key roles have top priority.
- *Husband*: my wife is the most important person in my life
- *Father*: I want to promote the capabilities and creativity of my children continuously and to help them reach a happy existence
- *Christian*: God can count on me to keep my duty towards others
- *Manager*: Help the organization where I work become successful and by doing this serve society
- *Student*: I want to learn something new every day, I will always be a scholar

Aligning your personal ambition and behavior ensures that your actions are ethical and in accord with your conscience. You thus obtain better insight into your own behavior, strengths, and weaknesses, as well as your personal goals. Moreover, your personal mission is thus not only based on insight into yourself but also on reality. Continuous learning and the gaining of knowledge about people, theories, techniques, methods, and so on are therefore also inevitable. Creating organizational harmony between personal and shared ambitions is discussed in the second half of this chapter, under "Formulating the Organizational Balanced Scorecard." Balancing these two types of ambition is the essential first step in the process of achieving durable organizational improvement and change. Unfortunately, these are steps that are often ignored by management.

To illustrate this initial step in the PBSC model, the personal ambition of Frank Jansen, the acting manager of Business Jet (an airline company for business people), is presented in Figure 3.3.

Defining Personal Critical Success Factors

The personal critical success factors can be derived directly from the personal mission, vision, and key roles. These factors form the

Table 3.2

Critical Success Factors of Frank Jansen	
Financial Perspective	**External Perspective**
• Financial health	• Be appreciated by family, friends, colleagues, and employer • Deliver high-quality work
Internal Perspective	**Knowledge and Learning Perspective**
• Working together harmoniously, helping each other, inspiring others, and sharing knowledge with each other • Strive for physical and mental health	• Take initiative, learn from my mistakes, continuously improve and develop myself • Learn something new every day and always be a scholar

realizable milestones in your life. They are related to the *financial perspective* (the extent to which you can you fulfill your financial needs), the *external perspective* (your relation with your life companion, children, friends, employer, colleagues, and others), the *internal perspective* (your physical health and mental state), and the *knowledge and learning perspective* (your capabilities or skills and learning ability). In essence, formulating the personal critical success factors is about answering the question: Which factors in my personal ambition are decisive for my personal well-being and success? Table 3.2 shows the most important critical success factors of Frank Jansen. These are derived from his personal mission, vision, and key roles. Figure 3.4 illustrates how the critical success factors in the Personal as well as in the Organizational BCS are linked, per perspective, to the objectives, performance measures, targets, and improvement actions.

Formulating Personal Objectives

Each personal critical success factor is linked to personal objectives, which are related to one of the four BSC perspectives. Your personal objectives describe a desired personal result that you want to achieve in order to fulfill your personal vision. The personal mission and vision are long-term goals, and the objectives are short-term goals. Your personal objectives emerge from your own evaluation of your strengths and weaknesses and are derived from your personal critical success factors. When analyzing your strengths, ask yourself the following

Figure 3.4

Linking Critical Success Factors to Objectives, Performance Measures, Targets, and Improvement Actions

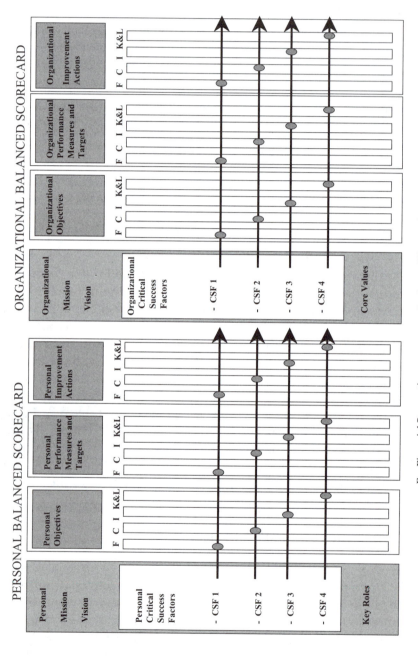

F = Financial Perspective

C = Customer / External Perspective

I = Internal Perspective

K&L = Knowledge & Learning Perspective

questions (see also McCall, 1998): What are some of the strengths that have contributed to your success up to the present time? How can these create problems for you? Which problems would you like to handle better? When analyzing your shortcomings the following questions are central: What do you think are your most important shortcomings? Has anyone ever mentioned one of these shortcomings to you? Can you describe a situation where one of these shortcomings would be a serious handicap? You can also ask yourself the following question: What is the most important change I face regarding my work and career?

Factors that may relate to these questions are, for example, aptitude, talent, ability, intelligence, being goal-oriented, perseverance, self-control, health, integrity, creativity, tolerance, enthusiasm, the situation at home and at work, more responsibility, prestigious job, status, power, being free, having more free time, having more time for the children, and so on (Wijngaards, 1988). A recent study on time management conducted by the Dutch magazine *Intermediair* (2001) shows that Dutch managers are dissatisfied with the way they spend their time, both at work and in their private life. They want to have time to:

- Think more (69.2% of the managers).
- Take more courses (69.9%).
- Take better care of their children (44.2%).
- Spend less time at the office (65.3%).
- Participate more in sports (75.1%).
- Have more time for social contacts (71.9%).
- Sleep more. On average, managers sleep 6.8 hours per night, whereas they would prefer to sleep 7.5 hours. Thus, they miss 40 minutes sleep every night; 33.6% say that they usually lack sleep.
- Have more time off; 38.8% of managers want a longer period of time away from work (they want to be on sabbatical).
- Have more time to spend on e-mail (60%); now they spend an average of 54 minutes per day on e-mail and 15.5 minutes on the Internet.

You will also have to face and include in your personal objectives the things that you are not good at doing. In addition, include any customs that restrict you or influence your life unfavorably and cause you to deliver poor personal results.

Defining Personal Performance Measures and Targets

Your personal objectives flow from your inner voice as well as from an analysis of your personal strengths and weaknesses. These objective might be, for example, raising and supporting a family; being helpful; enjoying mental and physical health; financial stability; enjoying things in life; being appreciated by others; having good friends and colleagues; having more time off; and so on. These are all related to the primary objectives of *becoming happier, having peace of mind, achieving something, and building relationships* (see also Maslow, 1970). Your performance measures make the personal objectives measurable. A personal performance measure is a measuring point with which your thinking and acting can be judged. To each performance measure you can link a desired value that can be used to measure it. This target is also dependent on your level of ambition. Performance measures and targets need to comply with SMART criteria. They should be:

- *Specific*. They must be specifically formulated so that they can also influence behavior.
- *Measurable*. They must be formulated in such a way that they can measure the objective.
- *Achievable*. They must be realistic, realizable, feasible and acceptable.
- *Result-oriented*. They must be related to concrete results.
- *Time-specific*. They must be time-constrained so that their realization may be tracked through time.

To illustrate the development of the PBSC, the personal critical success factors, objectives, performance measures, and targets of Frank Jansen are represented in Table 3.3. These PBSC elements have been derived from his personal ambition.

Formulating Personal Improvement Actions

The following step in the personal strategy development process contains the formulation of your personal improvement actions for realizing your personal mission, vision, and objectives. They involve continuous improvement of your competences, skills, behavior, and activities and are aimed at your personal well-being and success (also in your private life). Here the *how* is central: How do I want to achieve my personal results? How can I realize my personal objectives? How can I improve my behavior? How do I see to it that I learn

Table 3.3

Personal Critical Success Factors, Objectives, Performance Measures, and Targets of Frank Jansen, Acting Manager of Business Jet

FINANCIAL

Personal Critical Success Factors	Personal Objectives	Personal Performance Measures	Personal Targets
• Financial health	• More earnings • Reliable future earnings	• Salary increase • Employment contract	• At least 5% per year • From temporary (as acting manager) to permanent employment contract (for unlimited time) within two years
		• Pension • Disability Insurance	• 13% of gross salary • 5% of gross salary
	• Curbing spending	• Ratio of income to spending	• Increase of at least 5% within two years

EXTERNAL

Personal Critical Success Factors	Personal Objectives	Personal Performance Measures	Personal Targets
• Being appreciated by family, friends, colleagues, and employer	• Being appreciated by life companion	• Number of times being together in a charming atmosphere	• At least once a week
	• Being appreciated by own children	• Being cared for by own children	• Every time there is an occasion for it
	• Being appreciated by friends	• Number of real friends	• Increase depending on the circumstances

(continues)

Table 3.3 *continued*

Personal Critical Success Factors, Objectives, Performance Measures, and Targets of Frank Jansen, Acting Manager of Business Jet

EXTERNAL

Personal Critical Success Factors	Personal Objectives	Personal Performance Measures	Personal Targets
• Deliver high-quality work	• Being appreciated by employer • Improved level of satisfaction of employees • Greater trust of my employer in fulfillment of my job	• Level of reward • Number of authorities • Degree of satisfaction of employees • Level of satisfaction of employer	• Increase of at least 5% per year • Increase of 25% within two years • At least 80% within 1.5 years • At least 80% within 1.5 years

INTERNAL

Personal Critical Success Factors	Personal Objectives	Personal Performance Measures	Personal Targets
• Working together harmoniously, helping each other, inspiring others and sharing knowledge with each other • Strive for physical and mental health	• Improved level of satisfaction from others with respect to teamwork and personal contact • Satisfaction • Physically healthy and mentally strong	• Perception score from others with regard to teamwork and personal contact • Helping others • Percent of sick leave • Level of tension • Level of immunity to stress	• At least 80% within 2 years • To be determined • Less than 2% in 1 year • Decrease by at least 50% in 2 years • Decrease by at least 50% in 2 years

	Personal Objectives	Personal Performance Measures	Personal Targets
	• More time off	• Number of paid vacation days a year	• At least 17 days
	• Enjoying the good things in life	• Enjoyment	• To be determined

KNOWLEDGE AND LEARNING

Personal Critical Success Factors	Personal Objectives	Personal Performance Measures	Personal Targets
• Take initiative, learn from my mistakes, continuously improve and develop myself	• Higher labor productivity	• Labor productivity	• Increase by at least 25% within 2 years
		• Number of effective initiatives as a manager	• Increase by at least 30% per year
		• Number of successful strategic improvement proposals	• Minimal increase of 30% per year
• Learn something new everyday, and always a scholar	• Improved management competences	• Percent of available management competences	• 85% within 2 years
	• Opportunity for self-development in the field of business management	• Number of management courses followed	• 3 courses per year
	• Improved leadership skills	• Number of new management books read	• At least 10 per year
		• Percent of employees that feel they are working under effective leadership	• 85% within 2 years

continuously, both personally and within a team? How can I get to know myself better? During this formulation process it is advisable to brainstorm your intentions with a person you trust, one who will ask you questions and give you feedback. By doing this, you will gain deeper insight into your personal ambition. The implementation of the personal improvement actions is discussed in depth in Chapter 5. This implementation process is based on the Deming cycle.

Frank Jansen of Business Jet also formulated a few improvement actions in relation to his personal objectives. Due to the numerousness of his formulated improvement actions, he prioritized them. He gave the highest priority for implementation to those improvement actions that would make the greatest contribution to his most important critical success factors. One of Frank's most important improvement actions deals with *decreasing stress* by regular exercise, daily meditation, relaxation exercises, translating negative feelings into positive ones at every opportunity, and creating enjoyment at work for the sake of more laughter.

According to my own family medical practitioner the most important symptoms of stress are: a high level of sick leave, headaches, aggression, sleepless nights, nervousness, depression, high blood pressure, fatigue, fear, smoking and drinking heavily, lack of concentration, and memory loss. According to Deepak Chopra (1994) exercise is an essential element in the process of creating inner harmony and a very effective way to battle stress and to improving sleep. He gives the following related guidelines:

- Take daily walks of 30 minutes; the best time for this is from six to ten o'clock in the morning. Don't exercises after six o'clock at night, apart from quiet walks.

- You can also pick another kind of light to moderate uninterrupted exercise, such as cycling or swimming. A workout machine is suitable too. Wear easy, loose-fitting clothes.

- Don't exercise right after you've eaten; wait for two to three hours.

- During exercises hold every pose for a short time and then release it gently. Focus your attention and breathing on the part of your body that is being stretched.

- Use only 50% of your physical capacity, if you are able to cycle about 6 miles, instead cycle only 3 miles. By exercising regularly your ability will increase. Do not force your body.

- Do not exert yourself too much; during and after exercise you should feel energetic and strong, not fatigued and weak.

- If you are accustomed to exerting yourself a lot, reduce this to half during one month and see what this does for your sleep.

Stress endurance is one of the most important competences of the functioning assessment of John van Dam, leader of the Security team of Business Jet (see Appendixes A and B). The Business Jet case will be discussed in Chapter 6. Although Frank Jansen's other improvement actions have been left out here, it is useful to note that when Frank formulated these actions he also took into account aspects such as acceptance by others, feasibility, practicality, and time needed to implement the improvement action in question. In the next section a method used by Business Jet to select the most important organizational improvement actions for implementation is discussed. This approach is also applicable to personal improvement actions.

Formulating the Organizational Balanced Scorecard

> If a man advances confidently in the direction of his dreams to live the life he has imagined, he will meet with a success unexpected in common hours.
>
> *Henry David Thoreau*

The Organizational Balanced Scorecard includes the overall (corporate) organizational mission, vision, core values, critical success factors, strategic objectives, performance measures, targets, and improvement actions. These OBSC elements are discussed in greater detail in this section.

Formulating the Shared Organizational Ambition

Formulating the shared mission and vision as well as the related critical success factors and core values comprises the first step in the organizational strategy development process. The most important core questions are illustrated in Table 3.4. Together the organizational mission and vision form an important management tool that reflects the soul of the organization. They indicate what the organization stands for, why it exists, what its primary objective is, where it wants to go, how it plans to get there based on its values (its driving forces), and the important points everyone needs to concentrate on. Together they

Table 3.4

Core Questions to Be Used When Formulating the Organizational Mission and Vision			
Shared Organizational Ambition	Core Questions	Aspects	Implication for Employees
MISSION	**WHY DO WE EXIST?** Who are we? What do we do? Where are we now? For what purpose and why does our organization exist? What is our identity? What is our reason for existing? What is our primary function? What is our ultimate primary goal? For whom do we exist? Who are our most important stakeholders? Why do we do what we do? Which fundamental need do we provide?	• Ultimate primary goal • Primary function • Reasons for existence • Stakeholders The mission is not linked to a time horizon.	• Why do we work there? • Can we identify ourselves with the applied procedures and working methods? • Why do we find it meaningful and valuable that our organization exists? • What do we want to mean to each other and our surroundings? • Which value added do we want to deliver? Important issues here include motivation, identification, and single-mindedness.

VISION		
WHERE ARE WE GOING TOGETHER? What is the ambitious dream of our organization? What is our vision of the future? Where do we go from here? What are our long-term ambitions? What do we want to achieve in the long run? What changes lie ahead in the business landscape? What is our mutual image of a desired and reachable prospective situation, and what is the route of change needed to reach this? What is decisive for our success? Which factors make us unique? What do we stand for? What connects us? Who do we want to be? What is essential in our attitude? And what do we believe in?	• Developments • Ambitions • Core values • Critical success factors • Core competences Vision is linked to a time horizon, as well as to strategic objectives, performance measures, and targets.	• Where are we going together? • What is the required long-term organizational perspective? Important issues here include guiding personal ambitions and creativity, creating a climate for drastic change, self-guidance, strengthening the belief in the future and thus releasing energy, and strengthening single-mindedness and the unity of behavior.

produce the shared organizational ambition and have an important impact on the bonding of employees to the organization and to their performance.

A successfully formulated organizational ambition shows people how their activities can contribute to the whole, which allows them to work together with greater enthusiasm toward organizational objectives. Subsequently, they feel proud about making a useful contribution to something worthwhile. The organizational ambition only works in this way, however, when employees believe that management has a long-term commitment to it. The organizational mission and vision give direction to an organization and function as a compass or road map. The convincing articulation of a decisive, inspiring, goal-oriented, recognizable, challenging, and fascinating mission and vision through which people feel bonded and touched usually leads to more devotion, satisfaction, and commitment. After all, such a shared ambition inspires creativity and motivates and mobilizes people. It gives them energy and therefore leads to better performance.

This process is a way to create the future of the organization together. According to Peter Senge (1990), this future is positively influenced by a *creative tension* between where the organization wants to go (organizational vision) and where it stands now (existing reality). In this, the following principles play a role (Hargrove, 1995):

- *Aspiration principle.* What do we want to become?
- *Lever principle.* How can we apply our resources in such a way that they have the biggest effect?
- *Convergence principle.* What can we achieve together?
- *Concentration principle.* On which ambitious objectives should we concentrate?

Used as a management instrument, the organizational mission-vision gives the opportunity to create unity in the behavior of employees, allows them to be proud of their organization, and lets them focus on those relevant activities that create customer value and eliminate unproductive activities. An effective organizational mission-vision also provides a foundation for decision making and helps managers determine how to use available resources correctly.

Effectively formulated organizational mission and vision statements comply with the following criteria:

- The mission is short, concrete, and simple; it is understandable and clear to everyone in the organization so that it can be used as a concrete guide for taking action. It can also be visualized by means of a drawing.

- The mission is not focused explicitly on profitability or on any other financial element, and it describes the *why* rather than the *what*.
- The mission and vision appeal to the largest group of stakeholders and are formulated in positive terms.
- The mission and vision are realistic and recognizable for everyone; their feasibility is not open for discussion.
- The mission and vision are organization specific; their emphasis is on those elements that distinguish it from other organizations. At the same time the borders of the mission, specifically, are broadly defined to allow for the development of new initiatives.
- The mission and vision also include ethical starting points and cultural components, such as respect for the individual, contributions to society, helping people to develop their possibilities, and so on.
- The vision is ambitious and challenging; it inspires the employee, gives an attractive view of the final objective, gives guidance to initiatives and creativity, appeals directly to people, and joins forces within the organization.
- The vision gives direction; it determines today's actions in order to achieve an optimal future.
- The vision is complete; it takes into consideration all four scorecard perspectives financial, customers, internal processes, and knowledge and learning as well as society too.
- The vision advances; its elements are based on continuous improvement, learning, and development. The vision should be revised every ten years in order to keep it fresh. An effective vision can generally give the organization successful direction for decades.
- The vision is linked to time, and the mission is timeless.

Organizational Mission

The organizational mission encompasses the identity of the organization and indicates its reasons for existence: for whom it exists, why it exists, which needs it fulfills, what its ultimate objective is, what its primary function is, and who its most important stakeholders are. Related questions include: What activities are we occupied with? What kind of services or products do we provide? How do we define the customers we serve? On whose behalf do we make an effort? Which unique values do we give to our customers? A successful mission statement also describes to a greater extent the organization's activities and identifies the range of work in terms of customers, employees, services, and products. The mission determines the nature of the organization and is timeless. This *"genetic code"* of the organization is meant to help employees build a common understanding of the main objective, increase their devotion, and provide an explanation as to why their organization is different from the others. An effectively formulated and forcefully articulated mission creates unanimity in the behavior of employees, strengthens their single-mindedness, and improves the atmosphere of mutual communication within the organization.

Organizational Vision

The organizational vision includes the organization's long-term dream and indicates the route of transformation required to reach it. Besides that, the vision includes critical success factors, standards, and values. It also shows where and how the organization wants to distinguish itself from others. This implies that the organizational vision provides insight into *core competences*: the fields in which the organization excels, the reasons why customers use its products and services, and the principles of the employees (Hamel and Prahalad, 1994).

According to James Collins and Jerry Porras (1997), the vision helps the organization determine which core competences must be kept intact and saved, and in which future direction the organization should be worked. The starting point here is *cherish the core and stimulate progress*. The organizational vision is linked to a time horizon and its related strategic objectives and performance measures. Performance measures make the vision measurable. An effectively formulated and well-articulated organizational vision guides personal ambition and creativity, creates a climate for drastic change, strengthens belief in the future, and thus releases energy in the employees.

The vision also contains ethical starting points and is closely related to the organizational culture. Examples of these include *respecting the individual and the customer; contributing to society; helping employees develop their potentials; making customer satisfaction the most important goal; and teamwork*. Organizational culture is closely related to the behavior, standards, values, principles, emotions, and thought of the people who make up that culture (Lipton, 1997). These elements are determined by a number of factors such as education, religious beliefs, professional ethics, and so on. Research indicates that the

Figure 3.5

Mission and Vision of Business Jet

Mission
We are a safe and reliable airline company for business people.

Vision
In all aspects we want to be a professional organization, one that is the customers' first choice for business travel in all the regions where we operate. We want to achieve this by:

CSF Customer Perspective

1) Achieving excellent financial results and growing profitably, and through the successful introduction of innovative products and services;

CSF Financial Perspective

CSF Internal Processes Perspective

2) Offering our customers high-quality services and, due to our image, having a dominant share in the global market of business travel;

CSF Customer Perspective

3) Having airplanes depart and arrive on time, doing so more successfully than competitors, and creating an inspiring work environment that provides an atmosphere of team spirit, open communication, and process thinking;

CSF Internal Processes Perspective

4) Continuously developing our human potential, and, based on our knowledge, skills, and capabilities, acquiring competitive advantage.

CSF Knowledge and Learning Perspective

In order to be the most safe and reliable business travel company, everything within our organization will be focused on achieving top performances with a motivated working force that cares for the needs of the society we take part in.

CSF Internal Processes Perspective

Standards and Values

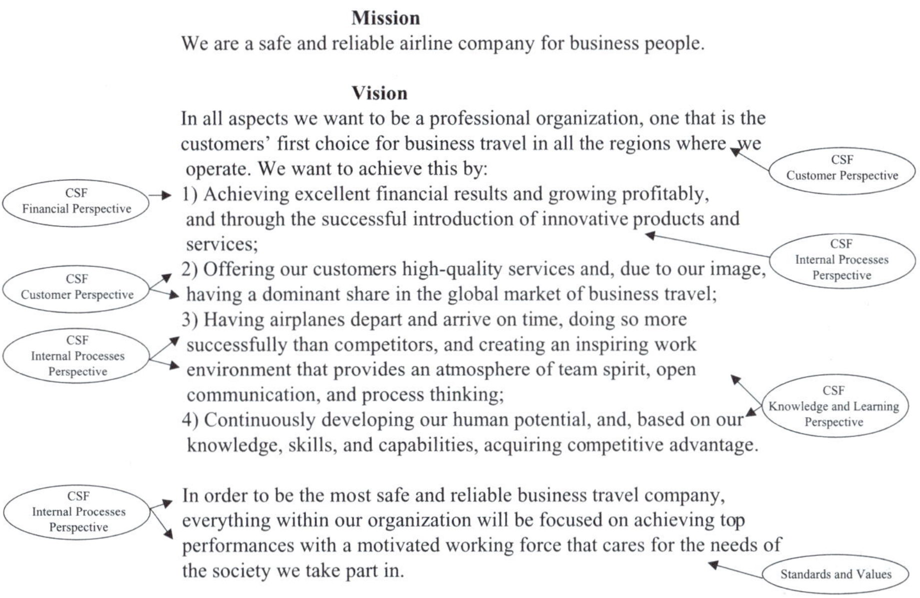

stronger the organizational culture is the more result-oriented employees are (Peters and Waterman, 1992). A culture is strong if the employees share many mental pursuits. Operational performance is usually positively influenced when organizational behavior is continuously aligned with organizational culture. Moreover, it seems that the commitment and involvement of employees is also optimal if their personal values and the core values of the organization match. When employees understand the organizational culture, they know what is expected of them. Core values function here as a foundation that supports and guides the job-related behavior of the employees.

To illustrate these points, the organizational mission and vision of Business Jet are provided in Figure 3.5. As can be seen, the vision of Business Jet consists of several critical success factors and a few elements regarding what the organization stands for. These organizational critical success factors will be discussed in detail in the next section.

The Mission-Vision Development Process

The mission-vision development process begins with the management team formulating the organizational mission and vision conceptually, and then communicating it during several sessions to all stakeholders. In practice, this dissemination of the shared ambition is done more and more through in-house conferences, where large groups of participants (30 to 80) are briefed, and then discuss the mission-vision with each other to learn how the strategy can be implemented. Based on this feedback adjustments are made and a definitive mission-vision statement is then formulated to which nearly everyone can subscribe. Afterwards, every business unit formulates its own vision based on the shared ambition of the organization. After employees have familiarized themselves with the vision of the business unit, they will use it as a guideline for formulating their own team's vision.

This process of mission-vision development is done at all organizational levels, with the active participation of all stakeholders at an early stage. This learning process is intuitive, iterative, and cyclic as well as democratic; it is based on the exchange of insight, creativity, and ideals. Peter Senge (1990) gives the following tips: treat everyone equally; strive for single-mindedness (absolute consensus is not required); stimulate interdependence and diversity; and concentrate on the process (not only on the formulation of the vision statement). With the development of the shared ambition, past and present insights and activities are aligned with future expectations. By exchanging thoughts with employees (*brainstorming* in a team, whereby each team is representative of the entire organization), employees and managers get better insight into the organizational course to follow; this will benefit the support and commitment within the whole organization.

The development process is therefore more important than the statement itself. When assessing the organizational vision, the following questions are central: *Does the vision give you direction, energy, strength, motivation, something to hold on to, and a feeling of warmth? Because of it do you feel like implementing your knowledge intensively and sharing it with others? Do you feel personally involved with the vision? Does it provide perspective to all stakeholders? Does it give an orientation to all key activities? Does the vision relate to you? Does it make you enthusiastic? Do you believe in it? Does the vision give you a feeling of direction? Will you work with all your might to realize the vision?* By asking and answering these questions you make choices that will gradually give greater and greater shape to the vision. This process consists of several diverging and converging cycles and proceeds spirally (see Figure 2.11). The phases of gathering information, making choices, and formulating the vision are hereby followed through cyclically. Top management starts this process, whereby the results are propagated from top to bottom. In order to do this, the management must give direction and support, as well as coach and think together with everyone instead of doing the thinking for the employees. When management then disseminates the shared ambition, it should do so not only with nice words and sentences, but also with feeling, decisiveness, enjoyment, pleasure, and passion.

Core Values

As we have seen, the organizational vision is based on a number of shared values that are used to strengthen the single-mindedness of the employees and positively influence their behavior. These values determine how people work to realize the vision; they express the behavior of all employees. The core values function as a foundation that gives direction and support to people at work. They relate to the way we treat each other and how we see customers, employees, suppliers, and society as a whole. According to James Collins and Jerry Porras (1997), the core values are the unchangeable guiding principles and fundamentals of an organization that are essential for its continuity. These include inner values, which determine where people within an organization stand. Some central questions here are: *Which values are precious to us? What do we stand for? How do we treat each other, and how do we work together? How do we think of ourselves? What are the desired characteristics of our cultural and leadership style?*

Thus, core values are related to the organizational culture; they are so fundamental that we cherish them even if we are not paid for them. Core values align people and function as the glue that binds the organization. They benefit commitment, loyalty, and devotion in all aspects of the organization, especially if these are in balance with the personal ambitions of people. As can be seen in practice, the effort and involvement of people are usually optimal when their own principles, standards, and values are aligned with those of the organization. It is therefore advisable to align the core values to the personal ambitions of individual employees and managers, and to then translate them to lower organizational levels. I will discuss this in more detail later. In general, organizations have three to six core values. Jack Welch formulated five core values to change General Electric: "loathing bureaucracy and all nonsense associated with it"; 'understanding what is meant by responsibility and devotion and decisiveness"; "determining aggressive objectives and realizing them with energetic integrity"; "having the faith to empower others"; and "nothing is a secret."

A set of core values of Business Jet is given in the following boxed text. Integrity and enjoyment play an important role here. Integrity deals with ethics, which I will discuss in the next section. Kamp (1999) writes the following about enjoyment:

> Richard Branson was being interviewed. He said that he dressed informally and made jokes to encourage his employees to do the same. He wanted them to consider enjoyment as an essential part of their job instead of something that only belongs to their private life. He believed he could encourage others to do the same if he approached work in a pleasant way.

Julie Bick (1997) made the following remarks based on her experiences at Microsoft:

> Team spirit is strengthened by shared experiences, irrespective if this is by working hard or by free time. Enjoyment increases companionship and morality. Therefore, regularly take time off to relax and make something worthwhile of special occasions.

Business Jet's Core Values

Business Jet is guided by the following core values:

Integrity: Doing business with integrity. Integrity is never compromised.

Enjoyment and Passion: Working with devoted people who enjoy their work, are passionate, and are driven to achieve superior performances in everything our airline company undertakes. Employee involvement is our way of life.

Customer Orientation: Listening continuously to our customers, discovering their expectations and providing them with the quality services they expect of us, and satisfying them constantly. They are the focus of everything we do.

Safe and Reliable: Being known as the safest and most reliable airline company for business people.

Linking the Shared Ambition with Ethics

Business ethics is an essential part of the Total Performance Scorecard concept. This implies that organizations must care about ethics and corporate social responsibility to ensure that their actions have integrity and reflect high ethical standards. The shared ambition should, therefore, be inspired by ethics. Ethics concerns human *duty* and the principles on which this duty is based (Thompson and

Strickland, 2002). Every company has an ethical duty to its shareholders, employees, customers, suppliers, and the community at large. Each of these stakeholders affects the organization and is in turn affected by it.

The duty to the shareholders arises out of the expectation of a superior return on investment and improved dividend payment. It is the moral duty of business executives and employees to pursue a profitable organization based on owner investment. A company's ethical duty to its employees arises out of respect for the worth and dignity of individuals who devote their energy to the business. Business executives also have the moral duty to promote employee interests such as competence development, career opportunities, job security, a safe and healthy workplace, and respect for the dignity and privacy due all human beings.

The ethical duty to the customer encompasses the provision of reliable products and services, at fair prices, that are delivered on time and within budget according to regulations. Organizations have the moral duty to protect customers: by voluntarily informing them about the ingredients in their products and whether they could have potential harmful effects; by recalling products they suspect have faulty parts or defective designs; and so on.

The duty to suppliers arises out of an organization's partnership relationship with them that is necessary to increase added value and realize a high-quality product. Companies confront several ethical issues in their supplier relationships. For example, is it ethical to purchase goods from suppliers who employ child labor, pay low wages, or have poor working conditions?

The ethical duty of the company to the community at large arises out of the fact that as a member of society, it is expected to be a good citizen. This is demonstrated by, for instance, paying taxes, being eco-conscious, supporting community activities, creating job opportunities, and operating responsibly.

A shared ethical ambition requires ethical behavior of everyone within the organization. In order to be successful, management and employees should act in accordance with the formulated principles and values. The boxed text discusses the infamous example of a successful company that had an effectively shared ethical ambition but nevertheless went bankrupt because it was undermined by the unethical behavior of its management (Thompson and Strickland, 2002). The Enron case stresses the importance of balancing the personal ambition of management and employees with their personal behavior and with the shared organizational ambition. The mutual alignment of the personal and shared ambition will be discussed in the next section.

The Enron Debacle: A Bold Shared Ambition Undermined by Management's Unethical Behavior

Until its crash in the fall of 2001, Enron was one of the world's largest electricity, natural gas, and broadband trading companies, with revenues of over $100 billion. Enron's strategic intent was to become *the* blue-chip energy and communications company of the twenty-first century through its business efforts in four core areas: Enron Wholesale Services, Enron Broadband Services, Enron Energy Services, and Enron Transportation Services. Enron management claimed that each of these business units supported the company's shared ambition, stated as follows:

Who Are We and Why Do We Exist?

We offer a wide range of physical, transportation, financial, and technical solutions to thousands of customers around the world. Our business is to create value and opportunity for your business. We do this by combining our financial resources, access to physical commodities, and knowledge to create innovative solutions to challenging industrial problems. We are best known for our natural gas and electricity products, but today we also offer retail energy and broadband products. These products give customers the flexibility they need to compete today.

What Do We Believe?

We begin with a fundamental belief in the inherent wisdom of *open markets*. We are convinced that consumer choice and competition lead to lower prices and innovation. Enron is a laboratory for *innovation*. That is why we employ the best and the brightest people. And we believe that every employee can make a difference here. We encourage people to make a difference by creating an environment where everyone is allowed to achieve their full potential and where everyone has a stake in the outcome. We think this entrepreneurial approach stimulates *creativity*. We value *diversity* and are committed to removing all barriers to employment and advancement based on sex, sexual orientation, race, religion, age, ethnic background, national origin, or physical limitation. Our success is measured by the success of our *customers*. We are committed to meeting their energy needs with solutions that offer them a competitive advantage. And we work with them in ways that reinforce the benefits of a long-term partnership with Enron. In everything we do, we operate safely and with concern for the *environment*. This is a responsibility we take seriously in all the different places around the world where we do business. We're changing the way energy is delivered, as well as the market for it. We're reinventing the fundamentals of this business by providing energy at lower costs and in more usable forms than has been provided before. Everything we do is about change. *Together* we are creating the leading energy company in the world. Together, we are defining the energy company of the future.

Our Core Values

Integrity: We work with customers and prospects openly, honestly, and sincerely. When we say we will do something, we will do it; when we say we cannot or will not do something, then we won't do it.

Respect: We treat others as we would like to be treated ourselves. We do not tolerate abusive or disrespectful treatment. Ruthlessness, callousness, and arrogance don't belong here.

Excellence: We are satisfied with nothing less than the very best in everything we do. We will continue to raise the bar for everyone. The great fun here will be for all of us to discover just how good we can really be.

Communication: We have an obligation to communicate. Here, we take time to talk with one another and to listen. We believe that information is meant to move and that information moves people.

But gaping flaws in Enron's strategy began to emerge in the Fall of 2001, starting with revelations that the company had incurred billions more in debt to grow its energy trading business than was first apparent from its balance sheet. The off-balance-sheet debt was hidden by obscurely worded footnotes to the company's financial statements involving mysterious partnerships in which the company's Chief Financial Officer (CFO) had an interest (and was apparently using it to make millions in profits on the side). After Enron's stock price slid from the mid-$80s to the high-$30s despite glowing earnings reports, the company's well-regarded Chief Executive Officer suddenly resigned for "personal reasons" in August 2001. Weeks later, the company's CFO was asked to resign as details of his conflict of interest in the off-balance-sheet partnerships came to light.

Meanwhile, top company executives continued to insist publicly that the company was in sound financial shape and that its business was secure, hoping to keep customers from taking their business to rivals and to reassure concerned shareholders. But Enron's crown jewel, its energy trading business, which generated about $60 billion in reported revenues, came under increased scrutiny, both for the debt that had been amassed to support such enormous trading volumes and for its very thin profit margins (some of which were suspect due to accounting treatments that had won the stamp of approval of Arthur Andersen, the company's auditor). Within weeks, Enron filed for bankruptcy, its stock price fell below $1 per share, its stock was delisted from the New York Stock Exchange, and a scandal of unprecedented proportions grew almost daily. Arthur Anderson fired the partner on the Enron account when it appeared that working papers

(continues)

relating to the audit were destroyed in an apparent effort to obstruct a congressional investigation of the details of Enron's collapse. Enron's board fired Arthur Anderson as the company's auditor.

Then Enron was caught destroying documents (as late as January 2002) in an apparent attempt to hide the company's action from investigators. Enron's chairman and CEO resigned; the company's former vice chairman committed suicide after it became public that he had vigorously protested Enron's accounting practices earlier in 2001. It also came out that senior company officers had sold shares of Enron stock months earlier, when the stock price slide first began. Enron employees—most of whom had their entire 401(k) monies tied up in Enron stock and were precluded from selling their shares, and 4,000 of whom were dismissed in a last-ditch effort to cut costs—watched helplessly as their retirement savings were wiped out by the crash. The extent of management's unethical behavior is still under investigation. But Enron management clearly did not act in accordance with the principles and values it espoused.

Source: Used with permission from A. A. Thompson and A. J. Strickland. *Strategic Management: Concepts and Cases*. Boston: McGraw-Hill, 2002, pp. 65–66.

A variety of methods can be employed to improve business ethics, such as (see also Miller, Catt, and Carlson, 1996):

- *Writing a code of ethics;* this tells employees and managers how to act in various situations, and makes clear to them that they will be expected to recognize the ethical dimensions of corporate policies and actions. This should always be included in the organizational shared ambition. Free and open communication is the key element in implementing codes of ethics. Steve Jobs, CEO of Apple Computer, stated the following about such communication:

  > I believe strongly in open communication within the firm. All employees have complete access to almost all information in the company, including other employees' salaries. Only when employees understand the entire master plan for the firm will they be able to make effective decisions that are in line with the company's values.

- *Commitment to ethical business behavior;* top management must be openly committed to ethical conduct and must provide constant leadership in tending and renewing the values of the organization. Everyone within the organization must be made aware of the core values of the firm's ethics program. Involvement and commitment of personnel at all organizational levels is important in order to develop higher levels of trust and pride in the business.

- *Setting up a permanent ethics committee.*
- *Employing an ombudsperson;* someone in the company who can go directly to top management with problems or complaints.
- *Establishing "hot lines" for comments and complaints regarding unethical acts;* to process reports of unethical behavior. Employees should feel it is their duty to report violations.
- *Conducting in-house ethics seminars.*
- *Developing communication programs that emphasize corporate ethics;* to inform and motivate employees, customers, suppliers, shareholders, and the general public.
- *Executing ethical audits;* to ensure compliance by personnel on at least an annual basis.
- *Introducing enforcement procedures;* including discipline and dismissal for violations.
- *Paying special attention to values and ethics in recruiting and hiring practices.*
- *Giving recognition and rewards;* for exemplary ethical employee or managerial performances.

Balancing Personal Ambition with Shared Ambition

In the first half of this chapter we discussed the alignment of personal ambition and personal behavior for the purpose of acting ethically, creating inner peace, developing personal charisma, and improving personal credibility. Here the alignment of the personal ambition with the shared organizational ambition is central for the purpose of stimulating the enjoyment, active participation, and motivation of employees. Once these two ambitions have been formulated there is the need for a period of reflection, a time in which to think profoundly about balancing these two scorecard elements. This process of balancing deals with obtaining a high level of concordance between personal and organizational goals and a mutual rise in value. People do not work with devotion and do not spend energy on something they do not believe in or agree with. Clarity and uniformity of personal and organizational values and principles are, therefore, essential for the active involvement of people. Experience teaches us that identification with the organization is the most important motive for employees to dedicate themselves actively to the organizational objectives. People all have different personal values and principles that we must try to understand and key to the values of the organization. Only by doing this will changes and improvements have a permanent nature. The questions that are central here are: Does your personal ambition match the shared organizational ambition? Do they balance? As summary:

> Personal (<Mission>, <Vision>, ≈ Organizational (<Mission>,
> <Key Roles>)   <Vision>, <Core Values>)
> Personal Ambition ≈ Shared Organizational Ambition
> Personal Balanced Scorecard ≈ Organizational Balanced Scorecard
> Individual Learning ≈ Collective Learning

Do you act in accordance with the formulated shared ethical ambition? Can you identify with the shared organizational ambition? In doing this, do you feel personally involved and addressed by the organizational ambition? Do your personal values and principles match the organizational vision and core values? If they conflict, is leaving the best answer? Do your most important personal values do justice here? Which points in your personal ambition are strengthening to and which conflict with the shared organizational ambition? Which ones are neglected? Is there a win-win situation between your own interests and the ones of your organization? Are your personal mission, vision, and key roles to be found in the shared organizational ambition? If not, do they have to be expanded or adjusted? Are they acceptable? How can they flourish within the organization? Does your level of ambition have to be lowered? Which skills do you need to be a pillar of the organization and thus realize the organizational mission? What do you want to gain yourself with this? Are your developmental expectations in tune with those of the organization? Do you have ethical problems on the job? Have you considered a job change because of this?

Miller, Catt, and Carlson (1996) introduce a personal way to deal with ethical problems on the job (when your manager asked you to do something unethical):

1. Make sure there is a conflict. Make sure both you and your manager have all the facts. Check the contract to see if the activity is permitted.
2. Decide how much you are willing to risk. Do a cost-benefit analysis. Look at everyone involved, and ask yourself what the harm and benefit is to each group.

3. Make your move. If the unethical action is important enough for you to take a risk, tell your manager you cannot do it. Do not make accusations to your manager. Let him or her save face.
4. If there is trouble, get help. If your manager says you have to do it anyway and you feel that you cannot, then you should go to some influential person in the company. Try not to go directly above your manager.
5. Consider a job change. If the people you turn to for help do not have a problem with the situation, then perhaps you need to quit. Evaluate your manager's personal ambition and the shared organizational ambition. If they conflict with yours, then leaving may be the best answer.

Balancing personal ambition with shared ambition deals with the mutual concordance of the Personal and Organizational Balanced Scorecards or individual versus collective learning (see Figure 3.6).

Figure 3.6

Balancing Personal Ambition with Shared Organizational Ambition

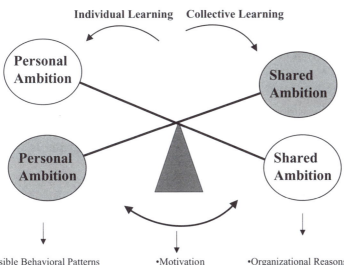

•Invisible Behavioral Patterns
•Higher Level of Consciousness
•Personal Intentions, Identity, Ideals, and Values
•Personal Driving Force/Inner Needs
•Self-Image and Self-Knowledge

•Motivation
•Self-guidance
•Enjoyment
•Motivation
•Participation
•Energy
•Added Value, Win-win
•Inner Involvement
•Ethical Behavior

•Organizational Reasons for Existence, Identity, Intentions, Values, and Interests
•Shared Image and Collective Knowledge
•Collective Behavior

The concordance of personal ambition and the shared organizational ambition should also take place at all lower levels of the organization. For this reason it is important to know which specific inner needs are behind the behavior of the employees, and what motivates them to remain with the organization or leave it. The boxed text shows the results of research into the turnover factors for information technology personnel in The Netherlands and what the individual interests are (Wanrooy, 2001).

Turnover Factors for Information Technology Personnel in The Netherlands

Reasons to Stay	Reasons to Leave
1. In substance an interesting position, a lot of variation	1. Little or no challenges anymore
2. New challenges	2. In essence an uninteresting position
3. Steady job	3. Low income
4. More money	4. Little chance for promotion
5. Favorable place of business	5. Unpleasant colleagues
6. Promotion and career possibilities	6. Too much pressure at work
7. Independence	7. Little or no salary perspectives
8. Pleasant colleagues	8. Leader who does not stimulate
9. Income perspectives	9. Unfavorable place of business
10. Opportunities to follow training	10. Very little freedom

Source: Wanrooy, 2001.

Evans and Russell (1991, p. 26) give an excellent example of erroneously interpreted motives:

A large software company had problems retaining some of its talented young programmers. It invested a lot of time and money in their education, but after one or two years they left to go to other companies. The company paid these people top salaries, provided an attractive working environment, and offered better than average secondary benefits. Still they kept leaving. The error the CEO made was to assume that those involved were primarily motivated by material needs. When they started to investigate what the real needs were, they found a great need for personal autonomy, creativity, and self-development. Because of the size and complexity of their usual projects, the teams consisted of at least 10 persons.

This meant that there was little opportunity to satisfy their personal needs. In the majority of the companies where the young programmers went to work, the projects were smaller and the working atmosphere was more personal; therefore, they could develop their creativity better.

Managers and their employees do not necessarily have similar perspectives on job-reward factors (Miller, Catt, and Carlson, 1996). Compared to employees, managers place greater importance on salary as a motivational tool. The boxed text outlines the differences between the factors valued by employees and supervisors. Many factors valued by employees are nonmonetary in nature (Kovach, 1987).

Motivation: Employees versus Supervisors

A sample of industrial workers in the United States was asked to rank ten "job-reward" factors. In addition, supervisors ranked the same factors, based on their perception of how workers would rank-order them.

Actual Worker Rankings	Supervisor Perceptions of Worker Rankings
1. Interesting work	1. Good wages
2. Full appreciation of work done	2. Job security
3. Feeling of being in on things	3. Promotion and growth in the organization
4. Job security	4. Good working conditions
5. Good wages	5. Interesting work
6. Promotion and growth in the organization	6. Personal loyalty to employees
7. Good working conditions	7. Tactful discipline
8. Personal loyalty to employees	8. Full appreciation of work done
9. Tactful discipline	9. Sympathetic help with personal problems
10. Sympathetic help with personal problems	10. Feeling of being in on things

Source: Kovach, 1987.

Defining Organizational Critical Success Factors

Organizational critical success factors are identified from the organizational vision. An organizational critical success factor (CSF) is one in which the organization has to excel in order to survive, or one that is of paramount importance to organizational success. These strategic themes are unique to the organization; in general they indicate an organization's strategy and determine its competitive advantage. They are the factors that are related to the core competences, which allow the organization to stand out in the market. These factors also guide the organization and may be critical to its success or failure of an organization. They should be documented by means of brainstorming among employees and managers, then organized hierarchically.

Critical success factors are not formulated in a quantified way. Later they will be quantified by means of performance measures and targets. Questions that are central to the formulation of organizational CSFs are: On what is our competitive advantage based? With what do we generate profit? Which skills and capabilities make us unique? How do shareholders see us? How do our customers see us? How can our primary business processes be controlled in order to make them valuable? How can we remain successful in the future? All these questions are related to the four scorecard perspectives. Examples of organizational CSFs are: *financially strong and healthy; well-motivated personnel; a stimulating working environment; skilled employees; teamwork; customer orientation; good customer service; top position in certain markets; image; high product quality; rapid introduction of new products on the market; efficient dealer organization; complete product assortment; and eco-consciousness.*

Table 3.5 shows the critical success factors of Business Jet that were derived from its shared organizational ambition. Figure 3.7, which shows the relationship between these factors, illustrates that all CSFs are interrelated. They all lead to the financial factor "good financial results and growing profitability."

Formulating Organizational Objectives

Formulating strategic objectives encompasses the third step in the OBSC process (see Figure 3.1). Strategic objectives are measurable results that are derived from critical success factors for the purpose of realizing the organizational vision. Using action verbs, they briefly describe the envisioned result so that it can be realized. Strategic objectives are effective only if they are formulated such that they are measurable and can exert influence by managers and employees. Each critical success factor has one or more strategic objectives that are related to one of the four scorecard perspectives (see Figure 3.4). Quantifying the objectives is avoided at this point, but it will take place at a later stage by means of performance indicators and targets. Insight in the strategic objectives is improved by first clearly

Table 3.5

Critical Success Factors of Business Jet	
Financial	**Customers**
• Good financial results and growing profitability	• Dominant share in the global market • First choice of customers for business travel • High-quality services • Image
Internal Processes	**Knowledge and Learning**
• Safe and reliable • Timely departure and arrival of airplanes • Team spirit (inspiring work environment) • Motivated workforce • Successful introduction of innovative products and services	• Continuous development of human potential • Competitive advantage based on knowledge, skills, and the capabilities of employees • Open communication • Process thinking

Figure 3.7

Relationships between the CSFs of Business Jet

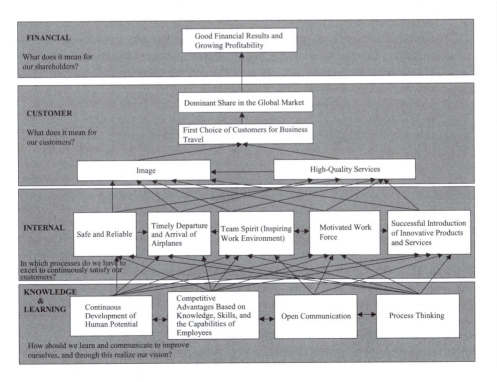

identifying the strengths and weaknesses of the organization (internal), and the opportunities and threats it faces from the environment (external). When formulating strategic objectives, all stakeholders should be considered. The most important objectives regarding the different stakeholders are presented in the following boxed text.

Strategic Objectives Linked to Each Stakeholder

- **Shareholders.** Increasing positive cash flow (= sales − {costs + taxes}), decreasing capital expenditure, paying a superior return on all investments and, due to this, an improved dividend payment. What do our shareholders expect of us? Which objective do we aim for to satisfy our shareholders on a continuous basis?
- **Employees.** Inspiring the competence of employees and improving the working environment; providing challenges and an enjoyable workplace. Focusing on increasing labor productivity, improving motivation, decreasing absence due to illness, and protecting the well-being of the employees. Which objectives do we want to achieve in order to improve the quality of the work?
- **Customers.** Strengthening our market position and increasing customer value; increasing leadership with respect to service level. Which products or services do we provide? How does the customer like our provision of the products and services? Which objectives do we aim at to satisfy our customers?
- **Suppliers.** Having an effective partnership with suppliers in order to increase the quality of the input, decrease purchasing expenditures, and eventually increase the value added. Which objectives do we aim for in order to increase our value added?
- **Community.** Operating in a responsible way. Paying attention to public trust, feeling responsible for the society, creating job opportunities, and being eco-conscious and conservative in energy use. Which objectives do we aim for in order to serve our community effectively and be a good citizen?

Formulating too many strategic objectives for the highest organizational level should be avoided. A maximum of 25 is usually more than enough. Select the most important objectives based on the following criteria: that they are measurable, open to influences, acceptable to different groups of people within the organization, and in alignment with the shared organizational ambition, business culture, and the available knowledge and skills to realize them. Too many objectives in the scorecard usually indicate a lower level of focus within the organization; it also means that the formulated objectives are not strategic for the level on which the scorecard is formulated. Tactical and operational objectives should be addressed in the scorecard of the underlying organizational sections. For the sake of clarity it is usually also wise to combine certain objectives. Experience has taught me that objectives are usually formulated, in practice, as strategies instead of concrete, sought-after results; in other words, the *how* is usually described rather than the *what.*

Table 3.6 outlines the strategic objectives of Business Jet as formulated by the executive team and in relation to the critical success factors and the four scorecard perspectives. The executive team, under the leadership of the acting manager Frank Jansen, decided to execute this strategy-forming process in part due to the heavy blows to the airline industry after the terrorist attacks committed by the Al-Qaeda network of Osama bin Laden in the United States on September 11, 2001.

Cause-and-Effect Relationship

All strategic objectives should be interrelated and affect one another. An objective is used to achieve another objective, which will result in the final organizational objective. The links between the different objectives are explained clearly in a cause-and-effect chain. The objectives that do not contribute to the final organizational objective are left out of the scorecard here. The cause-and-effect chain is a handy tool for communicating the BSC to lower organizational levels. Figure 3.8 shows the cause-and-effect chain developed by the executive team of Business Jet. In this figure, all first-level organizational strategic objectives are formulated and illustrated; they all lead to a final objective, namely, maximizing shareholders' value. The position of objectives within the four scorecard perspectives and their mutual relations are also clearly visible in Figure 3.8, as are the critical success factors in Figure 3.7. The executive team of Business Jet used both of these graphic displays to support the communication of the OBSC to all involved.

Defining Organizational Performance Measures and Targets

Defining the performance measures (PMs) and related targets encompasses the forth step in the OBSC process (see Figure 3.1). A performance measure is a measuring point, related to the critical success factor and strategic objective, by which the functioning of a process can be judged. It is the standard with which the progress of the strategic objective can be measured and with which the organizational vision and objectives are made measurable. A target is a quantitative aim of a performance measure. It indicates a value that must be met. Targets can be based on the expectations of management, the

Table 3.6

Critical Success Factors and Related Strategic Objectives of Business Jet

Financial

Critical Success Factors	Strategic Objectives
• Good financial results and growing profitability	• Maximizing shareholders value • Higher returns • Higher positive cash flow

Customers

Critical Success Factors	Strategic Objectives
• Dominant share in the global market • First choice of customers for business travel • High-quality services • Image	• Greater market share • Presence in global market • More insight in global market regarding business travel • Improved customer satisfaction level regarding our products, services, and employees • Greater degree of trust from our customers in the services we provide • Improved degree of familiarity with the public as a safe and reliable airline company

Internal Processes

Critical Success Factors	Strategic Objectives
• Safe and reliable • On-time departure and arrival of airplanes • Team spirit (inspiring working environment) • Motivated workforce • Successful introduction of innovative products and services	• Optimal safety and reliability • Reduced departure and arrival delays • Managers act as coaches • Effective teamwork • Improved employee satisfaction degree • Newly developed products and services

Knowledge and Learning

Critical Success Factors	Strategic Objectives
• Continuous development of human potential • Competitive advantage, based on knowledge, skills and the capabilities of the employees • Open communication • Process thinking	• Higher labor productivity • Improved manager competence • Improved commercial skills of marketing personnel • Improved access to strategic information • A customer-oriented culture • Openness and honesty when exchanging information • Active participation by everyone in improvement teams

Figure 3.8

Cause-and-Effect Chain Regarding the Strategic Objectives of Business Jet

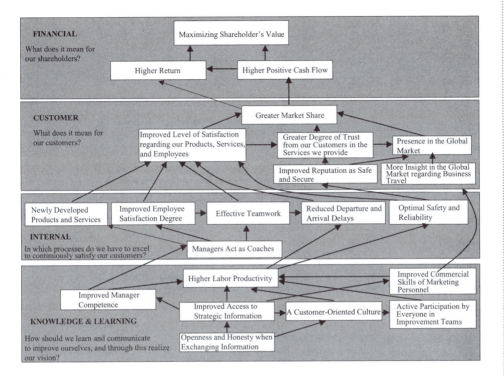

needs of customers, or the results of benchmark studies. PMs and targets provide management with timely signals that are based on the focused guidance of the organization according to measurements of change and a comparison of measured results against standards. It is advisable not to define too many PMs; two or three PMs per strategic objective are enough. Furthermore, they should also comply with the SMART criteria, which we discussed earlier in this chapter.

Table 3.7 shows an overview of possible performance measures per scorecard perspective. Throughout time, productivity, effectiveness, efficiency, and value added play an essential role here. The throughput time of a process is the sum of the time spent executing the work and the waiting periods in the process. Productivity is the ratio of output and input in a process, or the ratio between results and costs (Rampersad, 1994 and 1996). Effectiveness and efficiency also say something about productivity. Effectiveness indicates the degree to which the objectives are realized. Efficiency is closely related to the controllability of the process, the use of resources during the execution

Table 3.7

Examples of Possible Performance Measures per BSC Perspective	
Perspectives	**Performance Measures**
Financial	• Shareholders value • Return • Return on investment • Investment level • Cash flow • Revenue growth • Sales • Operational costs as a percentage of sales • Margin • Profitability = sales / costs + interests received • Percent of deviation from the budget • Productivity = output / input = result / costs • Actual productivity = actual result / actual costs • Expected productivity = expected result / expected costs • Result = output = (all produced units × sales price) + dividends • Labor productivity = result / labor costs • Labor costs = man hours × hourly wage • Capital productivity = result / capital costs • Capital costs = annuity value of used capital goods • Material productivity = result / material costs • Material costs = purchased material − storage costs • Miscellaneous productivity = result / miscellaneous costs • Miscellaneous costs = energy, maintenance, insurance, etc. • Integral productivity = result / (labor costs + capital costs + material costs + miscellaneous costs) • Effectiveness = actual result / expected result • Gross value added = sales − used raw material, goods, and services needed to produce these products • Net value added = gross added value − depreciation (consumption of durable capital goods) • Value added per annual sales • Purchase share as percent of sales • Circulation velocity of stock • Percent inventory • Purchasing price versus market price • Purchase share in relation to sales • Number of suppliers • Percent revenue from new products
Customers	• Market share • Market growth • Percent of customers who terminate their relationship with the organization due to dissatisfaction • Number of highly satisfied customers • Degree satisfaction of customers • Number of potential customers • Potential revenues • Time needed to answer a complaint • Time needed to solve a complaint • Degree of customer loyalty • Number of "nonsales" • Costs associated with losing a customer or gaining a new customer • Sales loss as a result of dissatisfied customers • Number of visits to important customers • Number of meetings with customer groups to be informed about their demands, requirements, ideas, and complaints

Table 3.7 *continued*

Examples of Possible Performance Measures per BSC Perspective	
Perspectives	**Performance Measures**
Customers, cont.	• Number of concrete objectives with regard to customer satisfaction • Number of guidelines related to optimal customer satisfaction • Percent of cases where the telephone is answered within three rings • Accessibility • Costs of marketing • Sales marketing department • Level of satisfaction of internal customers • Delivery time (between placing an order and delivery) • Time needed to make an offer • Percent of orders delivered late • Response time to a service request • Number of customer contacts • Number of customer surveys • Number of warranty claims • Number of customer complaints • Percent customer returns • Percent customers satisfied with communication
Internal Processes	• Efficiency = expected costs / actual costs • Throughput time = processing time + inspection time + movement time + waiting/storage time • Manufacturing cycle effectiveness = processing time / throughput time • Down time • Number of breakdowns • Availability = MTBF / MTTR • MTBF = Mean Time between Failures • MTTR = Mean Time to Repair • Failure rate = (number of failures / total number of products tested) $\times$ 100% • Failure rate = (number of failures / operating time) $\times$ 100% • Actual processing times versus waiting times • Machine availability = {(production time − stoppage time) / production time} $\times$ 100% • Throughput time of failures = dispatch time − notice time • Invoicing speed • Delivery time (between order and delivery) • Time needed to present an offer • Percent of delayed orders • Response time to a service request • Lead time for product development • Percent sales from new products • Time needed to launch a new product on the market (time-to-market) • Percent of sick leave • Percent of latecomers • Satisfaction degree of employees • Percent of personnel turnover • Percent of personnel who find that they are working under effective leadership • Percent of personnel who find that they do challenging work • Percent of forms filled in correctly • Percent correctly performed function-oriented behavior • Quality grade = {(production quantity − number of defects) / production quantity} $\times$ 100% • Percent rejects or percent approved • Percent scrap • Percent damaged

Table 3.7 *continued*

Examples of Possible Performance Measures per BSC Perspective	
Perspectives	**Performance Measures**

Internal Processes, cont.	• Percent returned
	• Percent injuries due to dangerous work
	• Percent safety incidents
	• Percent environmental incidents
	• Percent of processes that are statistically controlled
	• Percent of processes with real-time quality feedback
	• Percent delayed orders
	• Delivery reliability; percentage deliveries completed on time and according to the specifications
	• Quality costs consisting of:
	  – *Internal failure costs*; costs linked to correcting mistakes before delivery of the product, such as scrap, rejects, adjustments, downtime of equipment, labor sitting idle while waiting for repairs, and sales discounts for inferior products.
	  – *External failure costs*; costs that regard the adjustments of malfunctions after delivery of the product, such as repair costs, travel and lodging expenses, replacement costs, stock spare parts, lost goodwill of customer, guarantee and warranty costs, and dispatchment costs.
	  – *Prevention costs*; costs that are related to occurrence of the above mentioned costs, such as designing the product and the related process for quality, planning the quality control process, preventive maintenance costs, capital costs, quality training, and standard working procedures.
	  – *Judgement costs*; costs that have to do with measuring and evaluating products and processes to guarantee that these meet certain standards, such as input check, laboratory tests, acquiring special testing equipment, receiving inspection, reporting on quality, and ISO audits.

Knowledge and Learning	• Labor productivity = result / labor costs • Value added per labor costs • Value added per number of employees • Value added per labor time • Revenue per employee • Sales per employee • Availability of strategic information • Experience level of employees regarding information exchange • Percent of communication failures • Percent of available competences • Number of necessary skills • Number of required or followed training courses • Percent of qualified employees • Percent of employees that are trained in essential skills • Percent of employees with the need for crucial skills • Training costs of employees • Training costs of executives and managers • Training costs as a percentage of sales • Number of solved problems • Number of suggestions per employee • Number of suggestions implemented • Usable strategic information as a percent of available information • Percent of employees with a competence profile • Degree of existence of innovative technology • Percent of available strategic skills • Average time that someone stays in the same position • Percent of personnel with personal ambition linked to shared ambition of the organization
Source: Rampersad, 2002.	

of the process, and the operational costs. The rule of thumb here is: The shorter the throughput time, the more efficient the process in question. Thus, being more effective has to do with being more goal-oriented, and being more efficient has to do with being faster, cheaper, and better controlled. Value added is the difference between the retail price of a product and the purchase costs of the raw materials, goods, and services needed to manufacture the product. Table 3.8 displays the performance measures and targets related to the strategic objectives defined by the executive team of Business Jet.

Formulating Organizational Improvement Actions

The formulation of organizational improvement actions or strategies encompasses the fifth and final step in the OBSC process (see Figure 3.1). These improvement actions are measures for the realization of the strategic objectives. From these actions are chosen those that contribute the most to the critical success factors. The improvement actions are strategic options aimed at the strategic, tactical, operational, and individual level.

There are many options that consider customers, competitors, and the company itself, such as the degree of specialization, the level of technological innovation, desired growth, and so on (see also DeKluyver and Pearce, 2002; Porter, 1985). Figure 3.9 provides an overview of possible organizational improvement actions or strategies for increasing competitive power—by becoming *smaller, cheaper, faster, better*, and *different*. These are all strategic options. I want to stress the following: *There is not one specific improvement action that leads to sustainable competitive advantage, nor is there one best strategy—there are many options*. In Chapter 5 and 7, respectively, I will introduce a customer orientation audit and a knowledge management quick scan that will assist you in formulating creative improvement actions.

Improvement actions should also comply with certain criteria. On the one hand, they should be specific, compelling, solid, and feasible; on the other hand, they should be connected with the related performance measures and targets. Furthermore, they must be implemented in stages and allow for follow-up.

Table 3.8 displays the Balanced Scorecard of Business Jet. As mentioned earlier, the executive team (under the leadership of acting manager Frank Jansen) decided to execute this strategy-forming process due to the deleterious effects on the airline industry from the September 11, 2001 terrorist attacks in the United States. They decided to add extra safety precautions on top of the already existing safety precautions at the airports. Specifically, additional safety measures were established in their airplanes and at the permanent gates

Table 3.8

The Balanced Scorecard of Business Jet

FINANCIAL

Critical Success Factors	Strategic Objectives	Performance Measures	Targets	Improvement Actions
• Good financial results and growing profitability	• Maximizing shareholders' value	• Sales growth	• 10% in 3 years	• Increase airline tickets price by 5% for business and first class travel on transatlantic routes
		• Occupancy rate of airplanes	• Increase of 30% in 3 years	• Expand service package • Introduce discount system • Intensify promotion campaigns • Reduced input of airplanes on Mid- and South Atlantic routes • Maximizing profits
	• Higher returns	• Net profits at constant equity • Gross margin growth	• Increase of 15% in 3 years • $15 million at the end of next year	• Close down unprofitable business units such as rental car • Decrease cost price for airline tickets
	• Higher positive cash flow	• Costs reduction due to lower maintenance inventory	• $3 million in the coming 3 years	• Redefine highest minimal maintenance inventory
		• Percent of decrease of operational costs	• Each year an average of 10% lower than in 2000	• Outsourcing catering activities • Execution of cost failure study • Introduction of departmental budgets • Reviewing purchasing process and executing it more efficiently

CUSTOMERS

Critical Success Factors	Strategic Objectives	Performance Measures	Targets	Improvement Actions
• Dominant share in the global market	• Greater market share	• Market share	• 10% increase in 3 years	• Expand our activities in North America through negotiation • Develop a program for goal-oriented marketing

	Measures	Targets	Initiatives
First choice of customers for business travel			• Develop a plan for direct marketing • Communicate with customers through e-business tools • Develop a plan for entrance into Asian markets • Build up strategic partnership relations with regional airline companies
• Presence in global market	• Number of potential customers reached	• 30% increase in 5 years	
• More insight in global market regarding business travel	• Potential incomes	• 20% increase in 5 years	• Conduct market research for previously mentioned markets • Set up a database that includes characteristics of potential customers
• Improved customer satisfaction level regarding our products, services, and employees	• Number of customer surveys	• At least 10 per year	• Routinely conduct surveys among passengers • Map travel habits of business people
	• Degree of satisfaction of customers	• At least 75% in 3 years	• Set up a customers' helpdesk • Develop guidelines for optimal customer satisfaction
High-quality services			• Give extra rewards to customer-oriented employees
• Greater degree of trust from our customers in the services we provide	• Number of customer complaints	• Decrease of at least 30% per year	• Formulate a customer complaints procedure and execute it routinely
	• Degree of customer loyalty	• Increase of 30% in 4 years	• Develop and implement a plan to improve client trust and loyalty • Measure the degree of customer loyalty • Benchmarking with regard to customer loyalty
Image			
• Improved degree of familiarity with the public as a safe and reliable airline company	• Familiarity level as safe and reliable	• At least 70% in 4 years	• Conduct image study

(continues)

Table 3.8 *continued*

The Balanced Scorecard of Business Jet

INTERNAL PROCESSES

Critical Success Factors	Strategic Objectives	Performance Measures	Targets	Improvement Actions
• Safe and reliable	• Optimal safety and reliability	• Investments in safety and maintenance of airplanes • Percent of safety incidents	• To be determined • Reduction by at least 70% in 2 years	• Introduce total preventive maintenance system • Equip airplanes with extra electronic safety systems • Purchase extra metal detectors, video systems, and special scanners • Improve safety awareness of employees through training and communication • Intensify safety controls on all operational levels • Development of a safety bulletin to be published quarterly • Benchmarking with "Best-in-Class" regarding safety • Execute risk analyses by Security Teams at airports • All bags will be subjected to search (no more random checks) • Training of cabin personnel in "Handling Aggressive Passengers and Hijackers" • Equip cockpits with bulletproof door • Put two air marshals (military trained and armed guards) on each flight. • Use of specially trained dogs to search for plastic explosives (e.g., Semtex and C4) • Stimulate alertness and passenger involvement regarding public safety through communication (use of brochures and videos) • Scan passengers' iris (colored part of the eye) and link it to an international database

Objective	Critical success factor	Performance indicator	Target	Action
On-time departure and arrival of airplanes	Reduced departure and arrival delays	• Check-in time	• Shorten with 20% within 3 years	• Describe check-in process and organize it more efficiently • Formulate and communicate work instructions • Purchase handling systems • Develop work procedures
		• Loading and unloading time of airplanes	• Shorten by 15% within 3 years	
		• Downtime of airplanes	• Shorten by 25% within 3 years	• Arrange maintenance organization more efficiently • Purchase more defrosting equipment and install it within 2 months
Team spirit (inspiring work environment)	Managers act as coaches	• Percent of personnel who find that they are working under effective leadership	• 85% in 3 years	• Formulate development plan for managers • Provide training for effective team coaching • Execute employee satisfaction study
		• Degree of satisfaction regarding feedback	• At least 80% in 3 years	
		• Labor productivity of teams	• Increase by 25% in 3 years	
	Effective teamwork	• Percent of personnel who find that they do challenging work	• 85% in 3 years	• Provide training in teamwork and team development • Define and communicate tasks, responsibilities, and authorities of all employees
Motivated work environment	Improved employee satisfaction degree	• Percent of sick leave	• Less than 2% in 2 years	• Study improvement of working conditions • Execute employee satisfaction study
		• Score survey degree of satisfaction of employees	• 85% in 3 years	
Successful introduction of innovative products and services	Newly developed products and services	• Percent of sales from new products and services	• Increase of 5% per year	• Offering Internet services on board our jets (Internet and e-mail in the air) • Develop a formula for extension service provided to businesspeople
		• Time needed to launch a new product and service on the market (time-to-market)	• Shortened by 15% in 3 years	• Arrange development organization more efficiently • Determine development criteria for new products and services

(continues)

Table 3.8 *continued*

The Balanced Scorecard of Business Jet

KNOWLEDGE AND LEARNING

Critical Success Factors	Strategic Objectives	Performance Measures	Targets	Improvement Actions
• Continuous development of human potential	• Higher labor productivity	• Labor productivity of personnel	• 25% increase in 3 years	• Make career development plans for everyone • Conduct planning, coaching, and appraisal interviews with employees based on individual performance plans and competence profiles • Connect performance rewards to appraisal system
• Competitive advantage based on knowledge, skills, and capabilities of employees	• Improved manager competence	• Sales per employee	• 10% increase in 3 years	
		• Percent of available competences • Percent of managers trained in essential leadership skills • Training costs of managers • Marketing training costs	• 30% increase in 3 years • 85% in 3 years • $1 Million per year • To be determined	• Develop competence profiles • Provide training in effective leadership (also for airport operation managers) • Determine training budget for managers • Determine training budget for marketing personnel
	• Improved commercial skills of marketing personnel	• Percent of qualified marketing employees	• 85% in 3 years	• Make inventory regarding knowledge and skills lacking in marketing personnel; upgrade knowledge and skills with training

• Open communication	• Improved access to strategic information • A customer oriented culture • Openness and honesty when exchanging information	• Availability of strategic information • Degree of satisfaction of internal and external customers • Experience level of employees regarding information exchange	• 30% increase in 3 years • 85% in 3 years • 85% in 3 years	• Introduce intranet • Introduce management information system • Measure degree of satisfaction regarding internal and external customers • Execute study of employee satisfaction regarding information exchange
• Process thinking	• Active participation by everyone in improvement teams	• Number of solved problems • Number of suggestions executed by improvement teams	• 25% increase per year • 25% increase per year	• Provide training on "Working in Improvement Teams" (problem solving, teamwork, and interpersonal skills) • Offer a prize for the *"Best Improvement Suggestion"*

Figure 3.9

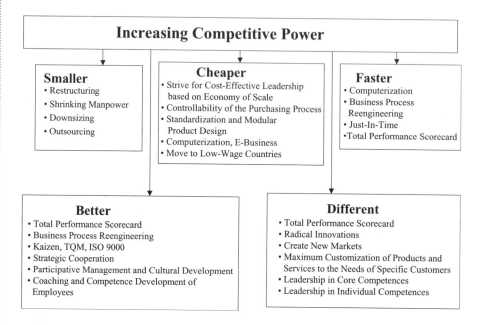

Possible Improvement Actions to Increase Competitive Power

used by Business Jet at a number of airports. This action reflected their strong image of *safety and reliability.*

Giving Priority to Improvement Actions

Due to the large number of formulated organizational improvement actions, which cannot all be executed at the same time, the executive team of Business Jet decided to give a priority number to each of these actions. The improvement actions that would make the biggest contribution to the most important critical success factors received the

Table 3.9

W1 and W2 Factors	
The W1 factors were scaled as follows: 1 = unimportant 2 = somewhat unimportant 3 = less important 4 = important 5 = very important	The W2 factors were scaled as follows: 1 = no contribution 2 = hardly any contribution 3 = average contribution 4 = high contribution 5 = very high contribution

Priority Number of Each Improvement Action of Business Jet Regarding Customer Perspective

Improvement Actions	Critical Success Factors	Weight of Critical Success Factor W1	Contribution of Improvement Action to Critical Success Factor W2	Priority Number of Improvement Actions P = W1 × W2
• Expand our activities in North America through negotiation	• Dominant share in the global market	4	3	12
• Develop a program for goal-oriented marketing	• Dominant share in the global market	4	4	16
• Develop a plan for direct marketing	• Dominant share in the global market	4	2	8
• Communicate with customers through e-business tools	• Dominant share in the global market	4	5	20
• Develop a plan for entrance into Asian markets	• Dominant share in the global market	4	3	12
• Build up strategic partnership relations with regional airline companies	• Dominant share in the global market	4	5	20
• Conduct market research for previously mentioned markets	• Dominant share in the global market	4	4	16
• Set up a database that includes characteristics of potential customers	• Dominant share in the global market	4	3	12
• Routinely conduct surveys among passengers	• First choice of customers for business travel	5	5	25
• Map travel habits of business people	• First choice of customers for business travel	5	3	15
• Set up a customer helpdesk	• First choice of customers for business travel	5	4	20
• Develop guidelines for optimal customer satisfaction	• First choice of customers for business travel	5	5	25
• Give extra rewards to customer-oriented employees	• High-quality services	5	3	15
• Formulate a customer complaint procedure and execute it routinely	• High-quality services	5	3	15
• Develop and implement a plan to improve customer trust and loyalty	• High-quality services	5	4	20
• Measure the degree of customer loyalty	• High-quality services	5	3	15
• Benchmark with regard to customer loyalty	• High-quality services	5	2	10
• Conduct image study	• Image	5	4	20

highest priority. The score for each improvement action was determined as follows:

- Giving a weight (W1) to the critical success factor in question.
- Giving a weight (W2) to the contribution of the improvement action in question to the critical success factor.
- Multiplying these two weights to obtain the priority score (formula: $P = W1 \times W2$).

The weights W1 and W2 were first individually estimated by the executive team members based on a number between 1 and 5 (see Table 3.9).

The more important the critical factor, the higher the W1 factor, and the higher the contribution of the improvement action to the critical success factor, the higher the W2 factor. The average weight number established by the entire executive team was then determined for both cases. The factor P was calculated by multiplying both average weights. The improvement actions with the highest P-factor received priority to be implemented first. The following aspects were also considered:

- A cautious start with the simplest improvement action that could provide quick results.
- Acceptability; should be accepted by different organizational groups (considering the business culture and possible organizational resistance).
- The costs associated with the problem.
- The costs associated with the improvement action.
- The global cost-revenue ratio.
- The chance of success (feasible and realizable).
- The time needed for implementation of the improvement action.

To illustrate this selection procedure, the priority number for each of Business Jet's improvement actions in relation to the customer perspective is displayed in Table 3.10. Only the improvement actions with a P-factor of 15 and higher were selected for implementation and further translated into the business unit scorecards.

In the next chapter I will discuss how the formulated Organizational Balanced Scorecard can be adequately communicated to all stakeholders, and how it can be translated to the scorecards used by the lower echelons of the organization.

Communicating and Linking the Balanced Scorecard

4

Giving people self-confidence is by far the most important thing that I can do. Because then they will act.

Jack Welch

Do you want to know who you are? Don't ask. Act! Action will delineate and define you.

Thomas Jefferson

This chapter focuses on how to communicate the contents of the Organizational Balanced Scorecard to everyone involved as well as how to link it to the scorecard of the business units and teams and to the individual performance plans of the employees. When the OBSC has been disseminated in this way, the entire organization will realize the importance of strategic thinking, continuous improvement, personal development, and learning. During this phase, the stakeholders are informed of the new business strategy and familiarized with it. This second phase in the TPS cycle (see Figure 4.1) is primarily concerned with aligning all the parties involved throughout the organization.

Communicating the Balanced Scorecard

Trust men and they will be true to you; treat them greatly and they will show themselves great.

Ralph Waldo Emerson

Figure 4.1

The Second Phase in the TPS Cycle

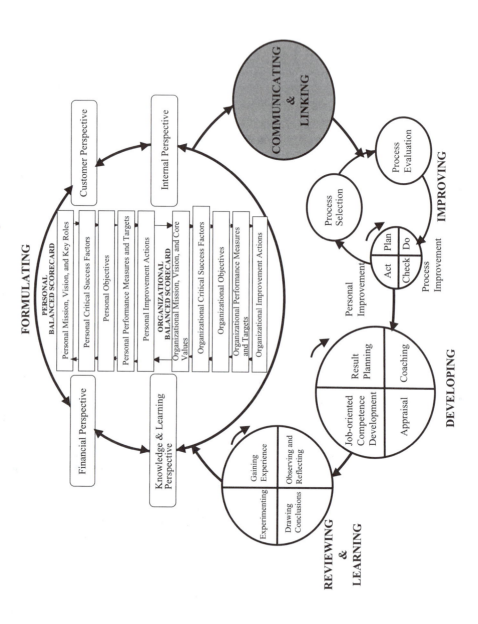

Communicating the formulated Organizational Balanced Scorecard to all stakeholders in clear, exciting terms is necessary in order to create organizational buy-in for it and to arouse organization-wide commitment. This can only be achieved if all stakeholders understand the OBSC and know which behavior is necessary to realize the organizational vision. The corporate scorecard has to be communicated to employees in a manner that is timely, honest, clear, correct, complete, structured, consequential, frequent, and preferably face-to-face. It is important that this communication does not happen too early, or the message may be forgotten by the time the goals of the message have been actualized. The OBSC should also not be communicated too late, or it may lead to mistrust. The amount of the information communicated at any time should also be balanced: there should not be so much information that employees do not have time to absorb it, but there should be enough information that they get the impression that something important is happening.

The OBSC should be communicated internally as well as externally. This process should be coherent, continuously informative, and handled in a systematic and structured way. The communicative objectives, core message, and medium for each stakeholder should be clearly defined beforehand. Use a communication matrix indicating all stakeholders: shareholders, CEO, middle management, team leaders, employees, customers, and suppliers (Kaplan and Norton, 1996). The communication process should include many means of communication, such as brochures, posters, monthly newsletters, monthly reports, e-mail, memos, video, electronic bulletin boards, and publication boards, as well as business meetings, conferences, office parties, staff meetings, shareholders meetings, and other gatherings. The frequency of communication should be indicated in the communication plan. Communicate the scorecard orally as well as in writing, top-down as well as bottom-up, vertically as well as horizontally (two-sided communication between sender and receiver) throughout the organization. The core message should deal with the formulated BSC. Also use the cause-and-effect diagrams in this communication process. Articulate the corporate scorecard with conviction, and create clarity about tasks, responsibilities, and authorities. Indicate what is open for discussion and what is not, such as the formulated scorecard perspectives.

The people within the organization must be convinced of the necessity for improvement, development, and learning. This may be accomplished by comparing the organization to its more successful competitors, by bringing into the open the dissatisfaction of customers, and by constantly emphasizing declining performance measures that are related to these factors. In extreme cases, make it clear that the long-term survival of the organization is at stake. By doing this last point, the skeptics may be convinced of the necessity to change. Employees should also be informed about the advantages of the improvement actions and how the gap between the actual and prospective situation can be closed. These suggestions for improvement should be structured well and clearly argued, whereby a concrete, improved result is promised to the employees. Also link the OBSC to the Personal Balanced Scorecard. Communicate not only the scorecard but also the complete TPS concept to colleagues, employees, and others. Everyone within the organization has to know about the content of the corporate scorecard, why it is important that the organization works in this way now, of which methods and techniques the TPS concept consists, and how these can be applied successfully. Communicate this information to your customers and suppliers as well, explaining to them why you are working this way and how it will affect them. The routine adaptation of the TPS concept can be encouraged by developing and distributing a pocketsize organizational TPS booklet.

As part of your continuous self-improvement, it is advisable to communicate your Personal Balanced Scorecard to others as well. As you learn from their feedback, you will improve your self-image and gain greater knowledge about yourself, which, in turn, is essential to learn, be creative, and improve your behavior. After all, your self-knowledge and self-image are not only determined by your inner voice but also by the image others have of you. That is why feedback is so very important.

Linking the Balanced Scorecard

> Most people do not really want freedom, because freedom involves responsibility, and most people are frightened of responsibility.
> *Sigmund Freud*

To put the strategic vision into action, it is necessary to link the corporate scorecard to the one of the business units and teams, as well as to the individual performance plans of the employees (see also Becker, Huselid, and Ulrich, 2001). Under the supervision of the business unit manager, each team determines its own specific scorecard, which is aligned to the OBSC. This is done in the manner described in Chapter 4, by means of a two day informal workshop. Each team develops a team scorecard based on the scorecard of its business unit. Then, with the help of the team leader, each team member translates the team

Figure 4.2

Linking the OBSC to the Business Units' Scorecard, Team Scorecard, and Individual Performance Plan

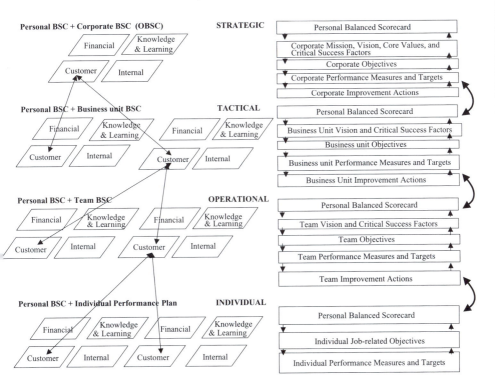

scorecard into his or her own individual performance plan. In this plan the emphasis is primarily on job-oriented results rather than tasks and improvements actions. Figure 4.2 illustrates the different cascading layers in this process. During this process participants also formulate their own Personal Balanced Scorecard, which is situated on a higher level of abstraction than the individual performance plan. With this approach, a bridge is drawn between the successive organizational levels; the message from top management is consistently articulated to the lower levels and vice versa. In Figure 4.2, for example, Business Jet's strategic objective for *optimal safety and security* can be translated into the objective of the Security team at Schiphol Airport to reduce the number of safety incidents on board airplanes departing from Amsterdam, or to improve the safety awareness of team members.

When the objectives are linked in this way, local efforts are aligned with the overall organizational strategy. Brainstorming with employees in several workshops allows them to gain better insight into the organizational course to be followed. This formulation process is identical for the strategic, tactical, and operational levels within the organization. The organizational mission formulated in the OBSC apply to all organizational levels. The organizational vision and linked critical success factors, objectives, targets, and improvement actions are then adjusted and fine-tuned to the related business units and teams. Here the OBSC is used as a frame of reference. Members of each lower level should also reflect upon the alignment between their personal ambition and the shared organizational, business unit, and team ambition.

The organizational objectives in the OBSC form the point of departure when linking the OBSC to the scorecards at lower organizational levels. For each objective it is determined whether the respective business unit influences this objective significantly, and if improvement actions can be formulated to directly influence the accomplishment of this objective. If so, the objective will be incorporated into the scorecard of the respective business unit. To finalize the business unit's scorecard, the remaining objectives and scorecard elements are formulated, based on the strategy of the respective business unit. This top-down and bottom-up process is executed iteratively in increasing detail at all successive organizational levels. In this manner the overall organizational strategy is systematically translated into more specific plans at each organizational level.

The level of detail in which the translation takes place depends on the organizational typology and the business size. Each department selects those objectives and performance measures from the OBSC that it influences, and then translates them into their own situation (see Figure 4.2). After this process, team scorecards are formulated that are in keeping with the business unit's scorecard. Then, the team scorecard is translated into the individual performance plans of the employees, which focus on the individual employees' jobs. The individual performance plan is part of the individual employee's competence profile and serves as the starting point for periodic planning, coaching, and appraisal meetings, as well as for his or her compensation and career planning (see Chapter 6).

Although the Personal Balanced Scorecard and individual performance plan are strongly interrelated, there are significant differences between them. With the Personal Balanced Scorecard the emphasis is on the personal life of people, their attitudes, skills, and behavior in society (also in their private life). The individual performance plan, on the other hand, is formulated at the operational level and focuses on the job to be done by the employee within the organization (job-oriented competences) and the improvement of the daily job-related performances. This plan is linked to the team scorecard and also contains ingredients of the Personal Balanced Scorecard. As a result of this policy deployment it is logical to also link the individual performance plan explicitly to the reward system, without losing track of intrinsic incentive compensation. Several organizations have linked part of their incentive compensation to the financial objectives in the OBSC and the remainder to the objectives related to the perspectives of *customers, internal processes, and knowledge and learning*, depending on reaching or exceeding related targets (Kaplan and Norton, 1996; Chang and Morgan, 2000). By appointing the different objectives a "weight" (priority number), the delivery of unbalanced performances will be prevented, as discussed in Chapter 3.

The linked scorecard framework consists of the following four levels (see Figure 4.2):

1. *Strategic*; formulation of the Personal Balanced Scorecard of the management team (including the CEO) and the corporate scorecard.
2. *Tactical*; formulation of the Personal Balanced Scorecard of the middle management and the business unit scorecard matching those of the corporate scorecard.
3. *Operational*; formulation of the Personal Balanced Scorecard of the team leaders and the team scorecard matching those of the respective business unit scorecard.
4. *Individual*; formulation of the Personal Balanced Scorecard of the team members and the job-oriented objectives, performance measures, and targets of individual employees matching those of the respective team scorecard.

The routine use of the scorecards and the individual performance plan can be encouraged by developing this framework in such a way that it is pocketsize. By doing this, everyone will have daily reminders of their own personal ambition and the shared organizational ambition, and both management and employees will have better insight into the results that must be gained to contribute to the realization of the organizational mission and vision.

Individual Performance Plan

As part of annual result planning, an employee and his or her manager together formulate the individual performance plan. Together they determine which results (job-oriented objectives, performance measures, and targets related to the team scorecard) will be expected

Table 4.1

Rollout of the Business Jet Corporate Scorecard to the Scorecard of the Safety Business Unit, the Security Team, and the Individual Performance Plan of Team Member John van Dam

	Organizational Unit	Objectives	Performance Measures	Targets
FINANCIAL	Safety Department	• Cost control	• Operational costs • Percent of deviation from department budget	• 13% reduction by end of 2003 • Maximum 10% per year
	Security Team	• Lower labor costs • Lower housing costs • Finalizing failure costs study	• Labor costs • Costs per m² • Failure costs	• 10% reduction in 2 years • 10% reduction as of August 2002 • 40% reduction in 16 months
	Individual (John)	• Working more cost consciously • Implement cost-saving measures • Contribution to failure costs study	• Efficiency • Number of implemented measures • Number of developed improvement proposals	• Increase of 10% in 2002 • At least 2 per quarter • Increase of 30% in 2002
	Organizational Unit	**Objectives**	**Performance Measures**	**Targets**
CUSTOMERS	Safety Department	• Improved level of familiarity among the public as a safe and reliable airline company	• Familiarity score as safe and reliable	• At least 75% in 15 months
	Security Team	• Improved satisfaction degree of passengers regarding flight security	• Number of customer surveys • Satisfaction score passengers at Schiphol Airport	• 10 per year • At least 70% at the end of 2002
	Individual (John)	• Customer friendly behavior while executing security tasks	• Number of complaints from passengers	• Decrease by at least 50% this year

INTERNAL PROCESSES

	Objective	Measure	Target
Safety Department	Optimal safety	Percent of safety incidents	Decrease by at least 75% in 2 years
Security Team	Conducted risk analysis	Number of developed and implemented safety suggestions	Increase of 30% per year
	Improvement safety awareness of entire security team	Percent of safety incidents on board our airplanes that have departed from Schiphol Airport	Decrease to less than 2% within 1 year
	Optimal labor conditions	Percent of sick leave	Decrease by at least 75% in 2 years
Individual (John)	Contribution provided to risk analysis	Number of developed safety suggestions	Minimum of 2 quarterly
	Develop safety procedures	Number of developed or updated safety procedures	8 procedures in 2002
	Less serious mistakes made during execution security tasks	Number of serious mistakes	Decrease of 50% by the end of this year
	Motivated	Labor productivity	Increase to 80% by December 2002 at the latest
	Contribution provided as chairman of project team "Improvement Security at Schiphol Airport"	Number of concrete safety ideas	At least 5 in 2002
	Physical and mental health	Percent of sick leave	Decrease of less than 2% by no later than November 2002
		Percent of stress	Decrease of at least 30% by the end of 2002
	Effective coaching of team members	Percent of employees who think that they are coached effectively	75% in 2002
	Trust of management regarding job fulfillment	Level of satisfaction of the safety manager	At least 75% by the end of 2002

(continues)

Table 4.1 *continued*

Rollout of the Business Jet Corporate Scorecard to the Scorecard of the Safety Business Unit, the Security Team, and the Individual Performance Plan of Team Member John van Dam

	Organizational Unit	Objectives	Performance Measures	Targets
KNOWLEDGE and LEARNING	**Safety Department**	• Improved competence of employees with respect to safety	• Percent of employees who have safety skills • Training costs	• Increase of 45% in 18 months • $315,000 per year
	Security Team	• Broader level of knowledge of team members regarding safety • Improved skills of team members regarding safety • Safety-oriented business culture	• Number of different safety tasks a team Member can do well • Percent of qualified employees • Training costs • Degree of satisfaction of internal and external customers	• Increase of 40% in 15 months • 95% in 15 months • $75,000 per year • 75% in 2 years
	Individual (John)	• Improved competence in the field of safety • Openness and honesty with knowledge exchange between colleagues • Active participation in improvement teams • Colleagues trained in "frisking of and dealing with aggressive passengers" • Improved coaching skills	• Safety certificate • Experience level of colleagues regarding knowledge exchange • Number of solved safety problems • Number of trained colleagues • Satisfaction degree of team members regarding way of coaching	• 30% of certificates obtained in 2002 • 75 % by the end of 2002 • Increase of 30% by the end of 2002 • 25 colleagues in 2002 • At least 75% by the end of 2002

from the employee during the coming twelve months in order to realize the team vision. At this time the Personal Balanced Scorecard of the employee should also be considered. The individual performance plan forms the starting point in the development cycle as well as part of the individual employee's competence profile. On the one hand it is aligned with the required job-related results (for the purpose of realizing the team objectives) and, on the other hand, to the individual's job-oriented competences (knowledge, experience, skills, and behavior).

The structure of the individual performance plan is similar to that of the team scorecard; it consists of the job-oriented objectives, performance measures, and targets, divided among the four scorecard perspectives (financial, customer, internal processes, and knowledge and learning). The emphasis in the individual performance plan is on obtaining results instead of on the tasks to be executed. A priority number can be set to the objectives, as described in Chapter 3. Objectives with the biggest contribution to the most important critical success factors of the team receive the highest priority.

Business Jet Case

To illustrate the above mentioned, the linking of the corporate scorecard of Business Jet to the underlying organizational units is given in Table 4.1. Here, the scorecard elements of the Safety business unit are rolled out into the objectives, performance measures, and targets of the Security teams active at Schiphol Airport. These teams consist each of eight to ten members. Each year, team members formulate their individual performance plans in consultation with their specific managers. For example, the scorecard of one of these teams is here matched to the individual performance plan of team member John van Dam, ingredients of whose personal scorecard are also incorporated. John is the leader of his Security team. He formulated his individual performance plan in January 2002 together with his manager (Steve Daniel). During that year John's plan was essential at the periodic result planning, coaching, and appraisal meetings he had with Steve, as it was at the related 360°–feedback assessment (see Appendixes A and B). The development cycle, which underlies this competence development process, will be discussed further in Chapter 6.

The following chapters will discuss the implementation of the Total Performance Scorecard concept. Improvement, which is the first step in the implementation process, is the focus of the next chapter.

Improvement

5

To improve is to change; to be perfect is to change often.

Sir Winston Churchill

There is only one valid definition of a business purpose: to create a satisfied customer. It is the customer who determines what the business is.

Peter F. Drucker

This chapter emphasizes the systematic execution of the formulated organizational and personal improvement actions. Figure 5.1 illustrates this third phase in the TPS cycle. The improvement of your behavior and the organization's business processes is central here, and is based on PDCA learning (see Figure 2.5): how to correct mistakes, improve what already exists, and to do things right the first time. When you are working on personal improvement this involves behavioral, communicative, and management skills; health; assertiveness; financial stability; personal value-added factors; and other issues. The organizational improvement actions relate to:

- *Improving*; this entails *doing existing things better*. Efficiency or doing things right is the pivotal issue here.
- *Renewing*; this deals with *doing existing things differently*. Here we deal with effectiveness or doing the right things.

Therefore, improving and renewing belong together. The interrelated improvement process, which is aimed at business processes, can also be broken down into the following three steps (Rampersad, 2001A):

- *Process Selection*; this is selecting and defining the critical business processes related to the improvement actions eligible for continuous improvement.
- *Process Evaluation*; this entails the description, evaluation, and documentation of the selected processes.
- *Process Improvement*; this is the continuous improvement of the evaluated business processes according to the Deming cycle.

The improvement process aimed at personal improvement (of the behavior, skills, and characteristics of individuals) is also based on PDCA learning. In order to realize the organization's strategic objectives, everyone should consider continuous improving, developing, and learning as normal. The TPS cycle provides an excellent framework for this to occur. By working continuously as a team according to this model and by familiarizing yourself with related skills, you will be able to constantly satisfy stakeholders. Consequently, problems will be systematically eliminated and employees will speak the same "*TPS language.*" The number of instances of doing things right the first time thus increases.

Process Selection

> Your most unhappy customers are your greatest source of learning.
> *Bill Gates*

In the first step in the organizational improvement process the emphasis is on the selection of the critical business processes eligible for improvement. The most important activities hereby are the following:

1. Form a steering group in which management also participates actively.
2. Define the critical business processes related to improvement actions; determine which business processes are relevant based on the CSF (critical success factor) standpoint. Select the improvement actions with the highest priority number.

Figure 5.1

The Third Phase in the TPS Cycle

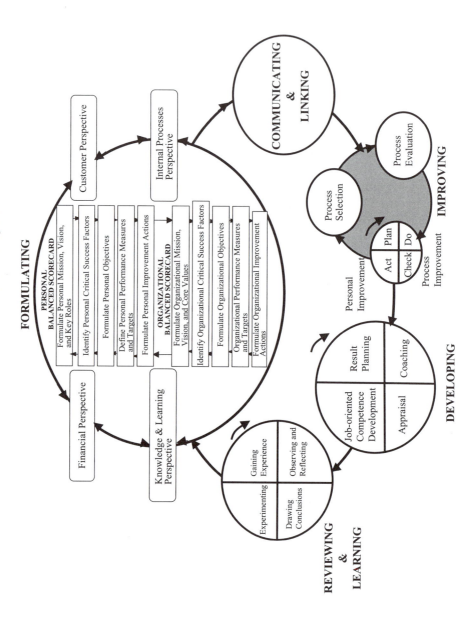

3. Appoint a process owner to each process selected. He or she is responsible for the improvement of the selected process and also functions as a sponsor, the person in the steering group who functions as the improvement project's counsel. He or she is aware that the project is important and, therefore, supports the improvement team, keeps the steering group up-to-date regarding progress, and supports result implementations.

4. Have the steering group or the process owner then install one or more *improvement teams* and appoint one or more team improvement actions.

5. Have the process owner and the team members define the appointed process together and see to process delineation.

6. Train the team in the use of improvement methods and techniques (e.g., brainstorming, benchmarking, making flowcharts and fishbone diagrams, having interpersonal communication, working in teams, etc.), and train the team leader in effective team coaching.

7. Discuss within the group the OBSC and related business unit and team scorecards.

8. Formulate an improvement plan, including, for example, the team mission, project title, improvement objectives, performance review measures, time planning for the execution of analyses, requested means, and aspects related to the creation of support for changes and improvements (such as buy-in from top-management, resistance from the employees, and consequences of introduction); this improvement plan will be updated and further developed in the *"process improvement"* phase.

9. Gather necessary information and analyze related customer data and complaints.

The output of this phase is the foundation for the improvement plan, which will be developed further in the *"process improvement"* phase. An important aspect of the process selection phase is defining the business processes related to improvement actions. A business process is characterized by:

- *An input*; for example, personnel, capital, materials, resources, etc.

- *A delineated process*; which deals with a series of interconnected activities.

- *An output*; products and services.

Figure 5.2

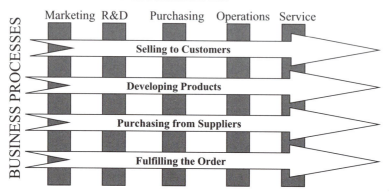

Business Processes of Jet Interior

Business processes form a series of activities executed by different departments.
These processes focus on delivering a product or service to an internal or external customer.

The most important business processes of Jet Interior are:
• Selling to customers; planning sales, making acquisitions, managing business relations, visiting customers, making offers, processing sales orders, invoicing orders, receiving payments, and matching these with unpaid claims.
• Developing products; communicating with customers, determining customer needs, product design, process design, and attuning the service process to customer needs.
• Purchasing from suppliers; selection of suppliers, negotiating, closing purchase contracts, placing purchase orders, receiving purchase invoices, receiving goods, reconciling payments, and paying purchase invoices.
• Fulfilling the order; receiving the order, processing the order, planning production, and handling distribution.

• *The possession of internal/external customers and suppliers*; a process without customers is unimportant.

An organization may be considered as a chain of interrelated activities. Here each business process forms a series of activities that are fulfilled by different business functions, such as making rooms available (at a hotel), developing products (in a production company), purchasing from a supplier (in a trading company), and data processing (in a bank). Here it is important to distinguish between key processes (primary processes) and nonkey processes (supporting processes). Key processes start and end with a customer and are focused on adding value to the customer. Nonkey processes are supportive in nature. To illustrate these points, the most important business processes of Jet Interior, a producer of airplane interiors who is a supplier of Business Jet, are illustrated in Figure 5.2.

Table 5.1

CSF Matrix versus Business Processes of Jet Interior				
Business Processes	**Critical Success Factors (CSF)**			
	Motivated Employees	**Customer Orientation**	**Product Quality**	**Cost Control**
1. Selling				
1.1 Order Acquisition	X	X	X	X
1.2 Order Processing		X		
2. Purchasing				
2.1 Selecting Suppliers	X	X	X	X
2.2 Closing Purchase Contract	X		X	X
2.3 Placing Purchase Order			X	X
2.4 Receiving Goods	X		X	X
2.5 Paying Purchase Invoices	X			X
3. Manufacturing	X	X	X	X
4. Distributing			X	
5. Administrating	X			

To develop an effective process improvement plan, it is necessary to make a detailed division in subprocesses and process sections for each business process up to the action level. Start with the key processes. For example, the production process of Jet Interior is divided into the subprocesses of manufacturing, assembling, spray painting, testing, and packaging. The subprocess manufacturing is then subdivided into supplying, sorting, sawing, drilling, bending, sanding, and so on. Supplying can again be subdivided into the activities of picking up, moving, putting down, fastening, and other procedures.

With the aid of a matrix we can now determine which operational processes are relevant from the CSF standpoint. If a process is essential, it is indicated in the matrix. Nonessential processes (those with few marks in the matrix) can better be outsourced. Table 5.1 shows an example of this exercise with respect to Jet Interior. Outlining business processes in this manner provides an impression of the most important business processes that add value for the customer. Processes that create a high value-addition receive the most attention and are eligible for continuous improvement. From Table 5.1 it can be seen that order processing, distribution, and administration in this company are nonessential processes that hardly add any value; they are thus eligible for outsourcing.

Table 5.2

Matrix of Business Process/CSF and Performance Measures for Jet Interior

Business Processes	Critical Success Factors (CSFs)			
	Motivated Employees	Customer Orientation	Product Quality	Cost Control
1. Selling				
1.1 Order Acquisition	• Percent of sales per sales person • Percent of sick leave	• Percent of customers lost • Number of "nonsales" • Accessibility of sales department • Percent of available marketing competences • Number of customer complaints • Market share • Market growth • Degree of customer loyalty	• Number of customer complaints regarding product quality	• Percent of sales returns from new products • Marketing costs • Percent of decrease in marketing costs
1.2 Order Processing	• Labor productivity • Percent of personnel turnover • Process speed	• Completing rush orders • Throughput time of orders	• Number of processing mistakes • Percent of mistakes in customers' information	• Efficiency • Turnover of the marketing business unit
2. Purchasing	• Level of satisfaction of purchasing personnel • Training costs of purchasing personnel	• Delivery speed (time between ordering and delivering) • Time needed for supplier to make a firm invoice	• Percent of approved materials • Percent of returns	• Purchase versus market price • Purchase share as opposed to sales • Number of suppliers

• Percent of personnel who find they are working under effective leadership	• Percent of orders delivered too late • Percent of orders where too much or too little was delivered	• Delivery reliability of suppliers	• Number of suppliers supplying 1 article • Average order size per supplier
3. Manufacturing • Percent of sick leave of manufacturing personnel • Labor productivity • Value added per personnel costs • Percent of personnel turnover	• Number of customer complaints • Throughput time during manufacturing	• Percent of manufacturing waste • Percent of rejects during production • Effectiveness • ISO norms in manufacturing process • Value added • Quality grade	• Availability of machines • Quality costs • Percent of manufacturing waste • Efficiency • Integral productivity • Capital productivity • Material productivity • Value added/sales
4. Distributing • Percent of sick leave at distribution business unit • Labor productivity	• Percent of completed, on-time deliveries, according to specifications • Delivery speed	• Percent of damaged goods returned • Effectiveness	• Warehouse utilization • Stock levels • Circulation speed • Availability of transportation resources • Capital productivity
5. Administrating • Labor productivity • Percent of personnel who feel they have challenging work	• Time needed to fix a complaint	• Effectiveness • Number of administrative mistakes	• Billing speed • Age of accounts receivable • Efficiency

For each process-CSF combination, Performance Measures (PMs) related to the scorecards can be defined. These measure the activities that have crucial organizational importance and, as such, deliver a valuable contribution to the controllability of business processes. They give management timely signals regarding efficient organizational guidance based on measuring (process) changes and comparisons of the measurement results with the norms. For example, the following PMs belong to a *customer-oriented organization*: number of customer complaints; how fast complaints are handled; repair time; percentage of completed on-time deliveries handled according to specifications; and order handling time. The PMs linked to *high product quality* include: number of customer complaints; percentage of rejects; percentage of damaged returns; number of process interruptions; and quality grade. The following PMs correspond to *motivated employees*: percentage of sick leave; percentage of tardiness; labor productivity; turnover; and so on. Table 5.2 shows an example of the Jet Interior company where one or more possible PMs are presented for each process-CSF combination.

The other activities in this improvement phase of the TPS cycle deal with defining customers' needs in relation to improvement actions and making an inventory of customer data and complaints. The central questions at this point are:

- Which products and services do we deliver, and what do we have to offer?
- Who are our customers, and how do they get what we have to offer?
- What do they want, and what do they expect of us?

By answering these questions on an ongoing basis, we will understand the customer better, and the product or service will better match market demands. These questions were already addressed in part during the formulation of the strategic objectives.

Which Products and Services Do We Deliver, and What Do We Have to Offer?

It is important to define the product or service as concretely as possible. This definition indicates your actual function as a supplier. The more specific the definition, the better your customers' needs can be met.

What the company thinks its customer wants
is not necessarily the same as
What the company thinks it has to offer
is not necessarily the same as
What the company actually offers
is not necessarily the same as
How the customer experiences this
is not necessarily the same as
What the customer really wants

Source: Philips Electronics, 1994.

Who Are Our Customers, and How Do They Get What We Have to Offer?

In the framework of the TPS philosophy it is important to understand the entire customer chain; this means intimately knowing all your customers. The needs of each customer must be examined separately, and not only external but also internal customers should be considered. In fact, if the company does not satisfy the needs of its internal customers, how can the organization comply with the needs of its external customers? All employees determine the degree of customer satisfaction. Employees of different sections and within different business units must be considered as customers of and suppliers for each other. The customer is the next link in the chain of production activities. By bringing individual employees together as customers and suppliers, the traditional barriers between business units will be broken. Each employee delivers something to a colleague, whereby one functions as the internal supplier and the other as the internal customer. Figure 5.3 shows that department C functions as the internal customer of department B, and that department A is the internal supplier of department B. Strengthening this relationship results in an internal network of customer-supplier relationships, which is beneficial to the quality of services provided to the external customer. Everyone in the organization must learn to think in terms of: *Who are my internal customers, and how can I satisfy their needs?*

To illustrate this approach, the internal customer checklist of Hewlett-Packard is shown in the boxed text (Rees and Rigby, 1988). Here it is expected that each section of the organization asks itself seven questions, which are regarded as fundamental to the operation.

Figure 5.3

Internal and External Customers

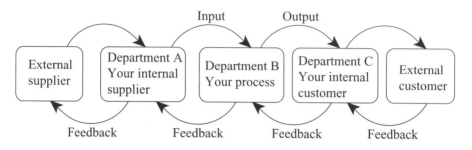

Customer-supplier-relationship

Hewlett Packard's Internal Customer Checklist

1. Who are my customers?
2. What do they need?
3. What is my product or service?
4. What are my customers' expectations and measures?
5. Does my product or service meet their expectations?
6. What is the process for providing my product or service?
7. What action is required to improve the process?

Problem-Solving Methodology

1. Select the quality issue.
2. Write an issue statement.
3. Identify the process.
4. Draw a flowchart.
5. Select a process performance measure.
6. Conduct a cause-and-effect analysis.
7. Collect and analyze the data.
8. Identify the major causes of the quality.
9. Plan for improvements.
10. Take the corrective action.
11. Collect and analyze the data again.
12. Are the objectives met?
13. If yes, document and standardize the change.

Source: Rees and Rigby, 1998.

What Do They Want, and What Do They Expect of Us?

As a supplier, you should try to determine what the customer needs and wants. Here communication is very important. Talk to your customers: ask them what they think of your product or services; try to figure out how they use it; try to find out what they really want—which gains they are looking for in your product, which needs your product satisfies, and what motivates them to keep buying your product and stay loyal to you. Ask these questions: Which needs or expectations do your customers have? Which ones are you aware of? To what extent do you comply with the needs and expectations of your customers? If you do not satisfy their needs, what are the reasons according to your customers? Listen attentively to what they have to say and indicate which customer-supplier relationships need improvement.

Making an inventory of customer information and complaints, benchmarking, and systematically using Quality Function Deployment (QFD) are important methods for improving customer orientation. Due to its complexity, the promising QFD method is rarely understood in practice and therefore seldom introduced within organizations (ignorance creates unpopularity). I have explained this method in detail elsewhere (Rampersad, 2001A; see also Hauser and Clausing, 1988). An abbreviated introductory explanation of this method is presented in the boxed text.

Quality Function Deployment

What Is It?

Quality Function Deployment is used to systematically and structurally convert customer wishes into critical product and process aspects at an early stage. In this approach, which originated in Japan, customer wishes are addressed with the help of matrices that use detailed technical parameters and project objectives (see Figure 5.4). Due to the form of the matrix it is called the "quality house." Using three "sequel houses," the critical product specifications (technical parameters) are translated into the necessary process. This detailed translation allows the process to be executed in a controlled fashion for the purpose of achieving stable and acceptable product quality (see Figure 5.5). In the first house, customer wishes are linked to product specifications. In the second house, the relationship between these product specifications and the characteristics of the product parts is central. In the third house, product parts and process characteristics are linked. As a result, the performance measures of critical processes are established. Finally, in the fourth house, the process characteristics are translated into the manufacturing process operations that are to be executed in a controllable way—that is, manufacturing specifications. Among

(continues)

Figure 5.4

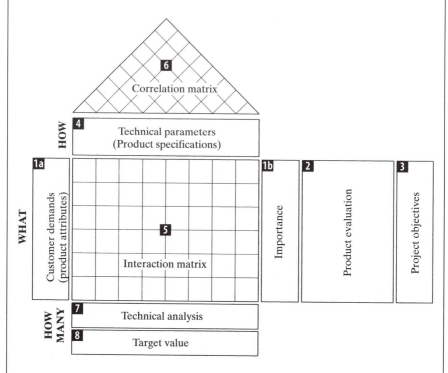

Fundamental Building of QFD Scheme

other things, this results in standard working procedures for each process step. For the purposes of this book, the emphasis is on the first quality house, which focuses on the relationship between customer wishes and product specifications.

When Do You Use It?

QFD is used to improve your understanding of the customer and to develop products, services, and processes in a more customer-oriented way. The objective of QFD is to allow the "voice of the customer" to be heard more clearly in the development process of new products and their related processes, and also to comply with the "*do it right the first time*" principle.

How Do You Execute It?

Put together a multidisciplinary expert team coached by a team leader and assisted by a QFD facilitator. When dealing with product development, the

Figure 5.5

Steps within the QFD

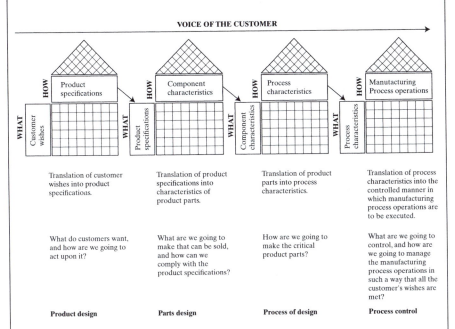

team leader should preferably be a *product manager* or a *product engineer*. The QFD facilitator is someone who is an expert in this area. He or she acts as the source of information and advises the team regarding the effective use of this method. In this preparatory phase, also formulate the objectives and *scope* of the QFD project. The central questions here are: Is top management committed? Which important product are we going to improve? Which target markets do we focus on? Who are our customers? To which competing products are we comparing ours? How long will the project's execution take? Which milestones can we distinguish? What does the reporting structure look like?

Steps to be used for constructing the first quality house, which is aimed at product development (see Figure 5.4):

1. Define who the customer is, make an inventory of customer wishes, and measure the importance (priority) of these wishes with the help of weighing scores. We can make an inventory of customer wishes (product attributes) through interviews, inquiries, and other endeavors such as visiting trade shows, the experience of sales associates, customer registration, direct contact with customers, and contact with the competition. These are all important information sources for appraising and mapping customer wishes. *Benchmarking* can also be of use here.

(continues)

2. Compare your product's performance to that of competitive products. Evaluate your product and note the strong and weak points according to the customer.
3. Identify and quantify the improvement objectives. Determine which customer wishes need to be improved in relation to the competitive product and indicate this in a score.
4. Translate customer wishes into quantifiable technical parameters, that is, product specifications. State *how* client wishes can be used to your advantage. Examples of technical parameters are: dimensions, weight, number of parts, energy use, capacity, and so on.
5. Investigate the relationship between customer wishes and technical parameters. Indicate in the matrix to what extent customer wishes are influenced by technical parameters, and indicate this relationship in a score.
6. Identify the interactions between the individual technical parameters. Make the relationships between these parameters explicit in the roof of the quality house.
7. Record the unit of measurement for all technical parameters. Express these parameters in measurable data. For example, the dimensions of an object are 150 mm (l) × 320 mm (w) × 550 mm (h) and the weight is 15 kg (33 lbs).
8. Determine the target values of the new product design or indicate the proposed improvements of the technical parameters.

An overview of the QFD method indicates that gathering information about the opinion of customers regarding your product or service is of essential importance. This information can be obtained in several ways, such as customer surveys, phone interviews, and customer panel discussions. Customer complaints should be regarded as something positive—as a chance to learn from mistakes and, based on this, to improve the process in such a way that those complaints will not surface again.

Quick Scan Customer Orientation

Table 5.3 shows a customer-orientation audit consisting of 73 sometimes painful questions regarding your customer orientation (Rampersad, 2001B). The questions are divided into the following five dimensions: (1) *general*, (2) *management style*, (3) *strategic vision*, (4) *internal processes*, and (5) *human resources*. Based on your answers to these questions, determine your organization's customer orientation and try to determine as a team why it is characteristic of your organization. Afterwards develop a plan to improve your organization's

Table 5.3

Quick Scan Customer Orientation, Used on Business Jet			
	YES	SOMEWHAT	NO
I. General			
1. Do you know who your customers are and how many there are?		X	
2. Do you listen effectively to all your customers, and do you familiarize yourself with their situation?	X		
3. Do you routinely conduct surveys among your customers about your products and services?			X
4. Do all your employees know about the results of these surveys?			X
5. Did you segment your customers based on their needs?			X
6. Are more than 75% of your customers satisfied?			X
7. Do you anticipate customer needs?		X	
8. Do you consider each customer a unique partner?			X
9. Are complaints addressed within two business days and resolved within one week?			X
10. Do you encourage dissatisfied customers to notify you of their complaints?	X		
11. Do you undertake unsolicited additional actions, and do you provide additional unsolicited services to satisfy your customers?			X
12. Do you have a customer help desk or a call center?			X
13. Do you know the percentage of customers who terminate their relationship with your organization due to dissatisfaction?			X
14. Are complaints systematically registered and analyzed in your organization?			X
15. Have you established procedures for handling complaints, and are these routinely used in your organization?			X

Table 5.3 *continued*

Quick Scan Customer Orientation, Used on Business Jet	YES	SOMEWHAT	NO
16. Do you measure the degree of customer loyalty?			X
17. Do you regularly advise customers about your products/services that best fit their needs?		X	
18. Do you know what the costs are when you lose a customer?			X
19. Do you know what the costs are to gain a new customer?			X
20. Do you know how much you lose in sales due to dissatisfied customers?		X	
21. Do you maintain relationships with your customers, and do you expand these relationships?	X		
22. Do you regularly organize meetings with customer groups to learn about their needs, wants, ideas, and complaints?			X
II. Leadership Style			
23. Is there commitment to customer orientation in top management?	X		
24. As a manager, do you know how many complaints are received yearly?		X	
25. Is management convinced of the importance of satisfied customers, and do they act accordingly?	X		
26. Have you integrated customer satisfaction into your organization's vision?	X		
27. Has this vision been clearly communicated to all your employees and customers?		X	
28. Does management recognize notable trends, and do they anticipate these in a timely manner?		X	
29. Does management set a good example regarding customer-friendly behavior?	X		
30. Is management open to suggestions and ideas from customers?	X		

Table 5.3 *continued*

Quick Scan Customer Orientation, Used on Business Jet			
	YES	**SOMEWHAT**	**NO**
31. Does management personally reward those employees who deliver a valuable contribution to increased customer satisfaction?		X	
32. Are relationships of management with customers supported and warmly encouraged?		X	
33. Is management at all times available to the customer?			X
34. Do all managers have regular personal contact with customers?			X
35. Does customer satisfaction also belong to the evaluation criteria of management?		X	
36. Are the customer's wishes continuously taken into consideration when making decisions?		X	
37. Does top management also personally handle complaints of customers?			X
III. Strategic Vision			
38. Are there at least 5 customer orientation objectives and related performance measures formulated in the corporate, business unit, and team scorecard?	X		
39. Have all managers formulated at least 3 customer-related personal objectives and performance measures in their Personal Balanced Scorecard?	X		
40. Have you developed e-business strategies for the coming years to increase customer satisfaction?		X	
41. Is the strategy regarding customer orientation continuously communicated to all employees?		X	
42. Do you have a partnership relation with all your customers based on mutual respect and trust?			X
43. Do you guarantee your customers a minimal service level and/or complete satisfaction?	X		

Table 5.3 *continued*

Quick Scan Customer Orientation, Used on Business Jet	YES	SOMEWHAT	NO
44. Do you continuously benchmark with regard to customer satisfaction?			X
45. Do you involve your customers with the execution of improvement processes?			X
46. Are all of your employees involved with the improvement of customer orientation?			X
47. Do you have guidelines regarding the optimal satisfaction of the customer?			X
48. Do you consider customer information a strategic asset?	X		
49. Do you have an up-to-date databank in which all customer characteristics are registered?			X
IV. Internal Processes			
50. Have you appointed process owners for controlling business processes?			X
51. Are products/services delivered within the period expected by the customer?		X	
52. Do your phone, fax, Internet, and other e-business tools match the way your customers prefer to communicate?		X	
53. Is the phone in your organization answered within 3 rings in more than 80% of the cases?	X		
54. Is every process in your organization arranged in such a way as to optimally comply with customer expectations?		X	
55. Do these expectations form the basis for performance measures?		X	
56. Have you implemented a Customer Relationships Management (CRM) system within your organization?			X
57. Do you use measured customer satisfaction as an indicator for process improvement?	X		
58. Do you involve your customers in the development of new products/services?			X

Table 5.3 *continued*

Quick Scan Customer Orientation, Used on Business Jet			
	YES	SOMEWHAT	NO
59. Do you also measure the satisfaction of your internal customers?			X
60. Are employees personally responsible for solving customer problems?		X	
61. Do you translate customer needs into product and process improvements and the development of new products and services?		X	
62. Do supporting departments within your organization guarantee the quality of the work they deliver?			X
63. Are your marketing employees free to spend what is necessary to correct a mistake made with a customer?			X
V. Human Resources			
64. Does customer orientation belong to the competence profile of all employees?	X		
65. Do you give extra rewards to employees who continuously perform in a customer-oriented manner?	X		
66. Do you regularly organize trips to your important customers for your employees?		X	
67. Are your customer service employees free to make decisions in order to satisfy customers?			X
68. Are your employees' interests and the interests of your customers related?		X	
69. Do you encourage your employees to generate ideas regarding the increase of customer satisfaction?	X		
70. Do you have an introductory program in which new employees are also educated concerning the importance of satisfied customers?			X
71. Is training mandatory for each employee in your organization?			X
72. Are customer orientation and continuous improvement criteria for promotion?		X	
73. Do your marketing employees receive training of at least two weeks each year in customer orientation?			X
Source: Rampersad, 2002.			

customer orientation. The executive team of Business Jet completed this checklist (see their responses in Table 5.3) to gain insight into the organization's customer orientation on the one hand, and to fulfill the customer perspective in the Organizational Balanced Scorecard on the other. From the results of this quick scan it seems that the customer orientation of Business Jet leaves much to be desired on several points (see columns marked "somewhat" and "no" in Table 5.3). These points lead to improvement actions, which become part of the result area for "customers" in the Organizational Balanced Scorecard.

Many of the recommendations related to this checklist also apply to your relationships with external suppliers. Treat your suppliers as if they are an integral part of your organization. Listen to their ideas on how you can work closely and productively together; create joint improvement teams; invite suggestions; assist them in improving their own processes; build mutual trust and respect; reward them if they achieve improvements; let them participate in the celebration of success; involve them in the development of new products and processes; and become a better customer yourself. Expanding your culture of continuous improvement and learning to all your suppliers will ensure that the quality of your inputs is sufficient to meet your own improvement objectives. If possible, minimize the number of your suppliers; go with the few best, improvement-oriented suppliers who have a demonstrated TPS culture and effective leadership by top management, and collaborate with them based on a long-term partnership contract.

Process Evaluation

> Failure is simply the opportunity to begin again, this time more intelligently.
>
> *Henry Ford*

In this second step of the improvement process (see Figure 5.1), the selected process is described in detail, and whether the process is clearly understood is verified. We confirm, based on measurements, that there is a business process that can satisfy the needs of the customer. The defined process is mapped and the process performances are measured. The performance measures defined in the first step function here as a starting point. During this phase, intensive use is made of improvement methods and techniques such as flowcharts, fishbone diagrams, and so on (Rampersad, 2001A). Flowcharts in particular are used frequently to display business processes.

In this step it should also be determined where measurements must be taken in order to control and manage process variations, and to what extent certain procedures should be adjusted based on this process review. These procedures are necessary in order to ensure that the process can be executed in a similar way every time. The best working method that is currently used should be recorded extensively in order to prevent a reversion back to old habits. The working instruction should include relevant norms that are based on measurements and related to customer needs. Relevant control limits should also be determined for each measurement, based on customer information and process capacity. In this way the process performance can be measured and adjusted if needed. The essential points in the process evaluation step include:

- Communicating the procedures to employees and promoting the use of these instructions within the organization.
- Training employees in its use.
- Making procedures available and imposing their use.

The most important activities in this step are thus describing the selected process, measuring the process performances based on the described performance measures, analyzing the available process data, performing cause-and-effect analyses, and identifying root causes. An especially effective method for executing the cause-and-effect analysis, and thus deriving improvement actions, is *risk management* or *risk analysis*. This preventive approach is explained in detail in the following section.

Risk Management

What Is It?

Risk management is a preventive approach for systematically mapping the causes, effects, and possible actions regarding observed bottlenecks. This method is usually used to analyze products and processes. The emphasis here is on the analysis of processes, whereby answers to the following questions are sought in advance for each process step: How can the process execution fail? What are the possible causes of this? What happens if the process execution fails? How can we prevent this? How important is this prevention? Who is responsible for the implementation of the solution? When will this be executed?

When Do You Use It?

In view of the TPS concept, risk management is used for systematically identifying failures in critical business processes and then eliminating them. This results in a list of critical points with instructions on what should be done to minimize the chance of process failure.

How Do You Use It?

Risk management is executed as a team. The chairperson is responsible for forming the team, gathering relevant information, organizing and planning the analysis session(s), leading the discussions, documenting the results, and providing feedback regarding the continuation of the actions. To identify as many potential bottlenecks as possible, the team should have a broad, multidisciplinary composition with team members who have extensive subject matter experience. A session should take no more than two hours, depending on the problem formulation, knowledge, and experience of the team members, and on the preparation of the session.

The steps for the implementation of a risk analysis are displayed in Figure 5.6:

1. Form a multidisciplinary, expert team of five to eight participants and call a brief kickoff meeting. Make relevant information available to team members in advance, so that it can be studied by the team members before the meeting. At the meeting, explain the objective of the session, the approach, and the role of the team members. Select the most critical process; in other words, define the problem area.
2. Map the process and make an inventory of all relevant process steps (subprocesses).
3. Determine for each process step the possible failure modes. Anticipate possible failures in the process in relation to the rest of the process steps.
4. Indicate what the cause of each failure mode is and what the effects of the failure modes are on the controllability of the process.
5. Judge the risks; quantify the weak points in the process by estimating the probability of occurrence (P) and the severity of failure (S) for each failure mode (see Table 5.5). The multiplication of these two factors is the risk factor (R). The chance of discovering the error on time is expressed in the factor (S). The more difficult it is to discover the error in advance, the higher this factor will be.

Figure 5.6

The Risk Management Process

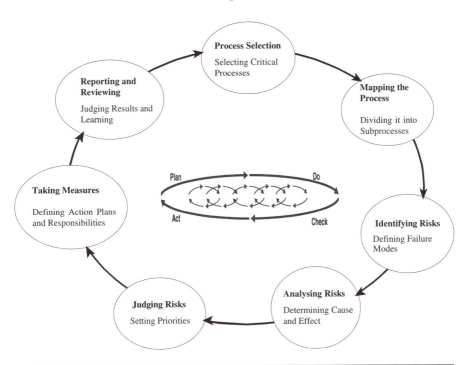

Source: Rampersad, 2002.

Table 5.5

Factors P and S	
Factor P (Probability of Occurrence)	**Factor S (Severity of the Failure)**
Factor P can be determined with the following scale: 0 = Impossible / hardly ever 1 = Very low 2 = Low 3 = Not as low 4 = Less than average 5 = Average 6 = Above average 7 = Rather high 8 = High 9 = Very high 10 = Certain	*Factor S* can be scaled as follows: 0 = Not a problem 1 = Very low/hardly a problem 2 = Low/to be solved through employee intervention 3 = Less serious 4 = Less than average 5 = Average 6 = Above average 7 = Rather serious 8 = High 9 = Very high 10 = Catastrophic / dangerous to people

6. Determine for each failure mode the actions necessary to improve the weak points in the process. The failures with the highest R factors have the highest priority (for instance R-values >20). Appoint a responsible problem solver to resolve the highest risk cases.

7. Report and review the results. Give feedback to the team members about the status of executed actions.

Case Risk Management at Business Jet

Immediately after the September 11, 2001, terrorist attacks by Al-Qaeda, Business Jet decided to implement extra strong safety measures in addition to the existing safety precautions at the airports. Thus, with the development of the Organizational Balanced Scorecard, several new improvement actions regarding safety and security were formulated, such as: equipping cockpits with an impermeable (bulletproof) door; putting in two air marshals (military trained and armed guards) on each flight; making scans of the irises of passengers; encouraging, through communication, the alertness and involvement of Business Jet passengers regarding public safety; risk analyses; and other measures (see Table 3.8). It was also decided to sharpen the safety measures at the Business Jet gates of the airports.

Schiphol Airport in The Netherlands received a high priority. During the past three years several safety incidents, such as an attempted hijacking, fights between aggressive passengers and cabin personnel, confiscated weapons, and others, had been recorded onboard Business Jet flights departing from this airport. These were also accompanied by long delays. Consequently, Business Jet decided last year to place their own scanner and a metal detector at gate B–4 (where most of its flights originate) and to perform additional controls in order not to damage its *safe and reliable* image. One of the Business Jet security teams at Schiphol executed a risk analysis of this process, whereby the systematic approach described under "Process Evaluation" in this chapter was followed. For this purpose a team of six Business Jet volunteers was assembled under the leadership of John van Dam. His personal performance plan, which was discussed in the previous chapter (see Table 4.2), also includes the personal goals that resulted from this analysis. The other team members were Rita Reeves, Rodney Johnson, Warren Jackson, Robert Dean, and Danny Job, who were selected based on their knowledge and expertise in this problem area as well as their social and communicative skills. In this improvement circle (a concept that will be explained in detail in Chapter 9), Rita and Rodney played a facilitating role in the fields of Human Resources

Management and maintenance, respectively. The other group members belong to the Security team. John was in charge of preparing the sessions.

Three sessions were organized, each lasting 1.5 hours. During the first session the team formulated the following team mission: *The mission of our risk analysis team is the systematic identification and elimination of safety problems in order to secure the safety of our airline company.* The team members also defined the subprocesses related to the primary process "Supervision of Gate B–4 at Schiphol Airport." The process was displayed with flowcharts, whereby the following process steps were identified:

1. Passenger places hand luggage on scanner conveyor belt.
2. Hand luggage is scanned.
3. At the signaling or detecting of a suspicious item, search hand luggage and take measures if warranted.
4. Passenger passes through the metal detector gate.
5. If metal detector alarm sounds, search passenger and take measures if warranted.
6. Passenger removes hand luggage from the conveyor belt and boards the airplane.

The other process steps, such as passport check, handing over airline ticket, receiving torn ticket stub, and taking a seat in the airplane, are left out here for the sake of brevity.

The executed risk analysis resulted in several recommendations for flight safety improvement of Business Jet at Schiphol Airport, which were put into operation within six months. Table 5.6 shows the results of the analyses from the fist session. The teamwork process, which is discussed in Chapter 8, was reviewed after the last session.

Process Improvement

A cardinal principle of Total Quality escapes too many managers: you cannot continuously improve interdependent systems and processes until you progressively perfect interdependent, interpersonal relationships.

Stephen R. Covey

In the process improvement step the selected business process is continuously improved (see Figure 5.1). For this purpose Deming's PDCA

Table 5.6

Risk Analysis for Business Jet at Schiphol Airport

Date: October, 2001
Page: 1

Organization: Business Jet
Business Unit: Safety

Participants: John van Dam, Rita Reeves, Rodney Johnson, Warren Jackson, Robert Dean, and Danny Job
Prepared by: John van Dam

Primary Process: Supervision of Gate B–4 at Schiphol Airport   **Team:** Security Schiphol

Subprocess	Failure Mode	Cause	Effect	P	S	R	Action	Responsible	Date
Passenger places hand luggage on scanner conveyor belt	Hand luggage of passenger gets entangled in the scanner with that of fellow passengers	Passengers arbitrarily stack hand luggage on top of each other on the conveyor belt	Passengers take wrong hand luggage with them	6	5	30	Develop working instruction for effective scanner use	Danny	November 2001
							In consultation with Airport Maintenance examine adjustment of scanner conveyor system	Warren	December 2001
Scanner scans hand luggage	In certain cases scanner does not identify suspicious items	Curtains in X-ray equipment allow too much artificial and sunlight to enter the scanner	Increase of safety risks	2	10	20	No action	—	—
If suspicious item is signaled or detected, search hand luggage and take measures if warranted	Hand luggage is searched superficially	Large stream of passengers, great handling speed (time pressure)	Increased chances of successfully committed attacks	9	10	90	Investigate installation of a second scanner (and additional personnel) next to the existing one	Robert	December 2001

Process step	Problem	Cause	Effect				Action	Responsible	Date
Passenger passes though metal detector gate	The detection gate does not identify metal items	Metal sensor is damaged	Increase of safety risks	7	10	70	Consult with Airport Maintenance regarding this and replace sensors	Rodney	January 2002
	Plastic explosives (such as Semtex and C4) are not detected	Limited functioning of metal detector	Increased chance of success of committed attacks	10	10	100	Develop and implement preventive maintenance system	Rodney	February 2002
							Investigate use of tracker dogs specially trained to detect plastic explosives at airplane entrance	Warren and Danny	March 2002
When alarm of metal detector sounds, search passenger and take measures if warranted	Searching passengers is progressing with difficulty	Aggressive behavior of passengers	Long waiting lines in font of metal detectors	8	7	56	Instruct and train security personnel in dealing with and searching of aggressive passengers	John	March 2002
		Insufficient searching skills of security employees	Increase of safety risks	6	10	60	Organize passenger search training for security employees in question	John	February 2002
Passenger removes hand luggage from conveyor belt and boards the airplane	There is no final check at the entrance of the airplane	Does not belong to the assigned tasks of security employees	Increase of safety risks	4	8	32	Analyze and adjust tasks, responsibilities, and authorities of security personnel	Rita	December 2001

cycle is continuously undergone. This cycle consists of the following phases (see Figure 2.5).

- **Plan.** Update the improvement plan that was formulated in the "process selection" step and flesh it out based on the Organizational Balanced Scorecard. Determine improvement objectives, indicate the improvement actions, and indicate how they are related to the critical success factors. The expected results, effects, peripheral conditions, and control factors (time, money, quality, and organization) need to be addressed here as well. An adequate definition of the problem is essential. This aspect is explained in greater detail in the following boxed text. The problem-solving cycle on which this explanation is based is shown in Figure 5.7. Don't forget to take management into account in your analyses, because, according to Joseph M. Juran (1974), approximately 80% of all organizational problems are caused by management!

- **Do.** At first, execute the improvement plan on a limited scale: test the selected solutions, conduct experiments, and train team members in using the improvement methods and techniques.

Figure 5.7

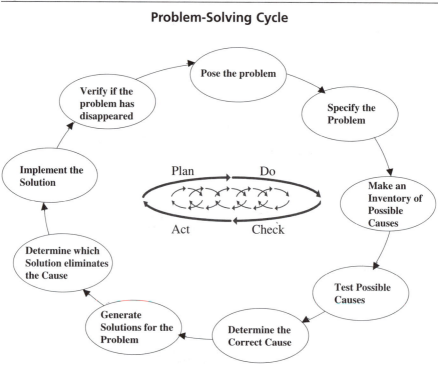

Problem-Solving Cycle

- *Check.* Review the results of these improvement actions based on performance measures; check to what extent improvement objectives can be realized with these actions; and compare the results with the norms or the theory. If necessary, start over.

- *Act.* Implement the results, that is, introduce the proven improvement, bring the process under control, asses the results, document the lessons learned in this phase, continuously improve and monitor the process, and standardize possible process changes. Such standardization implies that the existing working procedures should be adjusted or replaced and that all involved employees should know about these changes. As soon as possible, make these new procedures available to all employees and provide training in using them. Communication, giving feedback, and creating buy-in for the improvements and changes are essential in this step.

When the PDCA cycle is thus worked through repeatedly, the variability in the process decreases, and thus the results are improved continuously. In this phase ongoing rapport with the customer is essential in order to comply with their needs at all times. The cycle therefore begins again with the step *"process selection"* in order to keep track of significant changes in customer needs and to select the critical process to be improved next. This cycle is represented in Figure 5.1 by the line that returns to the starting point. The implication is that a new business process is selected and considered eligible for continuous improvement. Through this approach the customer is continuously satisfied, and the organization is able to come to know itself and its surroundings on an ongoing basis.

Problem Solving

Systematically solving problems encompasses a phased and cyclic process consisting of nine steps (see Figure 5.7). The first two steps in the problem-solving cycle, explained in detail below, relate to problem definition.

Formulate the Definition of the Problem

First of all, it is necessary to appoint an improvement team or an improvement circle, and to define the problem as a team. A precise definition of the problem is essential to find the exact cause for which an effective solution

(continues)

can be generated. For a clear problem description, the team needs to know which problems should be solved, where the problems occur, and which aspects play a role here. Try to get as much information as possible about the problem; consult several information sources regarding the subject, such as customer survey results, customer complaints, data regarding process performance, and discussions with internal customers. Gather all this information, analyze it, define the delineations of problem areas, define the problem as concretely as possible, and formulate the desired final situation (objectives). Discuss these with the problem owner so that you have an accurate problem description.

An inaccurately formulated definition of a problem may lead to ineffective solutions. An accurate problem definition, however, identifies problem characteristics, determines its consequences, focuses on the difference between how the current situation is and how it should be, and consists of a global measurement of the problem (how frequently it occurs, how many there are, when it happens, etc.). For an accurate definition of a problem it is also important to know how the process is presently being executed. Therefore, it is necessary to map the process in flowcharts, whereby all stages from input to output are illustrated. The team should also consult with employees who are directly involved in the process.

It is also important to know whether the measures taken resulted in an improvement. This will require taking measurements at different steps in the process as indicated in the flowchart. You can, for example, put down the number of complaints received daily. It is necessary to understand problem details and translate customer needs into measurable and concrete specifications. Brainstorm the problem from all angles. The five Ws (*When? Where? What? Who? Why?*) guarantee that all relevant questions about the problem are posed: When does the problem occur? When did it first appear? Where does it occur? Where is the biggest need for a solution? What is the problem? What are the causes? What are the boundaries? Who caused it? Who is currently struggling with the problem? Who is responsible for finding a solution? Why does it occur? Why must it be solved? By asking these questions you will get a clear specification of the problem.

Personal Improvement

> Don't bother to be better than your contemporaries or predecessors. Try to be better than yourself.
>
> *William Faulkner*

Thus far I have discussed (regarding your PBSC) who you are, where you want to go, and which personal results you wish to realize. In this phase of the improvement process I will discuss the implementation of your personal improvement actions. Here the focus is the continuous improvement of your skills and behavior, which are the foundation for your individual development, personal success, and well-being. This improvement is also linked to your Personal Balanced Scorecard. The following phases are repeatedly followed here, according to the Deming cycle (see Figure 5.1):

- *Plan.* Select an important personal objective from your Personal Balanced Scorecard (including matching performance measures, targets, and improvement actions) that you want to realize and share your good intentions with a trusted person (life companion, friend, colleague, or supervisor) or with your group. Choose the personal objective with the highest priority number, start off with it, and request feedback. Focus on the things that you are not good at and the habits that limit you, have an unfavorable influence on your life, and deliver poor results.

- *Do.* First, implement your personal improvement actions on a limited scale.

- *Check.* Review the results according to defined performance measures and targets, check to what extent you have realized your personal objectives and adjust your PBSC if needed. By reviewing your PBSC with your trusted friend and thus learning from your experience, your will improve continuously.

- *Act.* Implement the proven personal improvement (i.e., realize the behavioral changes), assess the personal results, document the lessons learned, and improve and monitor your actions and thinking continuously. Chapter 8 illustrates how certain competences (e.g., behavioral and interpersonal skills) can systematically be improved. Also consider balancing your personal ambition with your personal behavior.

When you follow through with the PDCA cycle continuously for the purpose of personal improvement, you both get to know yourself and your surroundings better and will perform better. Personal improvement is a cyclic learning process, which implies that, after the execution of your personal improvement action, you will again select a new improvement action (with the highest priority number) from your PBSC and start working on it. You will continuously satisfy yourself and others with this procedure, thus constantly improving your personal performances. In doing so, you create a stable basis for maximum individual development and personal well-being. For this purpose it is necessary to live according to certain principles. The Vedic principles of behavior according to the *Charaka Samhita*, shown in the following boxed text, can assist you with this.

Vedic Principles of Behavior

- Attention to the development of spirit, health, and useful activities.
- Speaking honestly and with softness.
- Speaking well of others at all times.
- Never getting carried away by anger.
- Avoiding extreme behavior.
- Remaining calm and without violence.
- Taking into consideration purity toward yourself and your surroundings.
- Being caring.
- Having respect for others.
- Cherishing love and having compassion.
- Developing a simple state of mind and innocent behavior.
- Staying in the company of wise people.
- Maintaining a positive attitude toward life.
- Being in control of yourself and living in harmony with your personal mission.
- Dedicating yourself to higher knowledge and to the development of a higher level of consciousness.

Source: Sharma and Clark, 1998.

These Vedic principles of behavior are related to individual learning and behavioral change. To promote collective learning or organizational change, I encourage you to apply personal improvement collectively as well, by organizing voluntary PBSC sessions. During these sessions of approximately two hours (possibly during a business lunch meeting), give each participant an opportunity to articulate his or her PBCS to the group and present the results of executed personal improvement actions. Based on the questions asked and the feedback received, people can gain more insight into their own personal ambition and will, therefore, be better equipped to review and adjust it.

The process of personal improvement discussed in the chapter deals with your personal characteristics and behavior, and focuses on your well-being and success in the community. The development of your competences, based on the expert execution of your job within your organization, is discussed in the following chapter.

Developing

6

Thinking is the hardest work there is, which is probably the reason why so few engage in it.

Henry Ford

In the past, discussing hierarchical relationships was a taboo. This is starting to change. People have more knowledge now and find that their needs are also important. Organizations that align personal and shared ambition, and link them to the competence development process, become more human.

Hubert Rampersad

In this chapter the development cycle is central. Here the emphasis is on the job-oriented competence development of individual employees and managers; this in turn enables them to do their job properly. Due to their gradual development and education the quality of their job performance improves and optimal use is made of their abilities to deliver the required organizational performance. Result planning, coaching, appraisal, and job oriented-competence development are continuously followed in this cyclic process (see Figure 6.1). Figure 6.2 shows the correlation between this cycle and other TPS elements. This figure also illustrates the personal and organizational alignment that is essential for the individual employee's competence development. Most organizations incorrectly implement the competence development system; frequently there is no clear connection between this system and the shared organizational ambition. Moreover, there is no connection

Figure 6.1

The Fourth Phase in the TPS Cycle

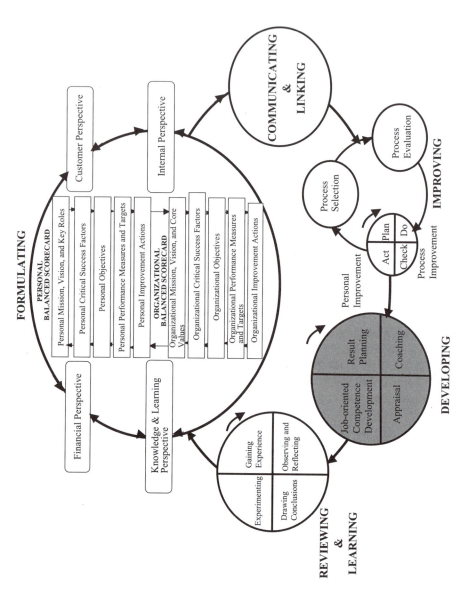

Figure 6.2

Correlation between the Scorecards, Competence Profile, and Development Cycle

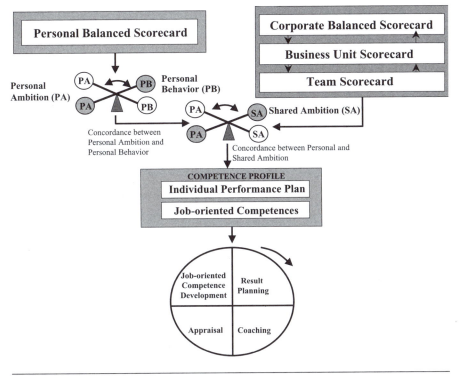

Source: Rampersad, 2002.

with the personal ambition of individual employees (see Figure 6.2). This does not stimulate learning, nor does it benefit sustainable organizational improvement and development. In HRM literature, the importance of these starting points is also usually ignored. This chapter shows how, based on the TPS concept, competence development and related appraisal can be handled more effectively from now on.

As I have mentioned before, result-oriented work is an essential part of the Total Performance Scorecard philosophy. We have seen in Chapter 3 how the requested results form the starting point for organizational activities. Through these, each employee knows what the shared ambition and the related organizational objectives are, and what is expected of each employee for the realization of these objectives. The next step in the TPS cycle is helping employees to develop their *job-oriented competences* and to improve their work. This happens in accordance with the four phases of the introduced development cycle (see Figure 6.3):

Figure 6.3

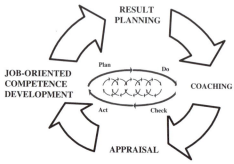

The Development Cycle

• Develop competence profiles
• Make agreements regarding the results to be achieved and the use of the competences
• How can the performance and development objectives be realized?

RESULT PLANNING

• Courses and on-the-job training
• Creation of practice situations
• Accompanying experienced colleagues
• Customer feedback meetings
• Traineeship
• Development tips
• Developing and implementing talent development programs

JOB-ORIENTED COMPETENCE DEVELOPMENT

Plan — Do — Check — Act

COACHING

• Help obtain the agreed upon results
• Assist with initiation of the agreed upon competences
• Discuss progress realization
• Test the agreements
• Give feedback

APPRAISAL

• Give opinion regarding the functioning
• Check if all agreements are complied with and the agreed-upon results are obtained
• Apply 360° feedback
• Evaluate result and career agreements
• Final review

Source: Rampersad, 2002.

- *Result Planning.* This phase deals with the creation of result agreements based on performance objectives and the selection of a set of job-oriented competences supporting these objectives. These two elements form part of the competence profile of the current job. In this phase the individual performance plan is prepared together with the manager. Based on the plan, periodic (usually annual) agreements are made between the manager and employee regarding the realization of the performances and development objectives. In this planning meeting agreements are made as well about the use of selected competences.

- *Coaching.* In this phase the manager and employee get together at fixed intervals to discuss the employee's progress; individual guidance takes place, agreements are tested and adjusted, and feedback is given.

- *Appraisal.* The formal appraisal takes place after a certain period (usually one year), to confirm if all agreements were met, if the agreed upon results were achieved, and if so, how they were realized.

- *Job-Oriented Competence Development.* This phase involves the competence development of employees through, for example, courses and on-the-job training, the creation of practice situations, accompanying experienced colleagues, customer feedback meetings, traineeship, development tips, and talent development programs.

Through the systematic development of these activities, it is possible to direct and control the development of job-oriented competences. Here a balance ought to be struck between the objectives, wishes, expectations, aspirations, and needs of the individual employee and those of the organization. See also Chapter 3 and Figure 6.2 in which I stress the necessity of a balance between the personal and shared organizational ambition.

Before employees and managers go through the four phases of the development cycle they should be thoroughly prepared. Advance preparation involves developing a function matrix, which contains the relationship between function families and levels, and formulating a linked training and career policy. In addition, other aspects, such as linking appraisal to reward, career planning, recruitment and selection, should also be taken into account. These are all part of the organizational HRM policy. As an example of such a policy, I direct the reader's attention here to the Five Es that form the foundation for Microsoft's effective HRM policy (see the following boxed text). Since it is beyond the scope of this book to explain all aspects of HRM policy, I limit myself in the rest of this chapter to describing the four phases of the development cycle as it is implemented at Business Jet (see Appendixes A and B). For detailed information concerning other HRM systems, please refer to the very extensive literature in this field.

The Five Es of the Human Resources Management Policy at Microsoft

1. *EMPOWERMENT*: Give people the power to initiate tasks they can execute from beginning to end.
2. *EQUALITY*: Treat everyone the same and demand that everyone else does this too.
3. *EMPHASIS ON PERFORMANCE*: Put a strong emphasis on performance and tell people ahead of time exactly what they are expected to do.
4. *E-MAIL*: Use e-mail to get messages to and from people and continuously use open and constructive deliberations about important and useful issues.
5. *ENRICHMENT*: Enrich people with rewards for success and do not only use financial reward for this purpose but also praise and recognition.

Result Planning

> All our dreams can come true, if we have the courage to pursue them.
>
> *Walt Disney*

Result planning is the first phase in the development cycle (see Figure 6.4). This phase consists of the drafting of the competence profile of the current job. Based on this result agreements are made that are related to the performance objectives and a set of job-oriented competence profiles. These aspects are central to the planning meeting between employee and manager.

Preparing the Competence Profile

In practice, the term "competence" is used in the following three ways:

1. Uniquely distinguished organizational characteristics that can be built upon and maintained by a combination of knowledge, technologies, and processes. These *organizationally oriented competences* are called *core competences* (Hamel and Prahalad, 1994). They are strongly related to the Organizational Balanced Scorecard.

Figure 6.4

The First Phase in the Development Cycle

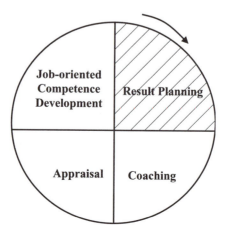

2. A collection of knowledge, experience, skills, values and norms, and behaviors of an individual employee that form the foundation of his or her personal success and well-being in society. These *individually oriented competences* are especially related to the Personal Balanced Scorecard.
3. A collection of knowledge, experience, skills, values and norms, and behavior required for adequately fulfilling the job. These *job-oriented competences* are related to the individual performance plan and are included in the competence profile. These are central to this chapter.

As you may recall, in Chapter 2 I defined the term "knowledge" as a *function of information, culture, and skills.* This implies that information, capabilities, experience, skills, attitudes, norms, values, opinions, and principles are also part of the definition of competence. The following boxed text illustrates the role of the PBSC, OBSC, and individual performance plan within the Total Performance Scorecard framework.

PERSONAL BALANCED SCORECARD → Personal improvement of associates related to *individually oriented competencses* and aimed at their personal well-being and success in society.

ORGANIZATIONAL BALANCED SCORECARD → Improvement and controllability of business processes related to the *core competences* and aimed at competitive advantage for the organization.

INDIVIDUAL PERFORMANCE PLAN → Gradual education and development of individual employees, related to the *job-oriented competences* and aimed at effective job fulfillment.

The job-oriented competences are part of the *competence profile,* which forms the input for following through the development cycle (see Figure 6.2). This profile encompasses the individual performance plan and a collection of knowledge components (including experience, skills, values and norms, and behavior) necessary to realize the job objectives and related results. The organizational critical success factors are translated here into the results and capabilities to be acquired by employees. The competence profile of the current job consists of:

1. *The individual performance plan.* This is an overview of the requested results (objectives, performance measures, and targets) belonging to the job, about which periodic result agreements are made. The result areas (*financial, customers, internal processes,*

and *knowledge and learning*) and the related result agreements form the starting point in the planning meeting between manager and employee.

2. *A set of job-oriented competences* (including subsequent levels per competence). This is what an individual employee must possess to realize the shared organizational ambition.

The preparation of the competence profile, and consequently the development cycle that follows, comes from the shared organizational ambition and partly from the employee's personal ambition (see Figure 6.5).

The Individual Performance Plan

The individual performance plan is derived from the team scorecard (see Figure 4.2). In this plan, managers and employees together indicate which job-oriented results are expected from the employee during the coming period. The joint preparation of this plan has a positive effect on the employee's motivation. It promotes self-guidance, due to the fact that the employee can influence his or her result achievements. The individual performance plan has almost the same construction as the BSC, with job-oriented objectives, performance measures, and targets that are divided over the four result areas (*financial, customers, internal processes,* and *knowledge and learning*). These are the essential areas that are derived from the organizational mission and on which employees should focus to realize the job objectives to be scored. The employee's objectives should be formulated in such a way that they are challenging, feasible, and acceptable. Therefore, the emphasis of the individual performance plan focuses on the results to be obtained instead of, as often happens, the tasks to be executed. A priority number can be assigned to the objectives, according to the approach described in Chapter 3. Here, objectives that deliver the highest contribution to the team's most important critical success factors get the highest priority.

To illustrate this process, I present the individual performance plan of John van Dam (Business Jet security team leader) in Table 6.1. John and his business unit manager (Steve Daniel) drafted this plan together in January 2002. It was derived from John's team scorecard (see Table 4.1) and includes what is expected from him in order to realize his security team's vision. This plan also includes some elements from John's Personal Balanced Scorecard. Together with his job-oriented competences, these were central in the planning, coaching, and appraisal meeting between Steve and John in 2002 (see Appendix A).

Figure 6.5

From Personal Ambition to Competence Development

Personal Ambition
•Who am I? For what reason do I live?
•Where am I going? What do I stand for?

Personal Objectives
• Which measurable short-term
personal results do I want to achieve?

Personal Performance Measures and Targets
How can I measure my personal results?
What makes my personal objectives measurable?

Shared Organizational Ambition
•Why does our organization exist?
•What is our identity? What is the purpose of our existence?
•Where are we going together?

Organizational Objectives
•Which short-term measurable results must we achieve?

Organizational Performance Measures and Targets
•What makes the organizational vision and objectives measurable?
•Which values must be obtained? What are the targets?

Improvement Actions
• How do we want to achieve the results?

Individual Performance Plan
•Which personal results must I achieve in my job and what must I do to realize the shared results?
•How can I measure my personal results?

Job-oriented Competences
•Which capabilities and skills must I have and which behaviors must I master to effectively fulfill my job, and through this try to realize the shared results?

Job-Oriented Competences

The job-oriented competences can be categorized as:

- *Competences related to the job and level of thinking.*
- *Knowledge competences*; what he or she must learn and know.
- *Skill competences*; what he or she must be able to do.

Table 6.1

John van Dam's Individual Performance Plan

INDIVIDUAL PERFORMANCE PLAN

Organization: Business Jet   **Department:** Safety   **Manager:** Steve Daniel
Employee: John van Dam   **Job:** Team Leader   **Team:** Security Schiphol Airport   **Period:** Jan. 2002–Dec. 2002

	Objectives	Performance Measures	Targets
FINANCIAL	• Working more cost consciously • Implementing cost saving measures • Contribution to failure costs study	• Efficiency • Number of implemented measures • Number of developed improvement proposals	• Increase of 10% in 2002 • At least two a quarter • Increase of 30% in 2002
CUSTOMERS	• Customer-friendly behavior while executing security tasks	• Number of passenger complaints	• Decrease of at least 50% this year
INTERNAL PROCESSES	• Contribution provided to risk analysis • Developing safety procedures • Less serious mistakes made during execution of security tasks • Motivated • Contribution provided as chairman of the project team "Improvement Security at Schiphol Airport" • Physical and mental health	• Number of developed safety suggestions • Number of developed or updated safety procedures • Number of serious mistakes • Labor productivity • Number of concrete safety ideas • Percent of sick leave	• Minimum of 2 quarterly • 8 procedures in 2002 • Decrease of 50% by the year's end • Increase to 80% at the latest by December 2002 • Minimum of 5 in 2002 • Decrease of no less than 2% by no later than November 2002

	Objective	Measure	Target
KNOWLEDGE and LEARNING	Effective coaching of team members	Percent of stress	Decrease of at least 30% by the end of 2002
	Trust of management regarding job fulfillment	Percent of Employees who think they are coached effectively	75% in 2002
		Level of satisfaction of the safety manager	Minimum of 75% by the end of 2002
	Improved competences in the field of Safety	Safety certificate	30% of certificates obtained in 2002
	Openness and honesty regarding knowledge exchange between colleagues	Experience level of colleagues regarding knowledge exchange	75% by the end of 2002
	Active participation in improvement teams	Number of solved safety problems	Increase of 30% by the end of 2002
	Colleagues trained in "frisking and dealing with aggressive passengers"	Number of trained colleagues	25 colleagues in 2002
	Improved coaching skills	Satisfaction degree of team members regarding way of coaching	Minimum of 75% by the end of 2002

- *Behavioral competences*; attitudes, principles, norms and values, demeanor, and the driving forces needed to hold the respective position.

Examples of job-oriented competences are: delegating, coaching, managing, working independently, acting in a customer-oriented manner, vision, cooperation, interpersonal skills, organizing, process orientation, acting proactively, inspiring, resoluteness, persuasion, and so on. For the effective fulfillment of one's job one should have different competences at one's disposal. The number of organizational competences differs and primarily depends on the nature and complexity of the job. In practice, between five and twenty competences are chosen for most jobs to be carried out. This number is higher for certain careers, such as consultants for organizational change for whom Doppler and Lauterburg (1996) recommended a long list of thirty-three competences (see Table 6.2).

It is important to be realistic and not to exaggerate with regard to the number of competences. Let the manager and the employee select five to ten competences together that are most relevant to the job, such as those where the organization wants to excel. The following questions can be useful for this purpose (van der Togt and Kemp, 1997):

- What are the critical job tasks that determine if someone delivers a performance that is considered to be successful and in accordance with the organizational norms?
- What should the employee be able to accomplish to execute tasks adequately (which skills)?
- What tranining should the employee have in order to do this (which knowledge)?
- Which demeanor or attitude is expected from him or her?

Judging the selected competences involves giving scores during the appraisal meeting. Using a separate form, point scales with two to five levels and different descriptions are used to indicate these scores. A four-point scale with the following description occurs frequently:

1. Above stated requirements
2. According to stated requirements
3. Not completely according to stated requirements
4. Below stated requirements

After defining the selected competences a description of the behaviors in each competence is given in four to seven levels, whereby the behavior for the respective competence is worked out along different angles. For example, the competence *creativity* can be subdivided into the following five levels, from low creativity to high creativity (Wanrooy, 2001):

Table 6.2

Competences of Organizational Changers

A. Personal Characteristics
1) Healthy physical constitution (self-confidence, stability, immunity to stress)
2) Fundamentally positive attitude (optimistic, constructive attitude)
3) Openness and honesty (direct, spontaneous, genuine)
4) Willingness to assume responsibilities (personal engagement)
5) Cooperative (opposed to elitist, hierarchical, authoritarian behavior)
6) Courage to take a personal stand and make own decisions (courage to stand up for your own convictions)
7) Meeting obligations (appointments)
8) Intuition (access to emotions)
9) Sense of reality (feeling for what is realistic)
10) Humor (ability to provide relaxation)

B. Special Skills
1) Ability to create an environment of openness and trust
2) Being able to listen well (listening actively)
3) Convincing people and enthusing them (so that they are motivated and can identify with themselves)
4) Ability to integrate (bringing people together in a team and also being able to let a team truly work as a unit)
5) Conflict handling (not being afraid to have your own point of view and enter into a confrontation)
6) Process competence (ability to understand and guide developments)
7) Chaos control (ability to keep working in complex situations)
8) Strategic competence (ability to see complex relations and thus take relevant measures)
9) Intercultural competence (ability to work in different social structures)
10) Communicating clearly (thinking clearly, being brief and to the point, formulating expressions in a way that is simple and understandable for everyone)

C. Specific Experience
1) Self-perception, observation of the "I" (being able to observe yourself intensively for long periods of time in order to understand your own personality, motives, and social behavior)
2) Individual mentoring (advising, guiding, and coaching individuals)
3) Teamwork and development (leading and developing small groups)
4) Providing guidance for communication within large groups (organizing and leading work meetings of groups of employees)
5) Project management (organizing and leading change projects)

D. Specific Knowledge
1) Basic knowledge of psychology
2) Fundamental knowledge of business economy
3) Systems and chaos theory
4) Group dynamics
5) Organizational theory
6) Organizational psychology
7) Establishment of organizational development (objectives, strategies)
8) Intervention in area of organizational development (tools, methods, and processes)

Source: Doppler and Lauterburg, 1996.

1. Thinks along with others about new ideas and solutions.
2. Comes up with new ideas and solutions.
3. Notices connections others do not see.
4. Develops innovative ideas and approaches.
5. Stimulates others to develop innovative ideas and approaches.

Table 6.3 shows the development of the competence *independence* in four levels, from somewhat below par (A) to excellent (D) (Broek, Giessen, and Oers-van Dorst, 2000). Figure 6.6 shows the characteristics of the competence *cooperation* in five levels, using a method that is applied frequently in practice. Appendix A shows the development of the competences *learning ability, problem solving, stress proof, coaching, customer-orientation behavior, listening, persuasiveness,* and *vision.*

At the end of the appraisal period the manager addresses the levels of each competence, based on the observed job performance. A judgment for each competence is determined, which results in the final judgment. In certain cases a weighing factor is assigned to the competences whereby, after multiplication and addition, a final result is reached.

The Planning Meeting

In the planning meeting between the manager and employee agreements are made regarding the result areas, objectives, performance measures, and targets on the one hand, and the use of job-oriented competences for adequate job fulfillment on the other. During this agreement meeting between the two partners, pertinent opinions and

Table 6.3

Elaboration of the Competence *Independence*			
Independence			
Frequently needs help, correction, supervision, and additional instruction. Plans and organizes own work insufficiently.	Executes tasks independently. Divides own work efficiently. Only needs help with nonroutine work.	Executes nearly all tasks independently. Only needs assistance with very difficult situations.	Usually acts independently, very systematically, and efficiently, even under pressure and in very difficult situations.
A	B	C	D

Figure 6.6

Elaboration of the Competence *Cooperation*

> **Definition: Delivering a contribution to the realization of the shared team objectives**
>
> Levels:
>
> 1. **Participates:** Participates in team activities. Does his or her part of the job. Abides by team decisions. Channels relevant information to others. Offers to help when asked.
> 2. **Encourages others:** Encourages the strong points of team members and supports them with shortcomings. Inspires others and gives them the feeling that they are important. Reacts constructively to the ideas of others. Improves mutual communication.
> 3. **Creates involvement:** Expresses appreciation of others and shows them respect. Involves others and through this tries to create self-esteem. Participates actively and is helpful. Listens to the problems of colleagues.
> 4. **Stimulates team learning:** Continuously focuses on the development and mobilization of the knowledge of team members. Values the input of others and learns from them. Also learns from his or her own mistakes. Shares knowledge with others. Evaluates ideas and suggestions from others. Interprets information. Gives tips to colleagues on how to handle things. Gives suggestions. Provides constructive feedback.
> 5. **Provides team spirit:** Creates an environment of enjoyment, passion, devotion, and enthusiasm. Gives form and direction to the effort of the team and creates an environment in which team members trust, help, accept, and appreciate each other, as well as are strongly motivated. Is aware of his or her own team role and core qualities as well as those of other team members. Keeps team moral high, avoids conflicts, and can negotiate well. Knows internal customers and suppliers well.

arguments are exchanged, expectations are expressed, and it is determined what each person will do to realize the results and to comply with the required competence demands. Here the employee will also indicate if all this is feasible, what he or she thinks can or cannot be realized, what his or her personal ambitions and aspirations are, what he or she will need in order to achieve these results, and what possible barriers there might be. On the result agreement forms, the following aspects are documented: name, occupation, and signature of the employee as well as the manager; the agreement period; the result areas; five to eight related agreements (with, for each agreement, its relative importance, one or more objectives, and the matching performance measures and targets); the manager's support for the achievement of the agreed upon results; and the date of the planning, coaching, and appraisal meetings.

The agreements regarding the behaviors (competences) supporting the results to be obtained are frequently written on a separate form. For each competence the following aspects are documented: definition; levels and their relative importance; the expected behaviors of the employee during the coming appraisal period; and the support to be given by the manager when the agreed upon competences are used. The manager and employee each receive a copy of the completed forms; the original is filed in the personnel dossier. Appendix A shows the completed forms used in 2002 at the planning meeting between Business Jet's John van Dam and his security manager Steve Daniel.

Coaching

> People are not an asset, not a resource. They are a treasure to be protected.
>
> *W. Edwards Deming*

During this second phase of the development cycle (see Figure 6.7), the manager helps the employee to achieve the agreed upon results and helps initiate the agreed upon competences.

Figure 6.7

The Second Phase in the Development Cycle

Two to three times a year the manager will conduct an open and two-sided progress meeting with the employee. Based on the copy of the completed planning forms, the progress towards realization, and the agreements made with respect to performance and development, employee's objectives are evaluated, tested, and adjusted if needed. Coaching occurs here in order to help improve job quality, develop the talents of the employee (long-term as well as short-term), improve the way he or she works, provide new challenges, and have a positive influence on his or her motivation.

The first coaching meeting deserves special attention. The objectives, rules, methods, and frequency of coaching must be clear to everyone. In the coaching section of the appraisal form, the following points are mentioned: what is going well, what can be done better, how it can be done better, which obstacles have been encountered, which situational factors have influenced the completion of the job, which training must be provided, and how. The questions that are central here are: How is it going? How can it be done better? What motivates you? What discourages you? Does everyone abide by the agreements made? Are the behaviors displayed sufficient to achieve the results? Where does the job constantly go wrong? What have we learned? Agreements are also made for the period up to the appraisal (who does what and when?).

In the coaching phase, interim reviews of the employee will also take place, with a presentation of the strong and weak points, if necessary. In this phase the manager works as a *formal coach*. In his or her daily role as manager the role of *informal coach* is also to be fulfilled, without the use of forms and strict procedures. This less formal role is discussed in Chapter 8, which also describes how effective coaching can benefit the self-guidance and learning ability of employees. After the formal coaching sessions, the partners (manager and employee) keep the report of the meeting until all agreements are realized. Appendix A reproduces the forms completed in 2002 for the coaching meetings between John van Dam and his security manager Steve Daniel.

Appraisal

> I have a different vision of leadership. A leader is someone who brings people together.
>
> *George W. Bush*

Appraisal is the third phase in the development cycle (see Figure 6.8). This takes place during the appraisal meeting at the end of the

Figure 6.8

The Third Phase in the Development Cycle

period. The 360°–feedback approach is used more and more often within the scope of appraisal, in order to obtain a more reliable image of behaviors. This system is a supplement to the appraisal, whereby the employee not only obtains feedback from his supervisor but also from colleagues, customers, and others. In this section the appraisal and the 360°–feedback system are discussed briefly.

The Appraisal Meeting

During the appraisal meeting the forms that were completed during the previous phases of result planning and coaching are discussed. This meeting takes one to two hours and, contrary to the coaching meeting, is one-sided. Here the manager gives his or her opinion about how the employee is performing, without input from the employee. This appraisal is based on an observation of the employee's behavior during the entire past period and the realization of the result agreements. The manager checks if all agreements are fulfilled, whether the agreed upon results are obtained according to the targets, and how they were realized. This assessment deals primarily with the results of the measurements. The result and career agreements that have been made are also evaluated. By giving feedback to the employee throughout the year, and by having frequent coaching meetings, the likelihood that the employee will accept the appraisal is positively influenced and surprises are prevented.

The manager gives his or her judgment regarding employee performance on the appraisal form, as per result agreement and competence. Based on these two opinions a final opinion is given. This form also registers the meeting date and development needs (education and training to be followed in order to improve employee performance and capability development). The appraisal meeting concludes with an explanation about the opinion, as well as the signature of the manager and the employee. The completed appraisal form is placed in the employee's personnel file, and both the manager and employee receive a copy of it. In Appendix A the report of the appraisal meeting between Steve Daniel and John van Dam concerning the period January–December 2002 has been included.

360° Feedback

The 360°–feedback method is an effective form of appraisal, whereby employees not only obtain feedback from the immediate supervisors regarding how they work (behavior and performance), but also from colleagues, subordinates, customers, suppliers, and others who have good insight on their daily activities. They function here as a provider of feedback and a point of reference, by completing a questionnaire about the employee's job-oriented competences. This list may also be completed by the employee, who functions here as the feedback receiver. The 360°–feedback system is a valuable supplement to the mixed appraisal system described earlier. It is a method used more frequently at middle management and operational levels to obtain a reliable picture of the employee's behavior. It is an effective method for learning, improving, and performing.

This approach results in a feedback report that is used as input for the appraisal and competence development of the employee. The development of a 360°–feedback system can be divided into the following phases:

1. Selecting the pertinent job-oriented competences from the prepared competence profile of the respective employee; these competences are related to the individual performance plan and the employee's Personal Balanced Scorecard.
2. Translating each competence into a number of postulations; for example, the following postulations can be formulated for the competence *"applying knowledge"* (Broek, Griessen, and Oers-van Dorst, 2000):
   - Often needs support with routine matters
   - Remains well-informed about developments
   - Needs professional support only with difficult cases
   - Possesses more than enough knowledge to perform all tasks
   - Picks up new tasks quickly
   - Is considered a source of information by others

3. Defining possible answers for the postulations; in general, the following five-point scale is used for this purpose: *completely agrees with, agrees with, somewhat agrees with, disagrees with,* and *completely disagrees with.*
4. Selecting feedback providers; together with the manager, the employee selects the people who have good insight into his or her work. These can be colleagues, subordinates, and even customers and suppliers.
5. Completing the questionnaire; responding to the postulations of the feedback providers.
6. Processing and interpreting the answers. The employee's own answers and those of the manager are compared to those of the rest of the feedback providers. This phase results in a feedback report that is discussed with the employee. At this point agreements are made and actions are planned regarding the work to be done in the coming year and further competence development. The central question here is: which behavior should not be displayed anymore or should be displayed more often in order to obtain higher performances?

During the appraisal of John van Dam at Business Jet, the 360°–feedback system was used to supplement the appraisal meeting and to create a solid basis for his competence development. For this purpose, only the competences *customer-oriented acting, coaching,* and *knowledge application* were judged with the aid of this system, because these are directly related to his position as team leader. These results are included in Appendix B.

Job-Oriented Competence Development

> The gift of fantasy has meant more to me than my talent for absorbing positive knowledge.
>
> *Albert Einstein*

Once the planning, coaching, and appraisal meetings have been conducted and 360°–feedback obtained, both the employee and manager know which job-oriented competences should be developed further in order to fulfill the job adequately and professionally. The fourth phase in the development process thus deals with promoting conscious and unconscious learning, which is central to the last phase of the cycle (see Figure 6.9).

A broad range of instruments can be used for the employee's competence development, such as:

Figure 6.9

The Fourth Phase in the Development Cycle

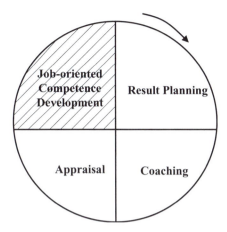

- Courses, workshops, conferences, and on-the-job training.
- Creation of practice situations.
- Individual guidance and coaching in the workplace.
- Accompanying experienced colleagues.
- Customer feedback meetings.
- Benchmarking.
- Traineeship, or having the employee do a work study in other business units or organizations.
- Development tips.
- Talent development programs.

In many cases it is mandatory to follow all these development routes, which are meant to give the employee the opportunity to develop the competences important to the effective fulfillment of his or her job. It is encouraged that these competences be developed in practice as much as possible, based on *"learning by doing"* and *"on the job"* situations. Obtaining and learning new insights and new skills, and integrating them into daily work, results in behavior change and in working more effectively. It is useful to observe here that knowledge and skills competences can be acquired. Behavioral competences, on the other hand, are partly innate and thus more difficult to acquire and learn. In most cases, however, they can be developed through individual coaching.

To effectively fulfill his or her job it is necessary that the employee have a stable knowledge base with continuous availability of the best knowledge. This may be accomplished through a *talent development program*. Doorewaard and Nijs (1999) mention the following requirements for on effective talent development program:

- Must relate to knowledge, skills, and attitude of the employee; must include learning from one's own strengths and weaknesses (reflection).
- Must match organizational objectives and strategies; the objectives must be translated into concrete development activities, whereby the employees themselves are responsible for their learning results.
- Must be adjusted to the specific learning situation.
- Must be embedded in the working situation; should not be separated from the working situation or the career. There must be a continuous interaction between working and learning.
- Colleagues and managers are in charge of this process too, not only the trainer.
- Development is a process that searches for direction, whereby the "best fit" between employee and organization may be found.

Weggeman (1997) also has an interesting view of talent development. He points out that such a program should be focused on:

1. *Transfer of explicit state-of-the-art knowledge*; among other things by:
   - Task-dependent organizing of multidisciplinary brainstorming sessions and problem-solving meetings.
   - Implementing a proactive education policy where internal and external courses, symposia, seminars, working conferences, and so on are included.
   - Introducing a series of lectures by external specialists.
2. *Sharing implicit knowledge*; among other things, by appointing mentors or coaches to junior employees; periodic rotation of carriers of valuable and scarce knowledge through different business units, or letting them participate in different teams; organizing internal project review meetings; and stimulating the use of gained knowledge by making available time, facilities, and rewards.
3. *Improving the skills to learn (learning to learn better)*; among other things, by making available self-assessment instruments where, for example, the employee's own learning style, behavior

type, team role, customer orientation, and other elements can be assessed; organization-wide synchronized planning of free time when professionals can share knowledge with each other; and offering a course on "learning to learn."

To benefit effective talent development it is also suggested to systematically include the employee's Personal Balanced Scorecard in the development process and align it with his or her competence development. In addition, encourage employees to bring into practice what they have learned from development efforts and to share their knowledge and experience with colleagues. When they do so, pay them compliments. Ask them in which area they wish to develop their learning possibilities and let them include these in their PBSC and individual performance plan. McCall (1998) gives an interesting overview of possible measures for stimulating the competence development process, as can be seen from the following boxed text.

Measures for Stimulating the Competence Development Process

Improving Information	Providing Incentives and Resources	Supporting Change
• Give specific feedback	• Formulate specific and measurable development objectives	• Give emotional support
• Give many examples	• Place development in the context of organizational strategy	• Look for change in the context of a system
• Give feedback on important criteria, possibly with regard to determined competences	• Find ways to assess progress in the scope of development objectives	• Determine what influence the requested change will have on others, on the nature of the job, etc.
• Give feedback about development, performances, and results	• Make people responsible for achieving development objectives	• Change the context if needed
• Expect business unit managers to acknowledge problems	• Involve the person in question with the formulation of objectives and norms	• Create an environment in which change is supported and encouraged

(continues)

- Use reliable sources

- Do not beat around the bush

- Give needed feedback, even if someone works properly

- Provide perspective when and if messages are confusing

- Interpret feedback in view of the future and the present

- Create a context for feedback that reflects the future organizational strategy
- Give feedback in a form that is acceptable to the receiver

- Increase the quality of the feedback coming from the work floor, customers, and others

- Make development a real priority
- Make a portion of employee wages dependent on personal development and functioning
- Promote or transfer people based on development considerations
- Promote those who serve as a role model for desired developmental behavior
- Provide, as much as possible, rewards and acknowledgement in order to attain growth
- Involve more resources when establishing development programs
- Before anything, see to it that the existing reward system is not in conflict with personal development
- See to it that there are role models
- Provide a safe environment in which to practice and try out new things
- Coach and train new people on how to acquire new skills

Source: Used with permission of M. W. McCall. *High Flyers: Developing the Next Generation of Leaders.* Boston: Harvard Business School Press, 1998.

Based on the planning, coaching, and appraisal meetings, and the 360°–feedback system, the appraisal of John van Dam of Business Jet has resulted in several actions and agreements to be applied to his continuing competence development. These are included in Appendixes A and B.

As this chapter has shown, continuously following the development cycle is essential for effective employee job fulfillment. Once the development effort has been complete, the cycle is traversed again during the following period, yet this time it is based on the updated competence profile. In this way employees constantly improve and are better able to fulfill their jobs. They continuously satisfy managers, colleagues, customers, and others close to them. Going through the development cycle also contributes to the realization of their Personal Balanced Scorecard. In short, the developing phase benefits both their own learning ability and the learning ability of the organization— which is the focus of the following chapter.

Reviewing and Learning

7

Anyone who stops learning is old, whether at twenty or eighty.
Anyone who keeps learning stays young. The greatest thing in life
is to keep your mind young.

Henry Ford

Where there is enjoyment, there is learning, and where fear
dominates, learning stops.

Hubert Rampersad

The last phase in the TPS cycle involves reviewing the scorecards,
updating them based on changing circumstances; identification of
improvement possibilities; and documentation of the lessons learned.
These learning aspects in the TPS cycle will be discussed in detail
in this chapter. They are related to David Kolb's learning cycle
(1984), which is part of the knowledge and learning perspective
(see Figure 7.1). I will discuss individual as well as collective learning,
and how, based on this, organizational learning capacity can be
increased. For this purpose a knowledge management audit is introduced to measure this ability and to develop a sustainable learning
organization.

Reviewing

He who learns but does not think, is lost! He who thinks but does
not learn is in great danger.

Confucius

Figure 7.1

The Fifth Phase in the TPS Cycle

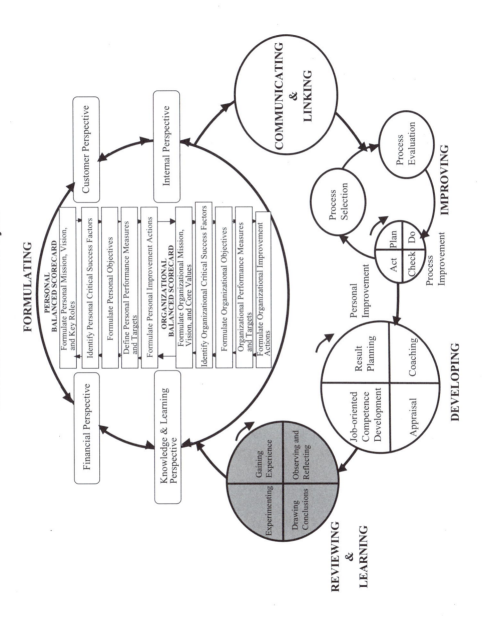

Reviewing involves checking what went right or wrong in the previous TPS phases. It is concerned with testing to what extent the formulated objectives have been realized. Depending on possible differences between objectives and results, the execution or the formulation of the scorecards can be adjusted. This last phase in the TPS cycle (see Figure 7.1) is linked to the formulating phase; is done in order to continually align the scorecards to the environment. Because of the learning effect created by this, the organization is better able to know itself and its environment on an ongoing basis. Of course, this phase also applies to the individual employee who continually reviews his or her Personal Balanced Scorecard and thus learns more about oneself. On the basis of both individual and organizational reviewing, the organizational learning ability continuously expands.

The activities in this phase of the learning cycle are also shown in Figure 2.10. More specifically, feedback from employees forms an important means of testing the organizational assumptions regarding the strategic objectives and improvement actions. For this learning process it will be necessary from time to time to reevaluate the scorecards on strategic, tactical, operational, and individual level, and to discuss the delivered performances periodically. Through periodic reflection on the executed improvement and development actions—and by checking if they really work—the organization can make conclusions regarding the realization of the strategic objectives. In this phase, deviations from objectives should be seen as opportunities to learn. In general, the corporate scorecard's review is performed annually. The business unit and team scorecard's review, on the other hand, is initially done monthly, then supplemented with quarterly and annual evaluations. At these reviews ideas are presented to the management team, strategic issues are discussed, and suggestions are presented for scorecard updates.

From time to time the Personal Balanced Scorecard must also be evaluated by the individual employees and adapted accordingly. The frequency of review depends on the individual person. It is recommended that you review your PBSC monthly or quarterly with a trusted person. By learning from your previous experiences, you will get to know yourself better and improve each time. Your performance plan should also be reviewed regularly according to the development cycle. As we saw in Chapter 6, this evaluation is part of the semiannual coaching and annual appraisal meeting with your supervisor.

Learning

> The only sustainable competitive advantage is the ability to learn faster than the competition.
>
> *Arie de Geus*

Learning is a cyclic and cumulative process of continually updating your knowledge by adding new things to your knowledge repertory. This is done in order to change your behavior, on the basis of which you can function better. Learning is a process of continuous personal transformation. A useful distinction can be made here between *conscious learning* and *unconscious learning*, which are often defined as learning through education and learning through experience, respectively. Conscious learning often leads to a higher capacity level than unconscious learning, because it offers the possibility to better guide and control the self-learning process. For this reason, it is necessary to have insight into your personal ambition (self-image and self-knowledge). People without such insight learn poorly. On the other hand, unconscious learning is repetitive. Here experience is obtained by doing (acting), which results in learning. This form of learning is also of essential importance, as the following percentages illustrate:

- After *reading* something, 10% is remembered.
- After *hearing* something, 20% is remembered.
- After *seeing* something, 30% is remembered.
- After *seeing and hearing* something, 50% is remembered.
- After *doing* something yourself, 90% is remembered.

In short, to achieve optimum learning, it is important that people have the opportunity to do things.

Learning can also be categorized as *individual learning* and *collective learning* (*team learning* or *organizational learning*). Individual learning is the source of all learning. Without individual learning, organizational learning cannot exist. With individual learning employees learn separately from each other and experience an individual behavioral change. With collective learning they learn together, with and from each other. When collective learning occurs the whole organization learns and undergoes a shared behavioral change, or organizational change. In both cases learning is usually based on experience. One learns from gained experience, for example, when reviewing the scorecards and the individual performance plans. Kolb's learning cycle is continuously followed during this process (see Figure 7.2). This cycle includes a horizontal and a vertical axis that allow one to discern at which of the poles learning customarily takes place. The axes and their poles are extend from *active* to *reflective* and from *abstract* to *concrete* (see also Senge, 1990). Kolb's cylce is a continuous process consisting of the following four phases (Kolb, 1984):

1. The gaining of tangible experience based on acting; by *doing* we experience.
2. The observation of this experience and thinking about it (*reflecting*) concerns the review and assessment of past appearances. How did it go? What went wrong? How do we look upon it now? Learning also happens through many small mistakes.
3. Drawing conclusions from the experience; trying to understand the experience through analysis and conceptualization (*thinking*). Converting gained impressions into experience, rules, hypotheses, models, and theories (making connections and generalizations), in order to draw conclusions from similar experiences. What new insights do we have now?
4. Testing these ideas in experiments (trying out the action in new situations). Based on this, *deciding* about what measures to take, which results in new behavior and new experiences.

According to Kolb, learning is thus a cyclic process of the skills *doing, reflecting, thinking,* and *deciding*. The attitudes and behaviors of people determine which form of learning they prefer, which is strongly related to the Personal Balanced Scorecard. Some questions that are central to this learning process are (Hargrove, 1995): Do I open up myself for learning? Do I want to be influenced? Do I really try to understand other views? Do I listen to, and really hear, what is said, and do I remain open to it? Do I explain my assertions? Everyone is different, therefore every PBSC will be unique. Consequently, everyone prefers a specific learning style. Thus, one person can prefer a top-down and integrated approach to a problem, but another prefers to use a bottom-up approach where every part is dealt with separately. One person prefers visualizing ideas, while another communicates them verbally. Peter Honey and Alan Mumford (1992) distinguish the following four learning methods or learning styles in relation to Kolb's learning cycle:

1. The *activist*. The activist yields completely to new experiences, and is broad-minded and enthusiastic about everything new. He has a tendency to act first and then think about the consequences.

As soon as the initial excitement of an activity fades away, he is already looking for something new. Implementation and consolidation quickly bore him. He is constantly relating to others, while making sure that he remains the center of activity.

2. The *thinker*. The thinker willingly distances herself to observe things from different angles. She gathers data from her experience and things that have happened, thoroughly thinks them through, and delays drawing a definite conclusion as long as possible. She carefully considers all possible angles and implications before taking action. She likes to study all possible consequences before acting. She prefers to remain in the background during meetings and discussions and enjoys watching other people work. She is usually distant, tolerant, and inconspicuous in the group.

3. The *theorist*. The theorist adjusts his observations and combines them into a logical theory. He likes to analyze and adores principles, theories, models, and systematic thinking. He solves problems step-by-step with a consistent logic. He frequently asks, "How does this match with that?" and "From what do you determine this?" He dislikes subjectivity and ambiguity and prefers the highest possible certainty. He tends to be a perfectionist with regard to putting his affairs in order.

4. The *pragmatist*. The pragmatist always wants to try ideas, theories, and techniques to see if they work in practice. She is practical and sensible, and likes to make decisions and solve problems. Endless discussions make her nervous. She has a practical nature and has "both feet on the ground." She sees problems and chances as a challenge. Her mottos are: "if it would only work," and "there must always be a better way." Pragmatists learn mostly from activities that have practical advantages and little theory.

Every learning style connects to the four phases in the learning cycle (see Figure 7.2). They all have strong and weak sides, and some do not relate well to each other. Thus, the theorist is the opposite of the pragmatist. For example, the theorist is especially interested in models, concepts, and theories, while the pragmatist is eager to try them out to see if they work in practice. This self-knowledge is necessary to increase one's learning capacity, and thereby to improve one's self-image. When improvement teams are put together, different learning styles need to be taken into consideration. An effective team learning process requires the presence of a balance of different learning styles and demands that every team member know his or her own favored style. The central question here is: how can we benefit from each

Figure 7.2

Kolb's Learning Cycle and the Matching Learning Styles

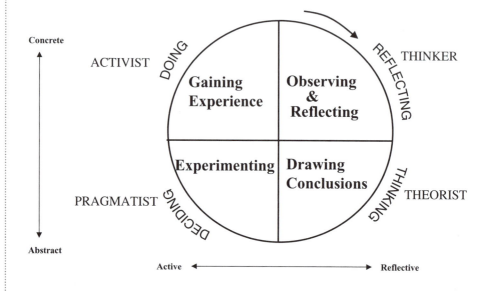

other's qualities and thus increase team performance? This is also important in the coaching of teams. The coach will have to see to it that the team members' activities are adequately connected to their particular learning style. He or she must understand which needs play an important role in each of the four styles in order to guarantee that learning indeed occurs. Table 7.1 illustrates how to accomplish these aims (Thomas, 1995).

Organizational learning ability is also increased when an inventory is made of each employee's learning style for alignment to the personal scorecard. Therefore it is important to know the characteristics of each employee's learning style and to align his or her learning process accordingly. Doing so thus favorably influences learning. To help you discover your own favorite learning style, complete the exercise in Table 7.2 (Thomas, 1995), then indicate the learning style that suits you best.

Learning Style Test

The following learning style test includes a handy aid that can be used to determine which learning style of each member contributes most to the team. Based on the division of the available learning styles, measures can be taken to balance the necessary learning styles in a

Table 7.1

How to Coach the Four Learning Styles	
Activist	*Thinker*
Support her enthusiasm, but encourage her to plan ahead. Offer her a variety of interesting tasks.	Allow him time to prepare himself, absorb things, and study the alternatives.
Theorist	*Pragmatist*
Give her time to study everything and draw conclusions. Give her plenty of opportunities to ask questions as well, and give her clear objectives and complex ideas to work on.	Give him the chance to work out implementations, give him plenty of opportunities to practice, and provide him with information and techniques.
Source: Thomas, 1995.	

Table 7.2

Which Learning Style Do You Prefer?
When you're go out to buy a new DVD set, what do you like to do?
(A) You do not worry about anything. You just have the equipment be wrapped and leave to play with it. You will soon find out how it works. You have no time to fuss with an instructional manual that is much too complex.
(B) You insist that the salesperson gives you an extensive demonstration and allows you to operate it by yourself before you buy it. When you are installing and operating the apparatus, the instruction booklet is next to you.
(C) Before you use it, you take the envelope with "read this first" on it and carefully read the instructions and directions.
(D) There are some similarities between this apparatus and its predecessor, which you recognize. Now you can concentrate on the new elements, try to figure out how it works, and then experiment with it. Later you'll read the manual to check if you were correct.
(A) = Activist   (B) = Thinker   (C) = Theorist   (D) = Pragmatist
Source: Thomas, 1995.

team in order to achieve adequate execution of the learning task. There are nine rules presented in Table 7.3, with four statements per rule (A to D). Continually compare the statements A, B, C, and D to each other. Give a 4 to the statement that you think fits you best, the next best a 3, and so on. Process the scores in the table as follows:

Table 7.3

Learning Style Test, Used on John van Dam				
Pronouncements	**A**	**B**	**C**	**D**
1. A. You look for differences. B. At first, you want to try things out. C. You feel involved. D. You are focused on the usefulness of practical applications.	3	4	1	2
2. A. You let things come to you. B. You immediately investigate what could be important. C. You analyze. D. You do not give a value judgment nor subscribe to a specific opinion.	2	1	3	4
3. A. You especially pay attention to what you feel and experience. B. You tend to look. C. You tend to think. D. You are particularly occupied.	3	2	4	1
4. A. You take things as they are. B. You take risks when you say or do things. C. You award value judgments. D. You continually try to be aware of what is happening.	4	3	2	1
5. A. You tend to work intuitively. B. You get fixed on doing something. C. You first try to think logically. D. You especially ask questions.	4	3	2	1
6. A. You find abstraction and general definitions important. B. You especially look and listen. C. You first try to think logically. D. You are particularly active.	1	4	3	2
7. A. You are chiefly focused on the present. B. You let everything go through your mind again and think it through. C. You are particularly focused on what is still going to happen. D. You are particularly tuned in to "doing."	4	2	1	3

Table 7.3 *continued*

Learning Style Test, Used on John van Dam				
Pronouncements	**A**	**B**	**C**	**D**

8.
   A. You are especially focused on having experiences.
   B. You are chiefly gathering information while listening and looking.
   C. You especially categorize symptoms in a coherent comprehension framework.
   D. You tend to test ideas and feelings, and experiment with your own behavior and with situations.
	4	3	1	2

9.
   A. You tend to experience what happens emotionally and intensely.
   B. You prefer to keep some distance from what is happening.
   C. You tend to approach what happens sensibly.
   D. You are actively co-responsible for what happens.
	1	3	4	2

Total Score	21	18	16	12
(A) = Concrete **(B) = Reflective** **(C) = Abstract** **(D) = Active**				

- Add column A; skip questions 1, 6, and 9.
- Add column B; skip questions 2, 4, and 5.
- Add column C; skip questions 1, 6, and 7.
- Add column D; skip questions 2, 4, and 5.

The total score per learning style is then presented and interconnected on four axes. When you do this for every member of the team, you are able to visualize the learning styles on the team and discuss them among team members. In addition, have members check to what extent their learning style connects to their formulated Personal Balanced Scorecards. John van Dam of Business Jet completed this learning style test for himself, and his test results are shown in Table 7.3. His individual performance plan has already been discussed in Chapter 6 (see Table 6.1). From his learning style diagram (see Figure 7.3) it appears that he is primarily focused on obtaining concrete experience. Consequently, he mainly fulfills the role of activist.

Figure 7.3

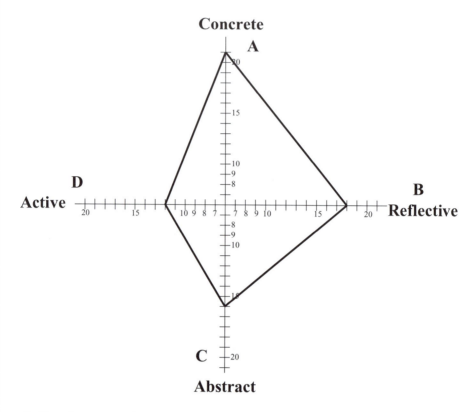

Learning Style Diagram of John van Dam

Collective Learning

Not only individuals but also whole organizations need to learn continually. Therefore, in addition to individual learning, collective learning or organizational learning is also necessary. An organization where learning also takes place collectively is called a *learning organization*. In this section, the issue of learning together and from each other, and knowing one another thoroughly, are the central issues. Learning organizations facilitate this process in all their divisions and thus continually transform themselves. The collective learning that takes place in teams is called *team learning*, which is more than the sum of the individual knowledge acquired by team members. According to Peter Senge (1990), the objective in team learning is to teach teams to think and act with synergy, coordination, and a feeling of unity. This sort of learning is generally more far-reaching than individual learning. Each phase of the learning cycle has an equivalent for teams, as can be seen in Figure 7.4.

Figure 7.4

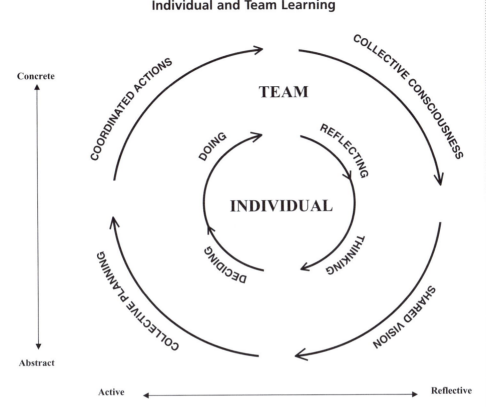

Individual and Team Learning

The individual employee's knowledge should be available and accessible to the entire organization. According to Argyris and Schön (1978), two basic learning forms can be distinguished within learning organizations:

1. *Single-loop learning*; the emphasis lies here on solving problems or identifying and correcting deviations. The organizational norms and practices are usually not adapted. The majority of organizational learning is of the single-loop type.
2. *Double-loop learning*; this becomes evident when the organization also critically analyzes its own actions and, based on this, changes its norms and practices. Here problems are integrally and more widely tackled. With this type of learning people also change their mindsets, which allows them not only to change their way of thinking but also their way of acting. This learning style plays a special role in learning organizations and is central to the TPS concept.

In an extension to the aforementioned Nonaka and Takeuchi (1995) distinguish four learning processes that are followed in a cyclic way:

1. *Socializing*; copying from, following, and imitating each other and, based on this, learning by trial and error.
2. *Externalizing*; orally expressing and documenting explicit knowledge in metaphors, analogies, theories, and so on (making knowledge explicit).
3. *Combining*; studying, sorting, classifying, and combining existing knowledge.
4. *Internalizing*; among other things, "learning by doing" and integrating the above three learning processes.

Argyris and Schön state that learning is promoted and new insights are established particularly when people are willing to lower their defensive shields, take off their blinds, acknowledge their own mistakes, and see things differently. To create a learning organization, the organization should create learning conditions and allow its employees to learn. This is not done only by means of education and training, but more importantly by offering a variety of challenging work, developing a vigorous shared organizational ambition, encouraging teamwork, and establishing a knowledge infrastructure (Internet, intranet, library, comfortable conference room, etc.). With such a culture and resources employees are given the opportunity to gain experience, experiment, take risks and openly review results, circulate tasks, manage knowledge streams, create opportunities for intensive knowledge exchange, organize voluntary dialogue sessions, and stimulate informal employee contacts, among other learning events. Researchers have noted that 70% of learning at work occurs in an informal manner (Pfeffer and Sutton, 2002). Another important condition for learning is making one's own knowledge common, that is, sharing it with others (see Figure 7.5).

Business literature mentions two basic types of learning strategies (Nonaka and Takeuchi, 1995; Doorewaard and Nijs, 1999):

1. *Organization structuring*; setting up the organizational structure in such a way that people have sufficient room and opportunity to gain experiences and learn. A socio-technical organizational structure is characterized by self-directing teams in which team members have broader tasks, responsibilities, and competences. These people are generalists instead of specialists, they are continually trained and there is an overlap in employee knowledge. By talking, discussing, and exchanging knowledge among themselves, people develop new views so that intensive cooperation

Figure 7.5

Sharing and Exchanging Knowledge

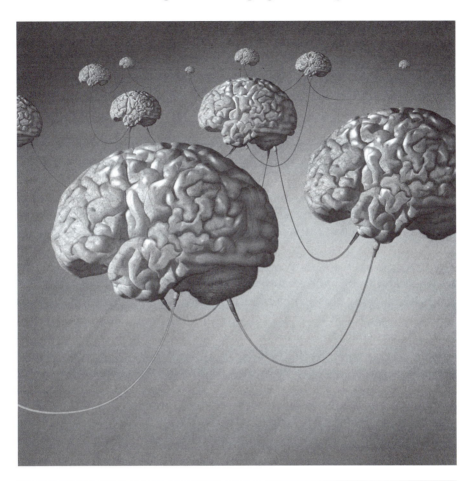

Source: Used with permission of Eiffel.

is spread out over the rest of the organization. Thus teamwork increases organizational learning capacity. An organizational form that also stimulates such learning is the organizational network. According to Nonaka and Takeuchi, organizational knowledge overlap facilitates mutual communication and knowledge exchange between employees. This simplifies making implicit knowledge explicit. In addition, an intermediate task is thus set for middle management: they form the bridge between top management's abstract and externally focused strategic vision and employees' practical and internally focused vision.

2. *Controllability of the management process*; this deals with measures to stimulate the organizational learning process. It concerns

the creation of conditions by management whereby people are willing to apply and share knowledge and exchange it extensively. A good way to do this is by socializing. Nonaka and Takeuchi recommend the use of images and metaphors while exchanging implicit knowledge, so that this knowledge can be imagined. Due to socializing, a mutual frame of reference is created; this stimulates generating new ideas. Here subjective insights and intuitions also deserve more attention, instead of only focusing on education and training.

In order to increase organizational learning ability, insight into the present knowledge and learning situation and related organizational barriers is also needed. For this purpose I introduce a knowledge management quick scan, shown in Table 7.4, which consists of fifty statements regarding your organizational *knowledge and learning orientation*, which are divided into the following five dimensions: *general*, *leadership style*, *strategic vision*, *internal processes*, and *human resources*. As TPS is implemented in your organization, judge the learning ability of your organization based on this checklist, and, as a team, check why this is characteristic for your organization. To this end, complete the survey in Table 7.4 by circling the number that best reflects the accuracy of the assertions in your organization. Use the scoring key (1 to 4) at the end of the table; 1 = never/no/not correct, 2 = once in a while/a little/less, 3 = frequent/usually, and 4 = always/yes/correct. Add these scores vertically. The closer your total score gets to 200, the more knowledge intensive your company is. A comparably high score is related to a learning organization with a large learning ability. The closer your total score is to 50, the smaller the organizational learning ability. Discuss your scores in your team and indicate what could have been done better in your organization.

Business Jet's executive team also completed this quick scan in order to comply with the corporate knowledge and learning perspective in the corporate scorecard. The shared evaluation results are marked (with black bullets) in Table 7.4. The total score was 138 points; this implies that, in the area of knowledge management, something needs to be done for Business Jet to be classified as a full-fledged learning organization. Statements with a score of 1 and 2 in the table suggest areas where improvement actions may be taken (see bottom of Table 7.4). These are part of the result area *knowledge and learning* in the organizational, business unit, and team scorecards, and in the individual performance plans. The following boxed text, "Strategies to Increase the Organizational Learning Ability," shows a summary survey of these improvement actions.

Table 7.4

Knowledge Management Quick Scan, Used on Business Jet				
GENERAL				
1. Making mistakes is allowed; failures are tolerated and not penalized. People learn from each other's mistakes, and errors are openly discussed.	1	2	3•	4
2. Employees know where particular knowledge can be found in the organization, and who knows what is transparent to everyone.	1•	2	3	4
3. Employees get the space to think, learn (consciously as well as unconsciously), act, make informal contacts, gain experience, experiment, and take risks.	1	2	3•	4
4. Management information systems are integrated and continually updated.	1	2	3	4•
5. The necessary knowledge for important decisions is usually readily available and easily accessible.	1	2•	3	4
6. There are no barriers to the use and exchange of knowledge.	1	2	3	4•
7. Employees have the skills to adequately categorize, use, and maintain knowledge.	1	2	3•	4
8. The organization has a network of knowledge workers.	1	2	3•	4
9. The organizational structure is simple, has few hierarchical levels, and consists of autonomous units.	1•	2	3	4
10. The organization is characterized by diversity (people with different cultural backgrounds and learning styles), a planned as well as intuitive approach, people with different team roles, etc.	1	2	3•	4
11. There is an active program for developing ideas. Based on this, new knowledge is continually generated.	1	2	3	4•
12. There is no competition between colleagues. Internal competition is not reinforced.	1	2•	3	4
13. An atmosphere of fear and distrust does not exist in the organization.	1	2	3	4•
LEADERSHIP STYLE				
14. Top management is committed to enlarging learning ability and creating a learning organization.	1	2	3	4•
15. Employees are continually stimulated and encouraged to identify and solve shared problems as a team, to brainstorm, to generate creative ideas, and to share these with each other.	1	2	3	4•
16. Managers have the knowledge that is important for organizational success.	1	2	3•	4

Table 7.4 *continued*

Knowledge Management Quick Scan, Used on Business Jet				
17. Managers fulfill the styles of *coaching, inspiring, and serving leadership* in an optimal mix. They stimulate a fundamental learning attitude, intensive knowledge exchange, and internal entrepreneurship, and they promote individual as well as team learning.	1	2•	3	4
18. Managers are continually focused on developing and mobilizing the knowledge of employees and regularly give constructive feedback about attempted improvement, development, and learning actions.	1	2•	3	4
19. Managers use simple oral and written language, are action-oriented, and facilitate the process of "learning by doing."	1	2	3•	4
20. Management knows which employees are the carriers of valuable and scarce knowledge. Sources of internal expertise have been mapped out.	1•	2	3	4
21. A knowledge manager, one who coaches and facilitates the learning processes, has been appointed. His or her most important skills are: understanding, processing, communicating, and sharing knowledge.	1	2	3	4•
STRATEGIC VISION				
22. Knowledge management is a strategic theme that is part of the shared organizational ambition.	1	2	3	4•
23. There is continuous collective learning in order to develop the core competences of the organization.	1	2•	3	4
24. There are a minimum of five knowledge and learning objectives and related performance measures formulated in the corporate scorecard.	1	2	3	4•
25. Managers have formulated a minimum of three knowledge and learning objectives and related performance measures in their Personal Balanced Scorecards that are aligned to the shared organizational ambition.	1	2	3	4•
26. Customer information is considered strategically valuable.	1	2	3•	4
INTERNAL PROCESSES				
27. Employees do not hoard knowledge but share it spontaneously with each other. Individuals, teams, and business units systematically and intensively exchange knowledge with each other.	1•	2	3	4
28. Knowledge growth is promoted through the organizational culture. This is a culture characterized by simplicity, open communication, and doing rather than talking too much.	1•	2	3	4

Table 7.4 *continued*

Knowledge Management Quick Scan, Used on Business Jet				
29. Problems are tackled holistically by a systems approach. For this purpose, procedures are drafted and used routinely.	1	2●	3	4
30. Knowledge gaps are systematically and continually mapped out, and measures are taken to narrow and eliminate them.	1	2●	3	4
31. Relevant implicit knowledge is made explicit through images and metaphors, reviewed, spread throughout the organization, and intensively exchanged.	1●	2	3	4
32. User-friendly communication and information systems are used to spread knowledge broadly among all employees.	1	2●	3	4
33. Obtained and developed knowledge is continually documented and made available to everyone in the organization.	1	2●	3	4
34. Employees with valuable and scarce knowledge rotate among different business units and participate in a variety of improvement teams.	1	2	3●	4
35. There is a learning environment characterized by positive thinking, self-esteem, mutual trust, willingness to intervene preventively, taking responsibility for business performances, openness, enjoyment, and passion. Employees are urged to continually study how they work and to adjust their work style if needed.	1	2●	3	4
36. The learning processes are initiated and guided by existing or expected problems. Problems are seen as a chance to learn or change. Conflicts are seen as unresolved challenges.	1	2	3●	4
37. People work and learn together harmoniously in self-guiding teams. Here team members have knowledge that overlaps; a balance of personalities, skills, and learning styles; and knowledge about their own favorite learning style and that of their colleagues.	1	2	3●	4
38. Knowledge is constantly being implemented and incorporated into new products, services, and processes.	1	2	3●	4
39. Benchmarking is done systematically to gain knowledge. Best practices within and outside the organization are identified and propagated internally. That which is learned is generalized.	1	2	3	4●
40. Knowledge and learning indicators are measured constantly and used as the starting point for process improvement.	1	2	3	4●
41. Organizational knowledge is shared through informal contacts, internal lectures, conferences, problem-solving and project review meetings, dialogue sessions, internal rapports, memos, etc.	1	2●	3	4

Table 7.4 *continued*

Knowledge Management Quick Scan, Used on Business Jet				
42. Knowledge sharing is facilitated through Internet, intranet, library, comfortable meeting rooms, auditorium, computerized archive and documentation system, etc.	1	2•	3	4
43. Employees have varied and challenging work. There is task rotation.	1	2	3	4•
HUMAN RESOURCES				
44. Job appraisal and competence development are explicitly linked to the personal ambition of individuals and the shared ambition of the organization.	1	2	3	4•
45. Managers and employees are judged by what they do, not by how smart they seem and how much they talk.	1	2	3•	4
46. Employee knowledge is developed constantly and kept up-to-date by means of training, coaching, and talent development programs.	1	2	3•	4
47. There is a proactive competence development policy, which includes internal and external training, courses, working conferences, symposia, and seminars.	1	2•	3	4
48. Knowledge and learning competences are part of every employee's competence profile.	1	2	3	4•
49. The knowledge of departing employees is passed on to successors.	1•	2	3	4
50. Employees who deliver collective learning performances for the sake of the entire organization's well-being and constantly share their knowledge with colleagues are rewarded more than others and have more promotion opportunities.	1	2	3•	4
Total Score: **138 points**				
Circle the correct number: 1 = never / no / not correct; 2 = once in a while / a little / less; 3 = frequently / usually; 4 = always / yes / correct				
Remarks/Suggestions: Improve localization of knowledge; improve availability and accessibility of knowledge; optimize organizational structure; develop leadership skills; create more insight with management about those who carry valuable and scarce knowledge; increase learning efforts; stimulate employees to share knowledge with each other and exchange it intensively; stimulate knowledge exchange between teams and business units; systematically map out and remove knowledge gaps; make relevant implicit knowledge explicit; improve user-friendliness of information and communication systems; improve learning environment; develop competence policy; and convey knowledge of departing employees to successors.				
Source: Rampersad, 2002.				

Strategies to Increase the Organizational Learning Ability

- Creating conditions whereby people are willing to apply their knowledge, and share and intensively exchange it with each other.
- Establishing the organizational structure in such a way that people get sufficient space and opportunities to gain experiences and think.
- Stimulating employees to formulate their own Personal Balanced Scorecard and through this cultivate a positive attitude toward improvement, learning, and developing.
- Letting employees reflect on the balance between their own personal ambition and the shared organizational ambition.
- Making an inventory of your learning style and aligning it to your personal ambition. Reviewing this periodically; aligning it to the planning, coaching, and appraisal meetings and the 360°–feedback system.
- Establishing improvement teams in which a balance of personalities, skills, and learning styles is present.
- Developing and accepting self-knowledge regarding your own favorite learning style and those of other team members.
- Giving people a sense of direction based on a shared organizational ambition and connecting them with each other.
- Working with teams where team learning is central—teams that think and act from a synergetic perspective, are well coordinated, and work with a feeling of unity.
- Using images, metaphors, and intuitions to share and exchange implicit knowledge.
- Working with self-directing teams in an organizational network that uses generalists with ample responsibilities and competences and in which there are knowledge overlaps and task rotations between employees.
- Stimulating employees to think about, identify, and solve common problems as a team, let go of traditional ways of thinking, constantly develop their own skills, acquire experience, and feel responsible for company and team performances.
- Having leaders who coach, help, inspire, motivate and stimulate, are action-oriented, and constantly evaluate processes based on performance measures.
- Having people who continually learn from their mistakes and openly communicate with each other, and who constantly apply Deming's and Kolb's learning cycles in their actions.
- Systematically working with problem-solving methods (brainstorming, problem-solving cycle, risk management, etc.).
- Giving feedback about improvement actions undertaken.
- Applying an integral and systems approach.

(continued)

- Implementing a knowledge infrastructure; Internet, intranet, library, evaluation sessions, etc.
- Stimulating informal employee contacts.
- Driving out fear and mistrust from the organization.
- Simplifying the organizational structure and the language of managers.
- Allowing mistakes; without mistakes, there is no learning.

Source: Rampersad, 2002.

Part One of this book concludes the discussion of the TPS-concept and the different phases of the Total Performance Scorecard cycle. In Part Two, I discuss a few subjects that guide and facilitate the related process of continuous improvement, development, and learning. These topics demand special attention for the successful implementation of the Total Performance Scorecard concept.

P A R T   T W O

Organizational Requirements

Teamwork

8

I am personally convinced that one person can be a change catalyst, a "transformer" in any situation, any organization. Such an individual is yeast that can leaven an entire loaf. It requires vision, initiative, patience, respect, persistence, courage, and faith to be a transforming leader.

Stephen R. Covey

Management deals with doing things right. Leadership deals with doing the right things. Efficient management without effective leadership is a waste of time. Leadership comes first and then follows management.

Hubert Rampersad

Teamwork entails sharing knowledge, the work, the thoughts, the feelings, the excitement, the happiness, the pressure, the pleasure, the emotions, the doubts and the success with each other. This increases the learning ability of the organization. For this reason, almost everything in the scope of the Total Performance Scorecard approach is done as a team. In order to achieve effective cooperation it is necessary to consider all the elements of teamwork shown in Table 8.1. All these elements will be discussed in detail in this chapter.

Team Composition and Team Roles

The only person who is educated is the one who has learned how to learn . . . and change.

Carl R. Rogers

Table 8.1

Elements of Teamwork	
SUBSTANTIVE FUNCTIONING • Defining problems and formulating team objectives • Generating and processing ideas and solutions • Team composition • Team development and team learning • Defining tasks • Budgeting time and resources	**PROCEDURE** • Following a method, such as brainstorming, problem-solving cycle, Deming cycle, risk management, etc. • Meeting procedure • Team review

SUPPORTIVE TASKS
• Keeping time (time keeper)
• Taking minutes (minute taker)
• Guarding and reviewing the teamwork process (process keeper)
• Making notes on a flipchart
• Organizing coffee, tea, cold drinks
• Booking and arranging the meeting room. Looking for an isolated location without distractions or interruptions.
• Making agreements about mobile telephone use, smoking, and breaks
	INTERACTION
	• Interpersonal communication:
	  • Listening
	  • Questioning
	  • Building on the ideas of others
	  • Constructive arguing
	  • Clarifying
	  • Summarizing
	  • Involving others
	  • Showing appreciation
	  • Giving and receiving feedback
	  • Constructive negotiating
	  • Conflict handling
	• Coaching

A team is *a group of people with complementary skills and personalities who feel committed to a shared objective and who need each other in order to achieve results.* It is not a good idea to put too many people on a team because this can work adversely. Having too many team members usually encourages conviviality, which is often mistaken for effective teamwork. To guarantee effectiveness, the team should ideally consist of five to eight members, should not have more than twelve members, and must have the correct composition. A balanced division of people with certain skills, learning styles, and different personal qualities, each aligned to the objectives to be realized and the improvement actions to be executed, is necessary here (see also Katzenbach and Smith, 2001). Effective teams are characterized by:

- Clear objectives that everyone wants to adopt.
- Coherence and harmony.

- Acceptance and acknowledgement of cultural differences as well as mutual respect and understanding.
- A strong foundation of trust between team members.
- The ability to solve problems and internal conflicts effectively.
- The ability to learn collectively from experiences.
- Team members who know their own learning styles and those of others within the team.
- A combination of, on the one hand, a number of different personalities and, on the other hand, the necessary competences, both of which are equally divided among all team members.
- Knowledge and acceptance of one's own team role and those of the other team members.
- A balance between ones's own team role and his or her function in the team.
- A harmonious work environment where people respect, trust, listen, and give each other useful feedback.
- Open communication, so that everybody has access to relevant information.
- Continuous training of team members.
- Leaders who inspire more creativity in the team (see Leonard and Swap, 1999).

Belbin's Team Roles

According to Belbin (1995), capacity and capability play an important role in team composition. Capacity deals with the knowledge and skills of people, made visible through diplomas, certificates, and experience. Capability, however, deals with the soft criteria such as people's strengths, behavior, character, and talent. Belbin distinguishes nine team roles in his theory of team role management. These nine roles are explained in Table 8.2. The team roles consist of the personality each team member contributes to the team. It is important that these team roles are divided equally among all team members so that there is a balance between the team role and the job of the individual team members. Team members must also know what their own team roles are as well as those of other team members and must accept these. Using a questionnaire (see Belbin, 1995), team members can check which team roles they more or less fulfill; based on this, they can then control team quality. John van Dam, team member of the Business Jet security team, filled out this questionnaire. From this it was learned that John primarily performs the role of *Shaper* in his security team and

Table 8.2

Belbin's Team Roles		
BELBIN Team-Role Type	**Contributions**	**Allowable Weaknesses**
Plant	Creative, imaginative, unorthodox. Solves difficult problems.	Ignores incidentals. Too pre-occupied to communicate effectively.
Coordinator	Mature, confident, a good chairperson. Clarifies goals, promotes decision making, delegates well.	Can often be seen as manipulative. Off loads personal work.
Monitor Evaluator	Sober, strategic and discerning. Sees all options. Judges accurately.	Lacks drive and ability to inspire others.
Implementer	Disciplined, reliable, conservative, and efficient. Turns ideas into practical actions.	Somewhat inflexible. Slow to respond to new possibilities.
Completer Finisher	Painstaking, conscientious, anxious. Searches out errors and omissions. Delivers on time.	Inclined to worry unduly. Reluctant to delegate.
Resource Investigator	Extrovert, enthusiastic, communicative. Explores opportunities. Develops contacts.	Over-optimistic. Loses interest once initial enthusiasm has passed.
Shaper	Challenging, dynamic, thrives on pressure. The drive and courage to overcome obstacles.	Prone to provocation. Offends people's feelings.
Teamworker	Cooperative, mild, perceptive, and diplomatic. Listens, builds, averts friction.	Indecisive in crunch situations.
Specialist	Single-minded, self-starting, dedicated. Provides knowledge and skills in rare supply.	Contributes only on a narrow front. Dwells on technicalities.
Source: Used with permission from R. M. Belbin. *Team Roles at Work*. London: Butterworth–Heinemann, 1995.		

secondarily the role of *Monitor*. This corresponds to his most important learning style: *activist* (see Figure 7.3).

When you are working on the development of team performance it is also important to take into account the recommendations presented in the following boxed text.

What Team Members Should Do

Team members should:

- Be encouraged to formulate their own Personal Balanced Scorecard and balance it with their behavior and the shared organizational ambition.
- Know their team role and as well as those of other team members, whom they should accept, value, and respect.
- Devote themselves to shared team objectives based on a shared organizational ambition.
- Consider themselves to be equal and responsible.
- Be interested and motivated.
- Give high priority to continuous improvement, development, and learning.
- Participate actively in the activities of the team.
- Know, trust, understand, complement, and help each other.
- Know their internal and external clients.
- Communicate openly and maintain an open mind regarding expectations about their surroundings.
- Use each other's information freely.
- Channel the experiences from the team back to their own working environment.
- Abide by the team's decisions.
- Be responsible for their own contribution as well as for team results.
- See problems as an opportunity for improvement.
- Be aware of their responsibility for improvement.
- Make personal improvement, development, and learning a routine a way of life.

Team Development

> Human progress is neither automatic nor inevitable. . . . Everystep toward the goal of justice requires sacrifice, suffering, and struggle; the tireless exertions and passionate concern of dedicated individuals.
>
> *Martin Luther King, Jr.*

Team development is organized in phases and cycles. Different aspects play a role during the initial phase (before the real team is formed), than during the process phase. Team development can be divided into four phases (see Figure 8.1), which are adapted from Tuckman and Jensen (1977):

1. **Forming.** Here we have a *collection of individuals*. In this phase team members get to know each other, test the authority of the team leader, take a waiting stance, are hesitant and unsure, observe the behavior of their colleagues, try to figure out their place in the team, and try to improve themselves. Due to defensive and sometimes hostile behavior, little or no progress may be registered at this point in time. In this phase, there is a lot of talk, but people tend not to understand each other. The preferred leadership style during this phase is directive (more task oriented than relation oriented). The leader must help the group with task implementation and the gathering of knowledge.

Figure 8.1

The Four Phases in Team Development

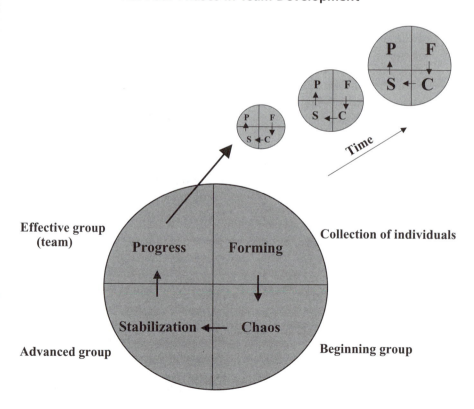

2. **Chaos.** Here we are dealing with a *beginning group*. In this phase, team members are aware of the long road ahead before the goals are reached. This phase is often coupled with feelings of dissatisfaction, resistance, and frustration. There may also be negative behavior, competition for attention, power conflicts between group members and management, mutual distrust, emotional reactions towards the tasks to be carried out, and doubts about their usefulness. The leadership style in this phase is guiding (strongly relation oriented). The team leader should take serious notice of the group's feelings of discontent, avoid taking them personally, and discuss them without being defensive.

3. **Stabilizing.** Here we see an *advanced group*. The atmosphere at this point is less tense. Cooperation and communication have improved. The members are getting used to each other, and trust, accept, and respect one another; at this time team spirit is gradually being formed and a sense of group unity develops. Now, constructive discussions take place. There is also more time devoted to work and less to conflict among team members, which has a positive effect on group performance. The leadership style in this phase is supportive (not very task oriented). In this phase, the leader must concentrate especially on the support and appraisal of everyone's efforts, improvement of the working atmosphere, communication, cooperation and further improvement of team relations.

4. **Progress.** At this time there is a *real team* (an *effective group*) with a creative working atmosphere, closely related unity, self-steering, good mutual communication, as well as hard and independent work being done to carry out tasks. The team members know each other's strong and weak points and feel involved; this results in a lot of progress being made. In this phase, the leadership style is advisory, accompanied by a continuous search for opportunities to improve cooperation.

The team development phases delineated by Tuckman and Jensen (1977)—*forming*, *storming*, *norming*, and *performing*, which are also useful for understanding and facilitating team effectiveness, are arranged in a sequential process. In reality, however, team development more often appear as a cyclic process in which the phases of forming, chaos, stabilization, and progress reappear in a somewhat different form (see Figure 8.1). The environment and team composition indeed change continuously, which has an impact on the team development process. Furthermore, after the progress phase, in which people count on achieved successes, teams tend to become lazy—at the cost of effectiveness. The coach should be able to recognize those moments when team development stagnates and tension builds up in the group, and then try to move the group to the next phase. Here attention should also be paid to negative team dynamics, such as manipulation, fear and distrust, resistance to action, and power plays. These can be solved by improving mutual trust, establishing codes of conduct, spontaneous feedback, informal association, and increasing involvement. It is important to remember that a working group should not be confused with a team, although this often happens in practice. Figure 8.2 shows the most important differences between the two.

Remmerswaal (1992) identifies three phases in the development of groups: the *beginning group*, the *advanced group*, and the *mature group*. According to Remmerswaal's point of view, a mature group is a team. Figure 8.3 shows a team scan that indicates the behavior these groups exhibit in the different phases of their development (Hoevenaars, van Jaarsveld, and den Hertog, 1995). This behavior is related to the following dimensions: *result oriented, involvement and loyalty, improvement and renewing ability, customer-supplier thinking, communication patterns, cooperation, conflict handling, guiding and coaching,* and *manners.* By filling out the team scan, the phase in which a group currently find itself can be determined. The scan also helps with what should be done to work as a mature group.

Complete this team scan and discuss the results in your group. Try to implement improvements using these results. John van Dam of Business Jet did so for his security team, and his current team profile is shown in Figure 8.3. In most dimensions, John's security team has not yet reached the mature phase and cannot, therefore, be classified

Figure 8.2

Differences between a Working Group and a Team

Working Group
- Individual goal
- Everyone is responsible for part of the result
- Cooperation is not necessary
- Little communication
- The whole is less than the sum of the parts
- Guiding, controlling leadership
- Open number of team members
- Individual learning

Team
- Shared goal
- Everyone is co-responsible for the end result
- Cooperation is necessary
- A lot of communication
- The whole is more than the sum of the parts
- Coaching leadership
- Clear number of team members
- Collective learning

as a real team yet. The improvement points derived from the checklist form the starting point for John and his colleagues to enhance their group effectiveness.

Interpersonal Communication

> Listening is the beginning of all wisdom; learning is listening effectively.
>
> *Hubert Rampersad*

Interpersonal communication is an essential element of teamwork and acts as the glue that binds elements of the TPS concept. Differences in style in interpersonal communications between colleagues, friends, and others are the source for lack of understanding, conflicts, disappointments, and missed opportunities. These are all wasted opportunities that have no place in the TPS concept. The primary goal of interpersonal communication is the creation of mutual understanding. Apart from that, the following communication goals also play a role:

- Stimulating collective learning; updating, sharing, and exchanging knowledge; keeping employees updated and creating transparency.
- Stimulating mutual organizational cooperation and commonality (we-feeling) and urging people into action.
- Articulating organizational norms and values; influencing people's views and attitudes; and cultivating an understanding of change and improvement.
- Developing skills such as the ability to listen well, set priorities, plan activities, and other abilities.
- Giving and receiving feedback.

Thus, interpersonal communication is concerned with broadening knowledge (learning) and, as a result, changing people's attitude and behavior. The following statement of top manager Robert Staubli illustrates the importance of interpersonal communication and related social skills:

> There are well-founded reasons to place more emphasis—some say perhaps a disproportionate emphasis—on the development of social skills. For an average company the estimated loss of potential business performance varies from 30 to 50 percent due to

Figure 8.3

The Development Stages of a Group, Used on Business Jet

Dimension	Beginning Group	Advanced Group	Mature Group
Result-oriented	One individual is well informed about the group's goals and performances and knows how to measure and improve performance.	A few people know the group's goals and performances and how to measure and improve performance.	Every group member is well informed about the group's goals and performances and knows how to measure and improve performance.
Involvement and loyalty	Group members are not very interested in how the company is functioning at this time, or how it will function in the future, and only do what is expected of them.	Group members read information sent to them and occasionally ask management a question about it. Sometimes they are willing to do something extra, but only for appropriate compensation.	Group members know their current organization well and are interested in how it will function in the future. They actively help and think about the organization and care about their work.
Ability to improve and renew	The group is not interested in improvement or renewal, does not offer ideas, and is not open to suggestions.	Sometimes the group comes up with an improvement proposal (e.g., through a suggestion box), but members remain standoffish when others have an improvement plan, and they blame others for their failures.	The group offers their own ideas and suggestions for the improvement or renewal of equipment, working methods, and/or products. They are involved with the process from start to finish.
Customer-supplier thinking	The group does not know its customers and suppliers, does not obtain or provide information about complaints, does not feel responsible for mistakes, and blames others for them.	The group knows the names of its customers through the indirect feedback of complaints, tries to avoid making the same mistake twice, and has a vague idea about customer scope. There is no contact with suppliers, but group members know what is wrong with the goods or services supplied.	The group knows. and visits its customers and suppliers, directly receives and gives signals about complaints, and holds discussions about customer improvement, wishes, and demands. The group feels responsible for the quality delivered.
Communication patterns	The group sees no need for consultations with group members or others in order to participate and help thinking. The group is hardly interested in how others handle matters and does not want feedback about its functioning.	The group meets on a regular basis "because it is expected" however, it does not really know what to discuss, does not yet take initiative to include or inform outsiders, but cries out for "more say in matters," doubts feedback about its functioning, and wants to learn from others when it suits them.	The group takes its own initiatives to deliberate, involves necessary persons or departments, wants to hear and learn from others how they handle certain matters, and wants feedback about its functioning.

(Left side vertical label: *Accent on care for production*)

Figure 8.3 *continued*

The Development Stages of a Group, Used on Business Jet

Dimension	Beginning Group	Advanced Group	Mature Group
Cooperation	The group fits together like loose sand. Members are not interested in each other and cannot replace each other. They merely work for themselves and do their own tasks. The group "leader" bears all the responsibility. New coworkers have to fend for themselves.	They are reasonably aware of each other's characteristics and capacities and take them into consideration, can partially replace each other, try to increase their exchange capacity, and try to teach new colleagues some activities. The rest has to be outsourced.	The group has strong ties, group members are considerate of each other, and can replace one another. New colleagues are welcomed and guided without any problems.
Conflict handling	Opposing group opinions and behaviors are not open for discussion; discussions regarding conflict are avoided. If they are unavoidable there usually is a quarrel. Group members do not give in to each other and stagnate.	Opposing opinions and behavior can sometimes be discussed, depending on the influence of different team members. Some members usually lose while others almost never do.	Opposing opinions and behaviors are open for discussion, are clearly discussed, and lead to improvement. Individuals are willing to make concessions for the benefit of the group.
Guiding and coaching	The group has a strong need for guidance on tasks and responsibilities. Corrective actions have to be taken from the top down. The group does not express the need for training, they only take part in obligatory training.	The group has regular doubts or disagreements and is, therefore, in need of management guidance to make its decisions. They go to all training programs suggested by management but do not come up with their own training ideas.	The group directs itself regarding tasks, responsibilities, and behavior. They correct each other when necessary, indicate educational needs, and are trained in a wide area.
Manners	How to behave is not open for discussion. Nothing is mentioned about rules and norms. There is no basis for trust; they do not dare to admit mistakes. They often speak slightingly of others. Personal interests prevail over group interests.	There are a few common rules and norms in the group, but not everything is open for discussion. Mutual trust grows, but certain mistakes are glossed over for fear of "slashing" or negative remarks. The vision, which combines personal and group interests, is strengthened.	Manners and behavior are open for discussion. The rules are clear to everyone. There is a broad basis of trust; mistakes are reported spontaneously and discussed in order to learn from them. Group interest follows naturally from personal interests.

Accent on care for people

Source: Hoevenaars, van Jaarsveld, and den Hertog, 1995.

mutual problems, unresolved conflicts, barriers, disrupted relations, not enough personal space, and lack of development possibilities. I think that this is a cautious estimation. (Metro, 2002)

The Communication Process

Learning requires controlling the communication process (see
Figure 8.4). This learning process consists of a sender who transmits a
message to a receiver, who interprets this message, and, in turn, the
reaction to this message from the receiver. This feedback gives the
sender the opportunity to ascertain that the message has been received
and understood. Communication is therefore a continuous cycle of
action and reaction. It is a constant process of two-way traffic. When
people communicate with each other, they are alternately the sender
and receiver of messages. Communication is only successful when the
receiver interprets the message according to the intention of the sender.
According to Evans and Russell (1991) communication gains depth
and value when we can create a sphere of openness, trust, and mutual
respect in such a way that we can also share our thoughts, feelings,
emotions, sensitivity, intuitions, excitement, happiness, ideals, and
truths with each other. This process can be hampered by differences in
the mindsets of the sender and receiver. This mindset, or the personal
way we look upon things, is created by things such as upbringing,
education, experience, norms, and values.

In the context of a team, interpersonal communication entails a
process of the exchange of messages between team members. This may
occur via talking or writing. The following list outlines key elements
of oral communication:

- *Spoken language (verbal).* This includes the ways in which words
  are used, such as in long, complex sentences or short, easy ones;
  the language (as in French or Spanish) in which someone speaks;

Figure 8.4

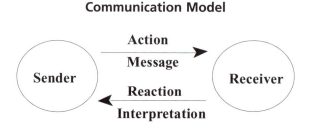

Communication Model

if someone speaks in the "I" or "we" form. Spoken language conveys, among other things, a person's level of education and intelligence.

- *Sound variations.* These are the sound elements that do not belong to the spoken language itself, such as volume, accent, clearness, pitch, speed of speech, laughing, crying, etc. From these elements we are able to deduce people's feelings. Nervousness, for example, is identified by high speed of speech and a quivering voice.

- *Visible information (nonverbal).* This concerns body language, such as blushing out of shyness, turning pale out of fear, frowning, laughing, head movements, crossing of arms, hand signals, clothing, personal care, scratching, playing with objects during lengthy stories, and so on. Research shows that more than 70% of all communication is nonverbal.

Nonverbal communication can be divided among the following categories:

- *Posture.* This includes postural indicators such as shoulders hanging (weak, sense of inferiority); head up (self-assured, proud); crossed legs (confident); feet under the chair (suspicious); slouching (not interested); leaning toward conversation partner (interested, enthusiastic); and other forms of body language.

- *Facial expressions.* These are facial expressions such as eyes wide opened (amazed, startled); eyes blinking (nervous); looking someone straight in the eyes (interested, attentive); avoiding eye contact (insecure); firmly closed mouth (determined); blushing (shyness, excitement); turning pale (fright, fear, rage); and other expressions.

- *Gesticulating.* These include actions involving the hands, such as hand on the hips (superior); hands on the back (pensive, passive); closed fist (angry, excited); hand on the mouth (shy, insecure); head resting in hands (pensive); movements with the index finger (drawing attention to); arranging ones glasses (hesitating); cleaning glasses (saving time); and others.

- *Distance.* The actual space between people during communication. Most interpersonal contact takes place at approximately an arm's length. Strangers usually keep a greater distance, while people who know each other well usually stand at half an arm's length.

Table 8.3 shows how negative nonverbal messages can lead to negative reactions (Barton, 1990).

Comprehension of the message from the *sender* can be improved by:

- *Simplicity of style*; comprehensible formulation, easy words, and short sentences.

Table 8.3

Nonverbal Messages That Can Produce Negative Reactions		
Nonverbal Message or Expression	Signal Received or Sent	Reaction of Receiver
Manager looks away when speaking to an employee.	I do not have this person's attention.	My superior is too busy to listen to my problem or simply does not care.
Failure to acknowledge greetings from a colleague.	This person is unfriendly.	This person is unapproachable.
Angry glance; that is, looks at the person angrily.	This person is angry with me.	Reciprocal anger, fear, or avoidance, depending on who is sending the signal.
Deep sighing.	Annoyance, aversion, or displeasure.	My opinions do not count. I must appear stupid or boring to this person.
Heavy breathing (sometimes accompanied by hand waving).	Anger or heavy stress.	Avoid this person at all costs.
Eye contact not maintained during communication.	Suspicion and/or uncertainty.	What does this person have to hide?
Manager crosses arms and leans back.	Indifferent and difficult to persuade.	This person has already made up his or her mind; my opinions are not important.
Manager peers over his or her glasses.	Skepticism or distrust.	He or she does not believe what I am saying.
Manager continues to read a report while employee is speaking.	Lack of interest and attention.	My opinions are not important enough to get my supervisor's attention.

Source: G. M. Barton. *Communication: Manage Words Effectively*. Costa Mesa, CA: Personnel Journal 69, 1990.

- *A recognizable structure*; a clear argument with a clear direction.
- *Conciseness*; stick to the essentials, be brief;
- *A stimulating style*; such as frankness, asking questions, joking, regarding the other person as valuable and equal.

Effective interpersonal communication is therefore an important aid for the successful implementation of the Personal and Organizational Balanced Scorecards. Communication skills are also a part of the competency profile of managers and employees. Interpersonal communication involves, among other things, asking the right questions, listening to the answers you get, and then responding to these answers. To achieve effective mutual communication *the receiver* should listen intently by, for example, questioning, summarizing, explaining, and being alert. It is the responsibility of the manager to create a working environment where effective communication can be developed. This can be done with the following methods:

- Be honest and open and give everyone the necessary information.
- Speak about *we* and not about *I* and *you*.
- Don't ignore your employees.
- Ask them about their opinions and views.
- Explain in advance why certain measures will be taken.
- Listen attentively and give constructive feedback.
- Put yourself in the other person's place.
- Understand your employees and meet them halfway.
- Avoid egotistical remarks such as, "My years of experience show that . . . ," "I know what I'm talking about . . . ," and so on.
- Emphasize the objectives.
- Don't look for a scapegoat.

Interpersonal Communicative Skills

The most important interpersonal communicative skills may be summarized as *listening, questioning, building on the ideas of others, constructive arguing, clarifying, summarizing, involving others, showing appreciation, giving and receiving feedback, constructive negotiating,* and *conflict handling* (Rampersad, 2001A; PA Consulting Group, 1991). These skills will be briefly described in this section.

Listening

What Is It?

Interpersonal communication starts with good listening. Listening is more important than speaking. There is a difference between listening and hearing. When someone listens, the words are actively registered and processed in the brain and then used. On the other hand, when someone hears, the words are registered in the brain but nothing is done with them. Listening can thus be summarized as hearing, understanding, remembering, and doing something with it. Thus good listening is effective learning. Table 8.4 displays the difference between good and bad listeners. As a result of bad listening billion of dollars are wasted annually due to: letters that have to be retyped, postponed appointments, labor conflicts, failed sales presentations, and so on (Evans and Russell, 1991).

Some other *bad listening habits* are (Thomas, 1996; Rampersad, 2001A):

- Not paying attention, thinking of something else, playing with papers on your desk or interrupting the conversation by answering the phone.
- Acting as if you are listening.
- Listening until you have something to say, then not listening and bracing yourself to interrupt the other person when the next opportunity arises.
- Emotional oversensitivity and prejudice.
- Hearing what you expect, thinking that you hear what you expected, or refusing to hear what you don't want to hear.

Table 8.4

Good Listeners versus Bad Listeners	
Good Listeners	**Bad Listeners**
Are quiet when someone else is expressing his or her opinions, tries to understand with the other person means, and asks questions for clarification.	Interrupt the speaker before he or she is finished.
Display nonverbal behavior such as nodding or looking straight at the person and leaning forward.	Display nonverbal behavior such as playing with objects, rocking, or looking at the time.

- Focusing on points of disagreement, looking for a chance to attack, listening intensively for something you don't agree with instead of concentrating on positive aspects.
- Being turned off by the other person and therefore being disinterested.
- Listening only to the facts, as opposed to listening to the whole message.
- Dropping out when something is boring and not interesting.

How Do You Use It?

Be quiet, make eye contact, relax and concentrate on listening when the other person is expressing an opinion. Allow the other person to finish, because people usually come to their point at the end of their story. Stay in tune with the speaker by using the "listening thought time" to review what has been said. The listening thought time is the gap between thinking speed and speaking rate, which gives you time to think while listening. In general, listeners think at a rate of about 500 words per minute, but the typical speaker talks at a rate of about 125 to 150 words per minute (Miller, Catt, and Carlson, 1996). Therefore, we mentally process words almost four times as quickly as people normally talk. Some other recommendations for effective listening are:

- Listen critically and intently to the whole message; listen for ideas, feelings, intentions, and facts, and extract the most important themes.
- Postpone your opinion; don't jump to conclusions before the other person has finished speaking.
- Don't be distracted by external disturbances and the manner of presentation; concentrate on what is said, pay attention to the speaker, and show that you are listening intently by making eye contact and showing through verbal and nonverbal means show that you understand what is being said.
- Concentrate on the contents and not on the "packaging."
- Wait before reacting; if you react too soon, you are liable to listen less intently and therefore to assimilate insufficient information. Don't be tempted to interrupt at the first opportunity.
- Be prepared to react to ideas, suggestions, and remarks without putting them down.

- Don't concentrate on what you expect to hear; don't anticipate what the other person is going to say; and let the other person finish talking.

- Don't listen impatiently, defensively, or aggressively.

- Suppress your prejudices.

- Suppress the need to react emotionally to what is said or to what you think is said;

- Try to organize what you hear.

- Take notes occasionally, but don't be distracted by constantly taking notes.

- Prepare yourself mentally to start listening.

Remarks That Show You Are Really Listening

- From your words I understand that . . . Is that correct?

- As I listen to you, it seems that you are very disappointed about . . .

- Do you mean to say that . . . ?

- If this is the case, then we must . . .

Questioning

What Is It?

Questioning gives you the opportunity to pursue factual information from the other person, or to find out what someone's opinion is about a certain subject. Two basic types of questions can be distinguished: *open* and *closed questions*. *Open questions* are meant to invite someone to give elaborate information about, for example, opinions and feelings. They are also used to involve people in a conversation. Open questions usually start with the words *what, when, why, who, which, where,* or *how*. Open questions invite and stimulate participation and involvement. By asking an open question, all possibilities for answering the question are available, which can result in broadening and deepening the contact. These questions are meant, for example, to ask for clarification and to stimulate one's own discovery. *Closed questions* are used to place emphasis on something or to get a *yes* or *no* answer. With these questions you can guide the conversation in a certain way. They can also be used to obtain specific information quickly. Unfortunately, they are less useful than open questions because the answer to them is usually only *yes* or *no*. To obtain a complete picture, it is important to ask mostly open questions.

Open and closed questions can be subdivided as the following types of questions:

- *Informative questions*; questions to receive actual information.
- *Specific questions*; questions that invite a person to think in a certain direction. This limits the answer possibilities, which means that limited information is obtained. With this questioning you prove your professional skill.
- *Multiple choice questions*; questions with alternatives.
- *Suggestive questions*; questions in which the answer is already suggested; these are based on the expectations and perceptions of the questioner.
- *Chain questions*; these are composed of several questions.
- *Opinion questions*; questions used to ask the opinion of the other person.

How Do You Use It?

Ask as many open questions as possible in order to increase involvement, prevent uncertainties, reveal valuable information and ideas, and correct outdated views. The results of such questioning are, for instance, more focused discussions, better supported decisions, and evidence of respect and interest. Questions to be avoided when coaching teams are (Pareek and Rao, 1990):

- *Critical and sarcastic questions*; to rebuke the other person or to call his or her ability in question, which develops a gap between leader and employees. These questions may lead to grudges, hostility, and the suppression of ideas. For example, "Why didn't you meet the deadline for this assignment?" contains criticism, whereas "Could you explain to me why it is that you did not meet the deadline?" is an invitation to search for the causes of the delay.
- *Annoying questions*; to check if the other person is right or wrong; this type of interrogation suggests a superior attitude on the part of the leader.
- *Suggestive questions*; to put the wrong answer in the employee's mouth and try to tempt the employee to give an answer. For instance, "Were you not able to meet the deadline because of other problems in the company?" This only leads to those answers the leader wants to hear and, consequently, hinders a closer examination of the problem.

Examples of Various Types of Questions

- Open questions: Can you tell me something about this? What do you mean? How does that work? What do you think? What is your vision on that? Why is it done this way?

- Closed questions: Did you or did you not receive the book? Is the work environment in our organization good or bad? Would you like a green or a blue one?

- Informative question: Since when have you been working there?

- Direct question: Are you satisfied with the delivery time-frame? What do you think about the work environment in our organization?

- Choice question: Do you want a red or a black pen?

- Suggestive question: Is it also your opinion that . . . ? Don't you also think that . . . ? You approve of the work environment, don't you?

- Chain question: How do you execute the process? Did you approach Frank about this? What does he think?

- Opinion question: Do you find this work meaningful?

Building on the Ideas of Others

What Is It?

People continuously generate ideas. It is important that you are able to build on the ideas of others; this results in an increase in the number and quality of ideas. Building on the ideas of others means that you adopt someone's suggestion and add something of your own to it.

How Do You Use It?

Give credit to the other person's idea and then suggest improvements and supplements. This way, fewer ideas are lost and more solutions that are thought through are obtained. Giving credit also produces a feeling of appreciation from the person who had the idea in the first place. The goal of building on someone's ideas is to elaborate, improve, and convert this person's idea into successful action. It is therefore important to always take ideas seriously. An internal reward given to the best idea may produce useful suggestions.

Examples of Building on Ideas

- Yes, because in the meantime we will have a chance to prepare ourselves better and analyze a few things more carefully.
- Good idea, Arnold. This gives us the opportunity to create the buy-in for . . .

Constructive Arguing

What Is It?

Constructive arguing makes differences in opinion known in a positive and constructive way; this results in a productive contribution to a discussion. The conversation is thus broadened, whereby new ideas and opinions can be created.

How Do You Use It?

Object in a positive and constructive manner. State another viewpoint and explain why, according to you, the first idea should not be accepted. Thus, correct inaccurate statements and offer different views. In doing so, you will obtain greater clarity, better involvement, and improved decision making.

Examples of Constructive Arguing

- That can be true, but look at it from the point of view of . . .
- In my opinion, it may not be such a good idea, because it is coupled with . . .

Clarifying

What Is It?

Interpret and repeat clearly and distinctly in your own words what the other person has said. Experience indicates that in approximately 50% of all cases misunderstandings occur because the other person's statement has not been clarified.

How Do You Use It?

Ask a question to be sure that you understood what the other person meant. Thus, interpret what the other person said, repeat this in your own words, and check if it is correct. This way you will have fewer misunderstandings, greater clarity, more objective discussions, and a better understanding of personal feelings.

Examples of Clarifying

- So as to leave no doubt, you say that . . .
- Thus, in other words, you mean that . . .
- If I understand what you've said correctly, this means that . . .

Summarizing

What Is It?

By summarizing what is said and repeating what is agreed on, you create order, clarity, structure, progress, peace, and more depth in the discussion. Clarifying involves a particular point in the discussion, whereas a summary encompasses an entire conversation.

How Do You Use It?

At the beginning of a meeting summarize the most important points of the previous meeting. From time to time during the meeting, give an impartial, noncritical review of the connection between the different items of the meeting. Ask as often as necessary whether your summary corresponds with what participants meant. Also, give a summary before going on to the next item on the agenda.

Example of Summarizing

- Okay, let's start. During the previous meeting, we discussed a couple of possible solutions and eliminated a few others, so that in the end three solutions remained. Rhoda was going to research the feasibility of the remaining solutions. Does this match with what we already discussed? Rhoda, could you please give us the results?

Involving Others

What Is It?

Involve the participants in a discussion in such a way that their active participation is encouraged and supported.

How Do You Use It?

See to it that no one is excluded from the discussion. Bring people who have been silent for a long period of time into the discussion by asking them a question. This way active participation is stimulated and a feeling of self-worth and strong motivation is created as well.

Examples of Involving Others

- John, we have not heard from you yet. What do you think of this solution?
- Fran, you're out of the spotlight. What is your plan regarding to . . . ?

Showing Appreciation

What Is It?

Show appreciation during a discussion in such a way that you stimulate improved performance, stronger motivation, and a feeling of self-worth.

How Do You Use It?

One method to encourage employees to improve performance is by expressing your honest appreciation every time someone endeavors something and gets results. Indicate clearly what you're showing your appreciation for and for whom it is meant. Do this when others are present and shortly after the delivered performance. Appreciation can be a word of thanks or a compliment for something someone has done or said correctly. The objective of this is to show that you have noticed someone's efforts, to stimulate people to repeat the effort, and to encourage others to deliver similar efforts. Don't focus exclusively on what employees do wrong. Catch them red-handed doing a good job and give them the benefit of the doubt.

Examples of Showing Appreciation

- Very good, Jane. That was a terrific speech. Thanks a lot.
- Finally, I would like to thank Fred for all the work he has done.

Giving and Receiving Feedback

What Is It?

Feedback is a form of communication whereby the receiver of the message lets the sender know how the message came across. As a result, the person will know the effect that his or her behavior has on others. Annoying behavior can be corrected and shaped into the required behavior. Giving and receiving feedback involves redirecting, correcting, and complimenting. As a result, group cooperation becomes more open and effective. This skill also fits within the framework of 360° feedback, an important means to improve the functioning of individual employees (see Chapter 6).

How Do You Use It?

Here are some general guidelines to follow. Feedback:

- describes the behavior that has led to the feedback; it does not make a description about the person.
- is not given to judge the person, it is just something that is mentioned in order to achieve improvement.
- is specific and not general; it is clear so that the receiver understands its message.
- is in the interest of both receiver and sender.
- is only meaningful if and when the receiver is open to it.
- should be given within five minutes.
- is not a discussion.

Apart from these guidelines there are certain rules for the sender as well as for the receiver. The most important rules for the *feedback provider* are:

- Clarify to yourself beforehand what you want to say and collect the necessary data.
- Start out with positive points.
- Present feedback in such a way that it is seen as an opportunity and not a threat.
- Be specific; make clear what effects the other's behavior has had on you: for instance, "The remark you just made irritated me, because I felt that I did not do my utmost to solve the problem adequately."
- Be open and honest.
- Make your observation of the other person's behavior descriptive (what you see) and not judgmental (giving assessments): "During the meeting you were not very talkative, why?" Not: "Your participation in the meeting was not up to par, were you not interested?"
- Convey what you observe in terms of specific behavior, not personal attacks or generalized judgments: "The remark you just

made irritated me." Not: "You're someone who always wants to be in the spotlight with your off-the-wall remarks."

- Refer to events that occur now or have happened recently, such as: "Your absence today was very annoying." Not: "In previous years you have frequently been absent too."

- Give the other person the opportunity to react; listen intently and keep an open mind to his or her opinion.

- Show that you trust the other person and end the conversation with some positive remarks about the future.

- Appreciate people for who they are, not only for their accomplishments.

- Be selective in giving feedback; only give feedback if the other person can benefit from it at this time.

- Draw conclusions and give specific examples.

The most important rules for the *receiver of feedback* are:

- Listen attentively and closely before you accept the feedback; ask for clarification when something is not clear.

- Don't go into a defensive mode or start attacking; don't look for explanations; feedback is a learning process.

- Accept the feedback and analyze why you're acting in the way that has been addressed.

- Know that the feedback giver is kindly disposed towards you; don't feel that you are being attacked.

- Don't express negative feelings; study the feedback with the sender.

- Don't try to be humorous or smart; concentrate on a change for the better.

- Summarize the feedback to be able to formulate your observations.

- Ask questions to clarify the feedback.

- Carefully evaluate the usefulness of the feedback.

- Don't react vehemently and aggressively towards negative feedback; get information from it.

- Don't consider the feedback to be criticism.

- Show appreciation to the feedback sender because he or she had the courage to help you.

Constructive Negotiating

What Is It?

Constructive negotiating is a process in which interdependent people with conflicting needs, interests, or objectives try to find a compromise through a good and tactical negotiation that will be acceptable to everyone. Such a negotiation is also characterized by a recognition of disputes, mutual benefits, possible use of pressure by the negotiating parties, and a willingness to bargain. Constructive negotiation is an essential part of teamwork. (See also Mastenbroek, 1996; Schermer and Wijn, 1992.) In fact, although team members have the same team objective, sometimes differences in opinion, contrarieties, and conflicts of interest can still develop. Through constructive negotiation team members can agree on how to reach the team objective.

How Do You Use It?

With constructive negotiation it is necessary to take into consideration the following rules, so that negotiating partners can enter into a good process that favors everyone:

- Adequately prepare the conversation.
- Look for the golden mean between hard negotiating (winning at the expense of mutual understanding) and soft negotiating (personal objectives are abandoned to maintain friendship with the other party). Continue to keep your own objectives in perspective, even if you make concessions.
- Attend to maintaining a balance in power and don't be completely dependent upon the other person; negotiations are not necessary when one party has more power than the other.
- Listen actively and put yourself in the other's shoes; try to understand his or her interests and perception on things. Say: "*I understand fully that you . . .*" Nevertheless, don't forget your own interests. Ask open questions and, when necessary, direct questions to find out the other person's interests. Also provide adequate information. Don't answer questions before you fully understand them; ask for an explanation.
- Strive for a compromise that benefits both parties; look for similarities in interests (mutual benefits) and combine them in a flexible way. Say: "*Can we share the work in such a way that everyone . . .*"

- See to a positive environment and good mutual relationship; separate the people from the problem. Be businesslike, not personal and emotional. Don't focus on the behavior of the other person. Focus on issues to which both parties are committed.

- Don't negotiate about positions and from one person's point of view but on the basis of interests; don't put your objective first, as if you are not about to give in an inch. A fighting attitude seldom rewards you, and forcing a point through does not lead to good results.

- Make choices from different alternatives, and use independent and objective criteria accepted by both parties to test these alternatives.

- Avoid a direct rejection of a proposal from the other person; get positive points out in the open, and express appreciation for these. If the other person proposes something, do not immediately make a counterproposal. React to the proposal by asking questions, and then try to present your proposal as an addition.

- Look for verbal and nonverbal signals from the other person, because these can be an indication of what the other person finds important or not.

- Be patient, optimistic, and friendly; have respect for the other person, and strive for a positive feeling in both of you.

- Give a summary; in this way any confusing or difficult situations or differences of opinion can be made transparent. In addition, summaries entail making concrete agreements, which creates continuity and order in the discussion.

Conflict Handling

What Is It?

If the differences between people are considerable, negotiations are generally useless and conflict arises. A conflict is a clash between people that is revealed by their behavior and attitude. Team conflicts arise when, due to irritation or differences of opinion, two or more team members are not willing to cultivate positive cooperation. Differences in speaking styles, conflicting objectives, differences in personal style, personal egos, differences in values and norms, differences in personal interest, lack of clarity, working under time constraints, and claims about scarce resources can all be the cause of conflict. Conflict handling, or the way in which we deal with differences, can sometimes be more harmful than the conflicts themselves. Conflicts can be positive in certain cases, however, because they force employees to reassess their own ideas and thus develop new knowledge (Nonaka and Takeuchi, 1995). If we were always to agree with each other, there would be no reason to challenge the status quo and benefit from the change. In conflict handling there must always be a continuous search for a balance between learning and escalation.

How Do You Use It?

In a conflict three phases of escalation can be distinguished (Bos and Hartig, 1998):

1. *Rational phase.* The case is still negotiable; the cause of the irritation is separate from the matter at hand; parties often reach a solution without outside help, provided that the conflict is recognized and there is willingness for constructive cooperation.
2. *Emotional phase.* Parties blame each other for the conflict, and efforts are undertaken to form coalitions.
3. *Fighting phase.* The relationship between the parties is in grave danger of being irreparably damaged. The parties try as much as possible to inflict damage, even at their own expense.

To effectively handle a conflict it is important to know the sensibility of those involved and in which phase the conflict is. Five styles of coping with conflicts have been outlined by Kor (1998):

1. forcing or enforcing your own solution if you are sure that you are right ("*stand firm*");
2. putting up with the other's ideas ("*keep the peace*");
3. reaching a compromise ("*pacification*");
4. denying that something is happening ("*play dumb*"); and
5. putting the problem on the table and together looking for acceptable solutions to benefit the team results ("*be open and above board in one's dealings*").

There is no ideal style for handling conflict. The preference for a certain style has more to do with your own personality and depends on the situation and the phase in which the conflict is. Good conflict handling requires application of all the aforementioned interpersonal skills as well as good negotiating. Some important rules for conflict handling include:

- Voice any irritations as soon as possible.
- If there are differences of opinion, discuss them quietly; do not react emotionally and become angry.
- Listen and evaluate before drawing conclusions.
- Search for points of agreement as soon as possible.
- Prevent the conflict between two persons from escalating into a team problem.
- Prevent emotional reactions; don't get angry, don't start crying, don't become jealous, and don't show hate. If necessary, go home to cool off.
- Don't make demands, and don't have an intractable standpoint.
- Don't linger too long on the past; look ahead.
- Be nice.
- Negotiate constructively.

A summary of the interpersonal skills discussed in the preceding sections is provided in Table 8.5.

Neuro-Linguistic Programming

Neuro-Linguistic Programming (NLP) is a theory of self-development. In this approach to learning the ways in which we communicate with each other are combined with elements of linguistics, neurology, and biology. Many books worth reading have been written on this subject. Here, I simply want to provide you with a short introduction to what NLP is and how it relates to the Total Performance Scorecard concept. NLP is a learning process that is an effective method for increasing the organizational learning capacity. The basic principles of NLP may be summarized as follows (Landsberg, 1999):

- We can attain each goal we set out for ourselves; by learning we can, for example, tackle problems more effectively, speak another language, play football, and so on.
- To develop in the direction of our goal, we must: (1) conjure up a crystal-clear image of our goal, and (2) move toward that goal by consciously following the paths that others or we have found useful in the past.
- We will only improve swiftly when we listen closely to the feedback from our surroundings and from ourselves, and if we then adapt our initiatives to this feedback. This principle also applies to the mental attitude that has a bearing on our personal ambition.

Table 8.5

Summary of Interpersonal Communicative Skills		
Goal	**Result**	**Techniques**
Listening		
Gather information.	Better understanding and being informed.	Be quiet, make eye contact, relax and listen attentively when the other person gives his or her opinion. Listen until the other person has finished speaking, and only reply then. Try to imagine yourself in the other person's position; this allows you to understand the subject of discussion better. Show interest, show the other person that he or she is being taken seriously and that you are trying to understand him or her. Ask questions for clarification, repeat what has been said literally or in your own words, and look for common interests.
Questioning		
Obtain valuable information and ideas; increase involvement.	Better decisions and focused discussions.	First, decide what you want to achieve with your question and then ask the right question. Second, ask questions in such a way that the other person feels comfortable and involved in the discussion.
Building on Ideas of Others		
Develop and shape ideas.	More solutions that are thought out, hence better, and a greater feeling of appreciation.	Express your appreciation for the other person's idea and then add something of your own.
Constructive Arguing		
State other views of the other person and correct wrong statements.	Transparency, better decision making, and greater involvement.	Analyze the other person's ideas and give an alternative view. Furnish reasons for why the idea cannot be accepted or explain why it would fail.

Table 8.5 *continued*

Summary of Interpersonal Communicative Skills		
Clarifying		
Be certain that you have interpreted what the other person has said correctly.	More transparency, fewer misunderstandings, and better listening skills.	Interpret what the other person has said and check if it is correct. Repeat the other person's words according to your understanding.
Summarizing		
Create insight on the most important points from the previous discussion.	Clarity and structure in the discussion.	Repeat the most important decisions and agreements from a previous meeting.
Involving Others		
Stimulate greater involvement and active participation.	Create better listening skills as well as self-esteem and stronger motivation.	Address the respective person by name and ask a question to involve him or her in the meeting.
Showing Appreciation		
Encourage someone to deliver the same effort and urge others to do the same.	Motivation and self-esteem; inspire higher performances.	Show your appreciation for good performance immediately and clearly. Preferably show appreciation in the presence of others and state clearly whom it is meant for.
Giving and Receiving Feedback		
Correct annoying behavior and adjust it to encourage the required behavior. Cooperation in the group becomes more open and effective.	More effective cooperation and open communication.	Decide for yourself if you will give the feedback or not and what you and the other will gain from it. If you will give and receive feedback, use the rules listed in the section on giving and receiving feedback, such as be specific, open, and honest; appreciate people for who they are; don't express negative feelings; don't consider the feedback to be criticism; etc.

Table 8.5 *continued*

Summary of Interpersonal Communicative Skills		
Constructive Negotiating		
After positive deliberation come to an understanding on conflicting wishes, interests, and goals; find a compromise that is acceptable to all parties.	More clarity, less irritations and differences of opinion, higher team performance, and a good relationship between the negotiating parties.	Provide good preparation, a balance of power, and a positive climate. Be patient and apply the rules mentioned for constructive negotiating, such as don't be completely dependent upon the other person; strive for a compromise that benefits both parties; be patient, optimistic, and friendly; etc.
Conflict Handling		
Reduce conflicts that result from irritations and differences of opinion.	More clarity, fewer misunderstandings, greater involvement, effective cooperation, and higher team performance.	Check in which phase the conflict is and acknowledge the sensibility of those involved. Then, apply the rules mentioned for handling conflict, such as listen and evaluate before drawing conclusions, search for point of agreements, prevent emotional reactions, be nice, etc.

- An important element of these principles is the ability to use all our senses. Clear communication with others and with ourselves requires more than simply the use of words.

To summarize, Neuro-Linguistic Programming involves all three of the following core principles:

Neuro: the way in which the senses are used when gathering, evaluating, absorbing, and digesting knowledge.

Linguistic: the use of language, symbols, and metaphors to form a mental picture.

Programming: developing new deep-seated principles, values, behaviors, and lively images and "programming" the mind with them.

These principles lead us to the conclusion that Neuro-Linguistic Programming is integrally embedded in the Total Performance Scorecard philosophy.

Coaching Team Members

> Much education today is monumentally ineffective. All too often we are giving young people cut flowers when we should be teaching them to grow their own plants.
>
> *John W. Gardner*

Coaching team members entails helping employees develop themselves and perform optimally in the team. The emphasis in coaching is on learning, dialogue, getting employees to broaden their views, and taking initiatives. The learning styles and interpersonal communicative skills that we just discussed are of decided importance here. The goal of coaching is to help team members gather knowledge and gain experience. It is a way to motivate people to perform to the best of their ability, and to develop the skills and insights that will lead to improved behavior. It is a learning process whereby Kolb's learning cycle is continuously repeated. With coaching, team members constantly learn as a result of self-discoveries, gain experience, receive feedback on team functioning, and learn about the effective use of everyone's skills and talents. The personal structured dialogue between the team leader and team member contributes to employee motivation, improved team performance, and a positive working relationship between coach and team members.

Coaching is a way to quickly transfer skills, knowledge, and experience and to get people to the point where they will perform to the best of their ability. Team member coaching is a success when people on the team achieve personal and professional growth through the encouragement, support, and guidance of their coach. For the coach it is a success when team members perform their tasks better and take on delegated responsibilities and authorities. The other advantages of coaching are: more creativity and teamwork, motivated employees, and higher labor productivity. To be able to coach effectively, the following conditions must be present (Thomas, 1996):

- A nonthreatening atmosphere.
- Helpfulness and sympathy.
- A climate of openness, trust, and respect.
- Personal dialogue that is focused on cooperation and teamwork.
- A focus on goals, improvement evaluation, and behavior feedback.
- The expansion of insight into tasks.
- An emphasis on the strong points of other people as well as points that are eligible for change.

- The identification of bottlenecks that hinder improvement and the realization of goals.
- Support to ensure that team members are willing to assume the responsibility for delegated tasks.

Coaching is also strongly related to delegating or empowering others. A good coach lets others do the majority of the work and places responsibility and power where it is needed most. The most important reasons why managers usually do not delegate are (Thomas, 1996; Rampersad, 2001A):

- The wish to continue to exercise authority and control.
- Wanting to have power over others.
- Lack of confidence in the ability of others.
- Fear that the other person will do the job better.
- The manager wants to attract the attention of his or her superiors.
- The manager likes to do certain tasks him or herself.
- Thinking that he or she can do it better.
- Being of the opinion that the job is too important to take risks.
- Thinking that others do not have the skills to coach.

The saying that "coaching has a positive influence on self-guidance" is an old one. It was Mary Parker Follet (1868–1933) who wondered as far back as the 1930s how it was that so many things went well in organizations. According to Follet, it was largely because the boss did not meddle! So, coaching also involves not meddling but empowerment. Empowerment entails giving employees within a certain framework authority, freedom, trust, and information. It makes them accept responsibility and develop skills in order to make independent decisions for performance improvement. Some important characteristics of empowered employees are that they:

- Feel responsible for their work.
- Align their personal goals to those of the organization.
- Continuously learn and share their knowledge with others.
- Are critical of themselves, have self-esteem, and are motivated.
- Are well-trained, creative, and customer-oriented.
- Monitor and improve their work continuously.
- Find new goals and changes a challenge.

Four Types of Behavior

To coach effectively it is important to have insight into the behavior of the team members. Business literature has numerous models to explain differences in behavior, which all have four main categories in common. The most popular personality theory that considers four behavior categories is the one by Geier and Downey (1989):

1. The *dominant-directive type*; these people are driven by an internal need to lead, and to take things into their own hands in order to achieve their goals. They have self-esteem, a positive self-image, and a strong ego; they also love a challenge, have a strong will, are independent, and goal-oriented. They have a tendency to criticize others and traditional working methods, and dislike routine work. They are pragmatic, reactive, and energetic. They like to feel important and impress people. They are also opinionated and impatient. They prefer to control others and can sometimes hardly bear the feelings, opinions, and shortcomings of others. They usually listen very poorly.

2. The *social-interactive type*; these people are talkative, popular, convincing, impulsive, enthusiastic, and like to be in the limelight. They have a lot of energy, need social acknowledgement, and like to be treated in a loving way. They try to influence others in an optimistic and friendly way that is focused on a positive result. What they fear most is public humiliation, and they will do their utmost to avoid this. In general, they work in a supportive, trusting, intuitive, and conciliatory manner toward solving problems. They like brainstorming and contacts with colleagues; enjoy not having to bother with supervisory duties, details, or complex matters; and prefer to participate in important projects and activities. Their weak points are a lack of patience and limited powers of concentration. They get aggravated quickly and sometimes neglect to check certain things. When they feel insufficiently stimulated or involved, they get bored and look for a distraction, which can result in superficial, inconsistent, and excessively emotional behavior.

3. The *uniform-stable type*; these people are generally quiet, calm, loyal, predictable, patient, persevering, goal-oriented, result-oriented, laconic, and modest. They don't express themselves easily, prefer a slower, easier pace than others, and are eager to finish things. They concentrate on building trust and strive for sustainable personal relationships and the preservation of a stable and well-balanced environment. They are friendly, helpful, and

rarely show rage or euphoria. They dislike sudden changes. Any interference with their fixed working method can make them lose their composure. They solve problems by observing and analyzing as well as applying solutions. They dislike taking risks and prefer repetitive activities. They also respect traditions, feel uncomfortable with conflicts, and enjoy formulating rules and implementing them.

4. The *thoughtful type*; these people are accurate, reliable, independent, careful, detached, introverted, inventive, perfectionistic, and resourceful. They take few risks, prefer to have clearly spelled-out priorities, want to know which pace is expected of them, and are eager to know how something works in order to judge everything correctly. Because they uphold their norms and values, they expect a lot from themselves and others. They will only go into action when they have determined which tasks and aspects will actually influence the desired results. Sometimes it can take a while before they bring certain matters into the open, because they usually need additional factual information.

Most people are a mixture of these four types. Decide which type you are and how this connects with your Personal Balanced Scorecard. In addition, represent your personal behavior type by means of a diagram and discuss this in your group. Figure 8.5 shows the behavior type of John van Dam of Business Jet. It reveals that John is mostly a dominant-directive type, which also corresponds with his learning style (activist) and his team role (Shaper) he performs in his Security team at Schiphol Airport.

How to Coach the Four Behavior Types

The manager needs to understand which behavior types are on the team in order to coach the employees effectively. A few interesting suggestions for the informal coaching of employees of each behavior type are shown in Table 8.6 (Thomas, 1996). Chapter 6 discussed how employees can be coached formally based on review forms and 360° feedback (see Appendixes A and B).

Leadership Styles

The most dangerous leadership myth is that leaders are born—that there is a genetic factor to leadership. This myth asserts that

Table 8.6

How to Coach the Four Types of Behavior	
Dominant-Directive Type • Show them how to win; give them new opportunities. • Bring variety into their way of working and look for possibilities to create variation. • Give them evidence of logic reasoning and develop their listening skills by letting them, for example, repeat in their own words what was agreed upon. • Give summarized information, facts, and crucial points. • Make agreements about the goals and let them be confirmed verbally. • Allow them to take initiatives within the correct framework. • Make them conscious of the effects of rushed conclusions. • Pay attention to what they have achieved, and compliment them about it. • Give them the lead when it is appropriate, but with relevant data. • Enter into a discussion about a topic that the two of you disagree on with conviction and a positive attitude, but based on facts rather than opinions. • Help them to be more considerate of the feelings of others.	**Social-Interactive Type** • Support their need for approval and making a good impression by enthusiastically expressing your belief in their ideas and your support of them. • Avoid complex details. • Give them evidence of logical reasoning and increase their listening skills by encouraging them to repeat everything that has been discussed using their own words. • Help them draft a coherent plan to obtain results based on objectives. • Set limits on the time available for discussions and tasks. • Make the job varied and avoid assigning tasks involving repetition. • Give them your sincere appreciation and compliment them on their performance and improvements. • Execute tasks together and coach them in logical decision making so that their ideas are converted into tangible results. • Don't be aggressive and avoid personal discussions. • Be active, stimulating, and maintain a fast pace.
Uniform-Stable Type • Warn them well in advance of eventual changes and new assignments. • Convince them with logical reasoning and provide the necessary information and proof. • Show that you are interested in them. • Give clear instructions and descriptions. • Compliment them on their patience and perseverance. • Don't behave aggressively toward them and avoid conflicts. • Let them serve and help others. • Provide a relaxed and friendly working environment. • Acknowledge their helpful manner and give feedback at the appropriate time.	**Thoughtful Type** • Approach them in an indirect, nonaggressive, and careful way. • Show the reasons for certain decisions, explain and give an interpretation of the underlying principles. • Let them study the improvements and results of others before they make their own decisions. • Compliment them on their thorough and correct way of working. • Allow them time to philosophize, reflect, and look for the correct answer within the available limits.
Source: Thomas, 1996.	

Figure 8.5

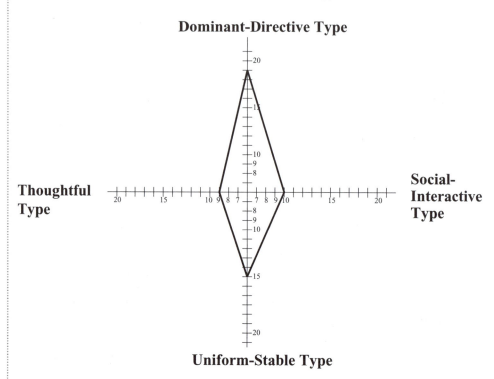

John van Dam's Behavior Type

Dominant-Directive Type

Thoughtful Type

Social-Interactive Type

Uniform-Stable Type

people simply either have certain charismatic qualities or not. That's nonsense; in fact, the opposite is true. Leaders are made rather than born.

Warren G. Bennis

Like teamwork, the leadership style also decides the success of the TPS concept and is a means of influencing organizational culture. In addition, leadership style influences employee health. A recent study at the British University Hospital in High Wycombe shows that not getting along with a manager raises one's blood pressure and, in the long run, is bad for your heart (Metro, 2002). These are just a few of the reasons to pay attention to leadership. Many books have been written on the subject, and their main theme is that the effectiveness of managers, is determined not only by their personal characteristics and behavior, but also by how much their leadership style is adapted to the situation. This is known as situational leadership. There are two basic leadership styles: (1) focus on tasks (work to be accomplished) and (2) focus on relationships. When focusing on tasks, managers concentrate on structuring tasks that need to be accomplished, indicating what and how the job must be done. This involves:

- Determining goals and targets for employees.
- Organizing and distributing work.
- Providing adequate resources.
- Instructing employees on how to execute their job.
- Checking the quality of work.

When focusing on relations, managers concentrate on improving employee satisfaction and cultivating a fundamental attitude about learning in the group. This involves:

- Expressing appreciation for employees.
- Providing support when necessary.
- Looking for tasks that fit the capabilities and the personal ambition of employees.
- Stimulating teamwork.
- Stimulating individual as well as team learning.

Effective leaders are those who are focused on both tasks and relationships and can perform a wide variety of roles. The literature on this subject includes many leadership styles and roles. Among the best known is the theory of Robert Quinn (1996). He distinguishes the following eight roles of leadership: *producer, director, coordinator, checker, stimulator, mentor, innovator,* and *negotiator* (see Table 8.7 and Figure 8.6). All these roles are strongly interrelated; they can be both in contrast with and supplemental to each other. They are classified in four quadrants divided by the vertical and horizontal axes of flexibility/stability and internally oriented/externally oriented, respectively.

Successful managers have the ability to execute all leadership roles in an optimal mix that balance them with each other. The following boxed text shows the relation between the different organizational functions and the required roles of the manager.

Functions	Roles Required of the Manager
Enterprising (production function)	→ Producer and Director
Organizing (control function)	→ Coordinator and Checker
Socializing (human relation function)	→ Stimulator and Mentor
Changing (improvement function)	→ Innovator and Negotiator

Illustrate in a diagram which roles you fulfill in your organization and discuss this with your employees and colleagues. You can also ask them to tell you which roles you fulfill in their eyes and what your weak points are; then try to make changes (360° feedback). Research shows that managers who allow employees to evaluate them generally score better on employee satisfaction.

Figure 8.7 shows the profile of Frank Jansen, the manager of Business Jet. This profile is based on the 360° feedback of his management team. Frank's profile shows that he is a *checker*,

Table 8.7

Eight Leadership Roles According to Robert Quinn	
Producer The producer promotes an active working environment, is deeply involved, motivated, and devoted, accepts responsibilities, and transforms assignments into acceptable results. For the producer, the only criteria for organizational effectiveness are productivity and profits.	**Director** The director sets the goals, chooses the right strategy, makes expectations clear, determines the policy and rules, identifies bottlenecks, selects solutions, defines tasks, and gives instructions. Thus, she is the organizational designer. For the director, the only criteria for organizational effectiveness are productivity and profits. When making a decision, the final result and maximum output are considered. Employees are only rewarded when they make a large contribution to the realization of these goals.
Coordinator The coordinator is mainly concerned with delegating tasks through the organization, arranging the efforts of the staff, and managing crises. He pays a lot of attention to technological and domestic issues. The leader in this role must be trustworthy and reliable. The coordinator emphasizes the maintenance and consolidation of processes. Here business management is mainly characterized by a hierarchical and bureaucratic structure.	**Checker** The checker knows what is going on in the company, checks if employees stick to the rules, takes care of details, does the administration and documentation, and performs inspection rounds. The checker emphasizes the maintenance and consolidation of processes; management is here characterized by a hierarchical and bureaucratic structure.

Table 8.7 *continued*

Eight Leadership Roles According to Robert Quinn	
Stimulator The stimulator incites cooperation, involvement, and solidarity, realizes teamwork, solves employee problems, contributes to moral development, displays great openness, and knows how to reach consensus. She is a coach, guide, and companion. She can initiate learning processes and strengthen the collective power of employees. The stimulator appreciates people for who they are.	**Mentor** The mentor is focused on the development of employee skills through a careful, helpful, and sympathetic approach. He also listens to his employees, expresses his appreciation, and gives compliments. The mentor helps employees structure their vision so that they can look beyond superficial circumstances. He values people because they are people. Business management is internally focused and flexible. Development of human resources and cultural change is central here.
Innovator The innovator makes continuous improvements possible, has a strategic vision of the future, recognizes important trends and demands in the market, sees ways to satisfy these demands, anticipates necessary changes, has insight into customer demands, and tolerates risks. Above all things, innovators are creative and clever people who can see into the future. With the innovator, competitive position, expansion, continuous improvement, adaptability, innovation, and creative solutions to problems are central.	**Negotiator** The negotiator is politically conscious, uses his power and influence, to obtain resources from outside, and can negotiate effectively. Reputation and image are very important here. The negotiator usually acts as an intermediary and spokesperson.
Source: Quinn, 1996, pp. 41–49.	

coordinator, *director*, *producer*, *negotiator*, and *innovator*. However, he is lacking in interpersonal skills. In his Personal Balanced Scorecard, which was already mentioned in Chapter 3, one of his goals is "improved leadership skills." Figure 8.7 clearly shows which areas need improvement. In particular, he needs to improve his abilities in the roles of stimulator and mentor, and balance them with his other roles.

Figure 8.6

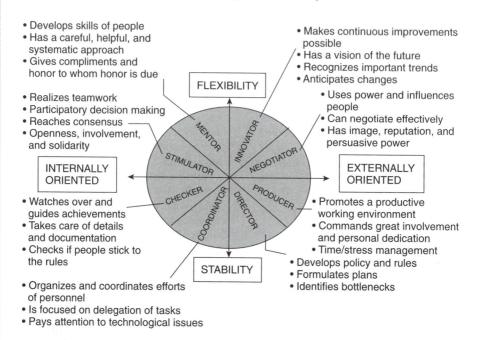

Robert Quinn's Eight Leadership Roles

- Develops skills of people
- Has a careful, helpful, and systematic approach
- Gives compliments and honor to whom honor is due

- Realizes teamwork
- Participatory decision making
- Reaches consensus
- Openness, involvement, and solidarity

FLEXIBILITY

MENTOR · STIMULATOR · INNOVATOR · NEGOTIATOR · CHECKER · COORDINATOR · DIRECTOR · PRODUCER

INTERNALLY ORIENTED

EXTERNALLY ORIENTED

- Makes continuous improvements possible
- Has a vision of the future
- Recognizes important trends
- Anticipates changes

- Uses power and influences people
- Can negotiate effectively
- Has image, reputation, and persuasive power

- Watches over and guides achievements
- Takes care of details and documentation
- Checks if people stick to the rules

STABILITY

- Organizes and coordinates efforts of personnel
- Is focused on delegation of tasks
- Pays attention to technological issues

- Promotes a productive working environment
- Commands great involvement and personal dedication
- Time/stress management
- Develops policy and rules
- Formulates plans
- Identifies bottlenecks

Figure 8.7

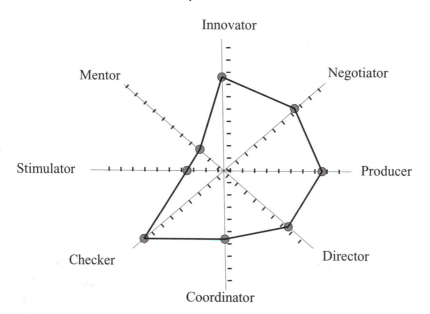

Leadership Profile of Frank Jansen

Innovator

Mentor

Negotiator

Stimulator

Producer

Checker

Director

Coordinator

Wanrooy (2001) mentions four leadership styles that are based on a situational approach and provide direction for managing professionals:

1. *Coaching leadership.* This includes helping, facilitating, supporting, and guiding employees to perform better.
2. *Inspiring leadership.* Charismatic, enthusiastic, and visionary leadership is central here; empowerment is also a part of this type of leadership.
3. *Serving leadership.* The leader is in the service of the employee; teamwork, a feeling of belonging, caring behavior, reflection, and altruism are central.
4. *Intrinsic leadership.* The most important characteristics here are personal leadership with intuition, dependability, openness, integrity, and spirituality. The best-known guru in this field is Stephen Covey (1993). In his vision, the effective leader grows from dependence to independence and then towards interdependence.

Fijlstra and Wullings (1998) mention a fifth leadership style, which they call *inspiring leadership*, that goes a step beyond those mentioned thus far and that is closely related to the TPS concept. An inspired leader is able to strengthen people's faith in their own capabilities, open up hidden possibilities, and thereby motivate them to deliver maximum performances. They are people who are characterized by wisdom, servitude, righteousness, moderation, innate refinement, ethical personal ambition, and respect for others.

Successful implementation of the TPS concept requires a balanced combination of all five leadership styles, with a strong emphasis on learning.

It is useful at this point to refer to the Philips Quality Leadership Role Model, which is shown in the following boxed text (Philips Electronics, 1994). This model is a comprehensive description of the variety of tasks to be accomplished by all Philips managers in order to ensure the implementation of Philips Quality in their area of responsibility. It is used

- As a source of inspiration in discussions of management teams.
- As a guideline for directing individual and team actions.
- As a support for management education.
- As a reference for appraisal and recognition of managers.
- As an input for action planning on management development.

Philips Quality Leadership Role Model

Customer First

Listen to customers and actively seek their opinion on the value of the products and services supplied. Make the customer visible, especially to those who are not in day-to-day contact with customers. Where relevant, develop a close link with customers and seek joint improvement activity. Lead the handling of complaints.

Demonstrate Involvement

Introduce and apply the Philips Quality principles and methodology. Participate in improvement activities and teamwork. Demonstrate the value of new methods and techniques. Benchmark the quality process.

Value People and Foster Teamwork

Take care of the development of people's skills and capabilities. Train for Philips Quality and coach the application. Enable people to be responsible for the result of their work. Monitor, appraise, and recognize people's performance. Advance teamwork and put team success ahead of individual achievement.

Build Supplier Partnership

Clarify Philips Quality to suppliers, audit their capabilities, give feedback, discuss improvements, and support them where needed. Recognize quality improvements made by suppliers and encourage joint improvement action.

Strive for Excellence

Hold the Philips Quality path, review progress of the improvement process and use conclusions to plan new initiatives. Actively seek best practices and use these to strengthen the approach.

Explain and Deploy Policy

Explain the Quality policy, as part of the business policy, to all involved. Set stretching targets and deploy these to business processes, to the functions within the organization, and to suppliers.

Manage Improvement through Processes

Demonstrate that the functional organization produces value for customers through processes. Make processes visible and manageable. Assess capabilities and measure performance. Seek ownership for process improvement and for process redesign.

In Table 8.8 at the end of this section, I provide a summary of the attitudes, tasks, and skills of leaders of learning organizations. This outline is a handy tool when developing competency profiles of leaders. It also functions as a checklist for managers who have lost touch. It is not, however, meant to generalize the characteristics of effective leaders. As Peter Drucker (1999) has pointed out, effective leaders reveal wide differences in their behavior. This makes it difficult to give general advice regarding this subject, and I will not attempt to do so. *Just as there is not one specific piece of advice to be given regarding the best organizational strategy, so this applies to the best leaders as well.*

Table 8.8

Summary of Attitudes, Tasks, and Skills of Leaders of Learning Organizations	
ATTITUDES AND TASKS	**SKILLS**
• Is honest, trustworthy, and consistent • Encourages a fundamental learning attitude • Teaches employees how to learn and encourages them to share their knowledge with colleagues • Experiences life as a permanent learning process; continually asking himself: "*What can I learn from this?*" • Stimulates working smarter instead of harder • Does not hide or try to get around problems • Gives others the recognition that is due to them • Listens actively to employees and respects them • Demonstrates constantly through his own actions and words that he is never satisfied with anything less than continuous improvement • Lets employees maintain their self-esteem and respect, and supports their skills • Helps employees take on responsibilities • Has the ability to bring out the hidden possibilities of employees • Is customer-oriented, decisive, goal- and result-oriented, energetic, and open to change • Is continuously focused on developing and mobilizing the knowledge of employees	• Has aligned her personal ambition to her personal behavior and the shared organizational ambition • Can make people believe in themselves • Thinks conceptually without losing contact with reality • Knows how to get the best out of others • Is well aware of her strong and weak points • Listens well • Can place herself in the position of others • Can carry out norms and values so that a "we feeling" develops • Can convince employees that the chosen way is the right one • Can build a confidential relationship • Can make decisions and carry them out • Can collaborate harmoniously, as well as transfer and

Table 8.8 *continued*

Summary of Attitudes, Tasks, and Skills of Leaders of Learning Organizations	
ATTITUDES AND TASKS	**SKILLS**
• Lays down the boundaries where employees can make independent decisions	mobilize knowledge and skills
• Encourages employee independence	• Can handle constructive confrontation
• Takes well thought-out risks, is innovative, and dares to accept mistakes	• Can plan, command, and improve activities
• Is patient, decisive, positive, and enthusiastic	• Can distinguish the important from the less important
• Has guts (sticks his neck out) and continuously takes initiatives	
• Keeps appointments and shows the drive to obtain results	• Can balance short- and long-term priorities well
• Has perseverance and the power of persuasion	• Can communicate clearly, openly, and at the right time
• Is immune to stress and radiates tranquility	
• Supplies employees with a feeling of safety	• Can solve problems systematically and structurally
• Builds trust and respect with employees, and cherishes them	
• Creates synergy and makes sure tasks are executed harmoniously	• Has the talent to identify notable trends and anticipate them ahead of time
• Has a feeling of responsibility	
• Shows vision and propagates this decisively	
• Shows involvement; gives people space but is visible	• Can activate, motivate, and stimulate people
• Stimulates teamwork, based on mutual respect, openness, and trust	• Can maintain organizational tranquility
• Shows appreciation for the contributions of others	
• Creates a climate of enjoyment, passion, devotion, and enthusiasm	• Can create cultural change focused on hard work, teamwork, and the active participation of everyone
• Is a sounding board, propagates knowledge, and learns from his own mistakes	
• Allows arguments to influence his decision making and completely devotes himself to the shared objective	• Has a personal vision and can translate the organizational vision into concrete objectives and vice versa
• Is accessible to all team members, inspiring them and giving constructive feedback	
• Delegates with complete trust; gives responsibility and authority and holds people accountable	• Is open and honest, without a hidden agenda
• Shows employees how their activities contribute to the greater whole	• Has the ability to decide where the organization should go and distinguish between dreams and hard facts
• Inspires employees to set concrete, practical, and measurable goals, and to accomplish them	

Table 8.8 *continued*

Summary of Attitudes, Tasks, and Skills of Leaders of Learning Organizations	
ATTITUDES AND TASKS	**SKILLS**
• Stimulates and motivates employees to take initiatives and serve the customer • Maintains and supports relations with employees, customers, and suppliers with understanding • Creates circumstances in which people are successful and where they are responsible for their work and that of others • Brings people together, stimulates individual and team learning, and inspires intensive knowledge exchange • Allows himself to be judged by employees based on 360° feedback and also gives feedback • Gets along well with people and knows how to inspire and motivate others • Lets intuition influence problem solving and decision making • Creates transparency in tasks and positions • Creates a community and working climate in which people with diverse cultural backgrounds can work together harmoniously, and accept, trust, and respect each other • Helps employees distinguish between primary and secondary issues and gives a helping hand when needed • Is serviceable and modest • Has high standards and values and actively promotes them • Uses a flexible, situational management style; takes personal circumstances into account • Praises employees who perform well, and pays attention to those with shortcomings • Stays ahead of problems and keeps the overall picture in view • Dares to accept mistakes and learns from them • Preferably communicates face-to-face • Is a proactive coach	• Is innovative and dares to accept mistakes • Gives direction but is open to the input of others • Can carry out norms and values so that a company feeling can develop • Can motivate, inspire, and make people enthusiastic • Is open and flexible but can at the same time take strong action • Can stimulate the learning process • Has a good sense of humor • Can create involvement and cultivate a culture of participation • Is charismatic • Can avoid conflicts and negotiates well • Believes in herself and others • Can conduct effective planning, coaching, and appraisal meetings with her employees; based on this, she can help them continually develop their potential and talents • Can adequately asses the talents and shortcomings of employees
Source: Rampersad, 2002.	

Conducting Effective Meetings

> In a good meeting you can solve problems, spread information, make parties come together, and develop new ideas. A poor meeting is a waste of time, boring for those present, and only makes things worse.
>
> *Julie Bick*

As we have seen in the preceding sections, team meetings are held regularly when following the TPS cycle. In practice, meetings often tend to be unstructured, chaotic, and too amiable; this usually means that they're a waste of time, money, and creative ideas—which does not fit into the TPS concept. It is useful at this point to refer to the results of a recent study regarding holding meetings in The Netherlands (see following boxed text). It is advisable to do away with the traditional way of conducting meetings. Holding a meeting is a learning process as well as a means of communication for the benefit of sharing, receiving, and exchanging knowledge, as well as solving problems and taking initiatives. A meeting consists of a group of people who discuss a previously scheduled item, under the supervision of a chairperson. For a meeting to be most effective, the following guidelines should be met:

- The objectives of the meeting are clear.
- There is open discussion.
- The right people attend the meeting; invite only those who are indispensable.
- The meeting is evaluated based on improvement possibilities.
- A chairperson is appointed to lead the meeting, a minute taker to record the minutes, a timekeeper to check the time, and a process keeper to guard the meeting process. This person sees to it that people listen to each other, do not speak out of turn, brainstorm in the correct way, and so on.
- There is a time frame for every item on the agenda.
- The minutes are available within a week.
- The meeting starts on time.
- The meeting is closed as soon as the objective of the meeting is reached.
- A clear agenda is formulated and its items divided into announcements, information items, and discussion items. These items should be separated during the meeting.

- The agenda is put together beforehand and circulated, so that everyone can prepare for the meeting.
- The agenda is followed.
- Consensus is not necessary; the eagerness to reach a consensus often leads to vague and slow decision making, stifles personal initiatives, and confuses where responsibilities lie.
- Learning themes should be discussed in every meeting.

The Dutch Hold Meetings to the Tune of 14 Billion U.S. Dollars

The Dutch hold meetings like crazy. On an average, a Dutch employee spends one-quarter of his time in meetings. With high-level managers this may even increase to 80 percent and the highest managers seem to do nothing but have meetings. This has become evident from a recent study of the bureau Van Vree in The Netherlands. The conclusion of this study is that the higher the job level, the more one attends meetings. The annual cost of meetings in The Netherlands amounts to approximately 14 billion U.S. dollars. This amount is based on the wages of the participants in the meetings; room rental fees and travel expenses are not included in this amount. Of all the employees, government workers are the worst offenders. A civil servant spends on an average 32 percent of his or her work time in meetings and a general manager in a government department spends almost half of his or her work time in meetings, about sixteen meetings a week. Including preparation time, about 70 percent of his or her work week is absorbed in meetings. From this study at different government departments it becomes evident that 40 percent of the civil servants think they meet too much. Even general managers at the government departments think that one-third of all meetings are superfluous. "But nothing is being done about it," says the director of Van Vree. "Perhaps they are afraid that their business right to exist will disappear if they meet less."

Source: NRC Handelsblad, Amsterdam, January 22, 2003, p. 18.

Answering a few technical questions are central to preparing and conducting successful meetings. These include:

- What subjects are going to be discussed?
- Who should attend and who should not?
- When and where will the meeting be held?
- What are the requirements for the meeting room?
- Should guest speakers be invited?

- Is the agenda made, and has it been sent to all participants ahead of time?
- Who is the timekeeper?
- Who is the process keeper?
- Who will take the minutes?

During discussion in the meeting, minutes should be taken. Someone who listens well, writes fluently, and can summarize the discussion quickly should be chosen to take the minutes. The purpose of the minutes is to register agreements and guarantee continuity for subsequent meetings. Important questions that the person who takes the minutes should keep in mind and try to cover are:

- Which questions were discussed?
- Which answers were given?
- Which arguments and considerations were important?
- Which problems were identified?
- Which mistakes were made, and what has been learned from them?
- Which decisions were made?
- Which actions will be undertaken?
- Which conclusions were drawn?
- Which agreements were made (who will do what and when)?
- Attendance registration.
- Date for the next meeting.

Table 8.9 provides an overview of the most important activities, tasks, and roles for conducting effective meetings in the context of the Total Performance Scorecard concept.

Team Evaluation

Leadership and learning are indispensable to each other.
John F. Kennedy

In the scope of the Total Performance Scorecard, the meeting process should be reviewed continuously, so that we can learn from it and control this process. To accomplish this aim an evaluation

Table 8.9

Overview of Activities, Tasks, and Roles for Conducting Effective Meetings

Chairperson

Prior to the meeting
1. Provide the right team composition.
2. Read the minutes of the previous meeting and formulate the agenda and objectives of this meeting.
3. Send invitations, agenda, and additional information to the participants on time and provide an adequate meeting room.
4. Prepare yourself.

During the meeting
1. Begin on time.
2. Ask if everyone has received the information and can be present during the entire meeting.
3. Discuss reporting (who will take the minutes), the objectives of the meeting, and the expected contribution of the participants.
4. Delegate supporting tasks to a time and process keeper.
5. Go through the agenda in order.
6. Guard the meeting process by: asking questions, summarizing opinions, asking silent persons for their opinions, clarifying opinions, stimulating listening, expressing appreciation, accentuating conclusions, and so on.
7. Give a summary of the most important points and encourage discussions focused on the realization of team goals.
8. Ask questions such as: Who has a suggestion? Who agrees and who disagrees? Who wants to comment on this? Who can complete or clarify this? Who has counterarguments? Who can summarize this? What mistakes were made? How can we learn from them?
9. Establish relationships between different ideas and stimulate open communication.
10. Ask for facts, suggestions, and information, and focus on what must be realized.
11. Do not tolerate latecomers, private discussions, and abandoning of the meeting.
12. Do not permit moving away from the subject; determine clearly who will do what.
13. Take stimulating actions to keep the meeting going if it threatens to deadlock.
14. See to it that all available information is accessible to all participants.
15. Stay neutral with respect to the subject and participants; treat everyone equally.
16. Do not discuss more than one agenda item at a time.
17. Maintain a relaxed, informal, and disciplined atmosphere.
18. Increase enjoyment and lessen tensions.
19. Encourage people to be open and take risks.
20. Consensus is not always necessary; strive for single-mindedness to achieve a particular goal.

Table 8.9 *continued*

Overview of Activities, Tasks, and Roles for Conducting Effective Meetings

21. Allow quiet time (for thinking).
22. Try to find a link between different ideas.
23. Make sure that decisions and actions are understood and written down.
24. Act as a coach; don't dominate or display an authoritarian attitude.
25. Interrupt small talk.
26. During the last ten minutes, give a short summary and note points of action.
27. End the discussion as soon as the subject has been treated exhaustively.
28. Evaluate the team effectiveness.
29. Document the lessons learned in this meeting.
30. Make an appointment for the next meeting.

Participants

Prior to the meeting
1. Read the minutes of the previous meeting, study the agenda, and prepare yourself.
2. Figure out what the objective of the meeting is, focus on it, and stick to it.
3. Be on time.

During the meeting
1. Make sure that your items are on the agenda and stick to the ones being discussed.
2. If you do not understand certain statements, ask for clarification.
3. Participate actively by listening well, summarizing opinions, asking for clarification, building on the ideas of others, making constructive arguments, not moving away form the subject, and so on.
4. Speak up if you have something to say, and be silent if you have nothing to say.
5. Avoid remarks that will divide the team and jot down the agreements.
6. Accept the chairperson.
7. Contribute to the solution and do not create more problems.
8. Don't be noisy; don't hinder progress or participate with a hidden agenda.
9. Don't be guided by emotions; remain objective. Keep personal feelings to yourself.

After the meeting
1. Do what was agreed upon, do not complain about the decisions taken, and do not try to reverse decisions outside the meeting; discuss disagreements in the following meeting.
2. Do not broadcast what was said during the meeting.
3. Evaluate the meeting.

Table 8.9 *continued*

Overview of Activities, Tasks, and Roles for Conducting Effective Meetings

Timekeeper

1. Monitor how much time the team takes to execute its tasks.
2. Give directions on how to spend time.
3. Discuss the planned duration of each agenda item at the beginning of the meeting.
4. Regularly announce the progress of time so that the team knows how far along they are.
5. Interrupt the team when it exceeds the allotted time.
6. Give suggestions about possible adjustments to the agenda.
7. Continuously guard the pace at which the different phases of the meetings are reviewed.
8. The meeting should not take more than one and a half hours.

Process Keeper

The process keeper is responsible for an efficient meeting.
1. Evaluative comments are not allowed during brainstorming sessions.
2. All participants must actively participate in the discussions.
3. All activities should be followed through in phases, such as the Deming cycle, problem-solving cycle, risk analysis, etc.
4. Do participants respect the opinions and suggestions of others?
5. Stop small talk or digressions to subjects that are beside the point.

Source: Rampersad, 2002.

form may be used, which is introduced and illustrated in Table 8.10 (Rampersad, 2002). After the meeting each team member should score the assertions in the Teamwork Evaluation Form (see scoring key at the end of Table 8.10 for guidelines), then add the scores in this form. The closer the total score is to 100, the more effective the teamwork process. The closer your score is to 30, the more inefficient the process. After you and others have completed this evaluation form individually, discuss your scores in the team. Indicate what could have been done better.

John van Dam's security team evaluated the meeting process during the execution of the risk analyses (see Chapter 5) with the aid of the evaluation form presented in Table 8.10. In this table the shared evaluation results are marked with black bullet marks. The total score came to 77 points, which implies that the meeting process went reasonably well. Nevertheless, there are a number of improvement points to be addressed, which are indicated by the statements with a score of 1 or 2 (see the bottom of Table 8.10).

Table 8.10

Teamwork Evaluation Form				
Company: Business Jet **Business Unit:** Security Team at Schiphol Airport				
We know our own team roles and learning styles as well as those of other team members. These were accepted, appreciated, and respected.	1	2	3	**4•**
We received support for our personal development and help with the generation of new ideas.	1	2	3	**4•**
Everyone listened attentively to each other until the end of the meeting. They listened to everyone's opinion, including minority points of view.	1	**2•**	3	4
Mostly open questions were asked.	1	2	**3•**	4
The ideas of others were built upon.	**1•**	2	3	4
There was constructive arguing.	1	**2•**	3	4
The remarks of others were clarified.	1	2	**3•**	4
Previous conversations were summarized.	**1•**	2	3	4
People who did not participate in the meeting were asked to become involved.	1	**2•**	3	4
Appreciation was expressed.	1	2	**3•**	4
Constructive feedback was given.	1	2	3	**4•**
There were no serious conflicts; there was no power struggle among team members.	1	2	**3•**	4
We exchanged knowledge spontaneously; we did not keep it to ourselves.	1	2	**3•**	4
The opinions of the team members were clearly expressed.	1	2	3	**4•**
We were in agreement and spoke the same language; we understood and complemented each other.	1	2	3	**4•**
We devoted ourselves to the shared team objective.	1	2	3	**4•**
The team objective was clear to us, and everyone found it valuable and approved of it.	1	2	3	**4•**
We each got the chance to openly express our opinions and ideas; we could say the things we wanted in a frank discussion and through open communication.	1	2	3	**4•**
There was no gossip in smaller groups.	1	**2•**	3	4
We respected and trusted each other; we felt comfortable, equal to each other, and responsible.	1	2	**3•**	4

Table 8.10 *continued*

Teamwork Evaluation Form				
Everyone had his or her own clearly defined task: timekeeper, process keeper, minute taker, data collector, etc.	1	2	3	4•
We followed a clearly defined method and had the opportunity to think and act creatively.	1•	2	3	4
What we were working on was transparent, and our discussions were purposeful.	1	2•	3	4
We stuck to the points on the agenda.	1	2•	3	4
We were clear about our responsibilities for the points of action taken; we committed ourselves to the team decisions.	1	2•	3	4
The team leader/chairperson was well prepared.	1	2	3•	4
We worked together harmoniously toward generating new ideas; we continuously looked for fresh points of views to tackle problems.	1	2	3•	4
Total Score:	77 points			
Circle the correct number: 1 = never / no / not correct; 2 = once in a while / hardly ever; 3 = frequently / usually; 4 = always / yes / correct				
Remarks/Suggestions: Improve listening skills; build more on the ideas of others; argue constructively; give more summaries; encourage those who are silent to participate more in the group; apply brainstorming techniques more systematically; communicate meeting objectives more clearly; follow the agenda during the meeting, and clearly communicate responsibilities regarding points of action.				
Source: Rampersad, 2002.				

Organizing Continuous Improvement

We gain strength, and courage, and confidence by each experience in which we really stop to look fear in the face . . . we must do that which we think we cannot.

Eleanor Roosevelt

Strength does not come from physical capacity. It comes from an indomitable will.

Mohandas Gandhi

The way continuous improvements are organized differs from organization to organization and is mainly determined by the business size and the complexity of the improvement needed. Depending on the nature of the problem, one can work with improvement teams or with improvement circles. The starting points of both concepts are the same, namely, systematic and structured problem solving based on the problem-solving cycle. Working with improvement teams and improvement circles requires the creation of an improvement infrastructure as well as the development of an improvement mentality throughout the organization. These two organizational structures will be discussed in detail in this chapter.

Improvement Teams

The life of inner peace, being harmonious and without stress, is the easiest type of existence.

Norman Vincent Peale

Figure 9.1

An Organizational Structure Based on Improvement Teams

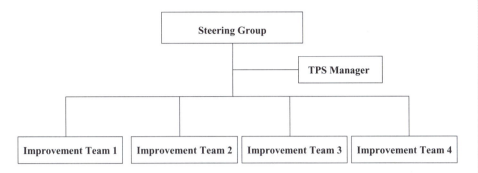

Improvement teams normally receive the task to implement a certain improvement action from management, as the result of a particular organizational strategy. After implementing this task the team is dissolved. In general, complex problems require an integrated approach. Such an approach requires a steering group, TPS manager, and improvement teams (see Figure 9.1).

Steering Group

The steering group of a complex improvement project can have the following composition:

- Chairperson: General Manager
- Secretary: TPS Manager
- Participants: Business unit managers and external advisor

Due to the involvement of management in the steering group, buy-in is created at this level. Management must completely stand behind the implementation of the improvement process by supporting, coaching, and guiding it. In this process the steering group fulfills two important functions, namely:

1. Leadership: Initiating, guiding, supporting, and promoting improvement activities as well as creating the necessary conditions.
2. Sponsorship: A sponsor is the steering group member who promotes the project. He or she is aware of the importance of the project and therefore supports the project team, keeps the

steering group informed of the progress, supports the implementation of results, and functions as the *process owner*. The process owner is the person in the steering group who is responsible for improvement of the selected process.

In larger organizations, several steering groups are usually appointed (one or more steering groups per each business unit), which in turn are coordinated by an overall steering group. The steering group meets usually once a month for one hour during regular working hours to discuss the implementation progress. The most important tasks of the steering group are:

- Documenting the scorecard-related improvement objectives and working out the improvement actions linked to them.
- Problem definition.
- Teaching teams how they should stay involved in the learning process.
- Seeing to a continuous learning process.
- Selecting critical processes that are eligible for improvement.
- Phasing the improvement process and determining milestones.
- Selecting team leaders.
- Formulating tasks for the improvement teams and functioning as their sponsor.
- Determining the progress of team activities.
- Creating buy-in for the organizational improvement actions.
- Initiating training activities.
- Creating conditions for the optimal functioning of the improvement teams.
- Leading, coordinating, and supporting the improvement teams and promoting the implementation.
- Reporting to top management.
- Advising top management regarding the policies in question.
- Determining and testing the progress of the implementation.

TPS Manager

The TPS manager is someone who is an expert in the field of the Total Performance Scorecard approach, and who is in charge of supporting the steering group, providing TPS training, and lending technical support to the improvement teams.

Improvement Team

An improvement team is a group of subject experts from different disciplines who have been put together by the steering group or the process owner for the purpose of addressing a certain problem (usually beyond the scope of business units) in a systematic and structured way. Improvement teams are separate from the formal organization and appointed on a temporary basis. They consist of a team leader, a TPS facilitator, and other team members. The team leader guides the team, consults with the sponsor or process owner, articulates the results, maintains contact with the steering group, and organizes regular meetings on a fixed day, time, and place. At the start of the project the meetings are held twice a week and later every week, for a period of one to one and a half hours. The steering group or process owner selects the team leader based on his or her competences in the following areas:

- Learning:
  - Stimulates a continuous learning process
  - Encourages learning how to learn
  - Stimulates intensive knowledge exchange
  - Stimulates team learning

- Management knowledge in:
  - Planning, organizing, and coaching
  - Decision making
  - Controlling and monitoring progress
  - Delegating

- Social relationships:
  - Customer-oriented action
  - Listening, giving feedback, constructive arguing, etc.
  - Convincing team members and actively promoting the team mission
  - Constructive negotiating, conflict handling
  - Influencing

- Personal competences:
  - Analyzing, systems thinking, and conceptualizing
  - Dealing with stress
  - Taking initiatives and risks
  - Confronting

The sponsor or process owner and the team leader set up the improvement team. Team composition depends on the skills needed (which depend on the problem definition) and on personalities. Improvement teams usually have a cross-functional composition. They consist of five to eight employees with knowledge and experience regarding the problem area, who are socially and communicatively skilled, have a positive attitude with respect to the problem to be solved, and are aware of their own and each others' learning styles and team roles. At this point we are dealing with a partially voluntary participation in the improvement team.

The rules to which a team member should abide have already been discussed in Chapter 8. The TPS facilitator in the team is someone who facilitates teamwork, functions as a mentor, fulfills the function of process keeper, advises the team about the use of TPS techniques and methods, and monitors the results. The TPS manager participates in the steering group and the TPS facilitator in the improvement team. The tasks of the teams are, among other things, brainstorming about problem formulation, mapping out the appointed critical process, conducting analyses and measurements, implementing improvement actions, adjusting working procedures, documenting the improvement process, and reporting the implementation of the improvement actions. Here management defines the problem formulation.

The improvement team should also have a clear mission and related concrete objectives, which may be formulated, respectively, by asking these two questions: *Why does the team exist?* and *What are the expected team results?* The answers to these questions are part of the project plan, in which the problem is also clearly defined, performance measures are determined, improvement actions are indicated, and how their relation to the Organizational Balanced Scorecard is made clear. The effects, limiting conditions, and control factors (e.g., time, money, quality, information, and communication) are addressed in the plan as well.

It is important to create time for the team and to provide all team members with the tools, required responsibilities, and authorities needed to adequately fulfill their tasks, which may involve training as well. After the team has completed its improvement actions, the team steering group makes a final presentation of the results. In some cases, the steering group certifies the process. In addition to a documentation of the lessons learned through a review of the teamwork process, an expression of appreciation for the results obtained is equally important at this point. In order to create a learning organization, it is recommended that every employee participate in at least one improvement team.

Improvement Circles

> To be idle is a short road to death and to be diligent is a way of life; foolish people are idle, wise people are diligent.
>
> *Siddhartha Gautama, The Buddha*

Figure 9.2

Organizational Form Based on Improvement Circles

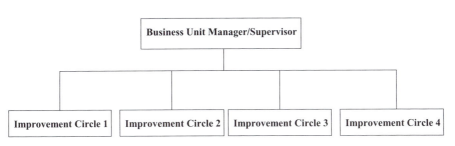

The concept of the improvement circle originates from the Japanese concept of the *quality circle* from the 1950s. Whereas the emphasis in an improvement team formed to solve a particular problem is usually on corporate level, the emphasis in an improvement circle is on the learning and participation of involved employees at lower organizational levels. Several process problems are thus solved at once. An improvement circle is a peer group of volunteers from the same level and business unit who are regularly involved during normal working hours, with the guidance of their supervisor, with the systematic identification and analysis of problems related to their own jobs (see Figure 9.2). The improvement circle thus discusses efficiency improvements, how to improve learning, and the sharing of knowledge. Here, the participants identify the problems themselves, and the solutions result in recommendations to management. The improvement circle also works towards implementing the final solutions. The knowledge gained is also shared intensively with others within the organization.

The assumption underlying this approach is that the employees involved are intimately aware of the problems related to their daily jobs. It is a form of participative management that stimulates the involvement of employees as well as team learning, which also benefits the communication between management and employees. An improvement circle usually consists of six to ten employees from the same business unit. In certain cases specialists from other organizational disciplines are also involved in the team to fulfill a facilitating function.

The improvement circle is thus part of the formal organization. The problems addressed by such circles corresponds to the field of expertise of the team. In contrast, the composition of improvement teams is adjusted to match the problem. For example, the executed risk analyses by employees of Business Jet's security team, under the supervision of John van Dam (see Chapter 5), represent the work of an improvement circle.

Managing Change

10

We cannot change the world, but if we change ourselves, the world will change with us. One who has established this transformation within him, no longer lives with false hopes. He sees things the way they really are and is set free.

Selvarajan Yesudian

Keep your mind open to change all the time. Welcome it. Court it. It is only by examining and reexamining your opinions and ideas that you can progress.

Dale Carnegie

Implementation of the Total Performance Scorecard is related to change. And, as I have stressed earlier, before there can be effective organizational change *you* should change first. You must learn new things and unlearn others before you can change yourself. This individual learning must then be converted into collective learning. Because learning is a behavioral change, individual behavioral change has to be converted into collective behavioral change, which leads ultimately to organizational change. Organizational change involves a process of collective learning and unlearning. This process generally is both inevitable and essential for organization growth. Some of the causes for change include market and technological developments increased competition, globalization, and other factors.

Despite the necessity for change, many people despise it. They are afraid of change and by nature resist it because it may affect their established ideas and opinions. Disappointments from previous experiences with altered activities, fear of the unknown, distrust, lack of information, and insufficient affiliation with the current culture are the most important factors that account for this resistance. In an organization, therefore, we can distinguish two kinds of people:

1. People who think they will be victims of change and who therefore resist, become angry, and get depressed; and
2. People who completely support, design, and plan the change.

Especially in the initial phase of the implementation of change, resistance to change seems very high because certain people in the organization, due to their own uncertainties and insecurities, see the proposed change as a threat. Conflicts then emerge in which the old trusted situation is frequently referred. Examples of expressions of resistance include:

- Let's just stay with both feet on the ground.
- I do not see why we have to change—everything is going so well as it is.
- It is going well—why should we do it differently?
- We are already the best in the market.
- Organizationally, this is absolutely impossible.
- This is ridiculous.
- We have always done it this way without any problems.
- It has always been like this, and we have always done it like this.
- At the moment, we are too busy to do this.
- This will be costly; do we have the money for it?
- Is this necessary? We have already tried this numerous times before and it hasn't worked.
- Do those managers know how busy we are?
- Stop it; it will never work.
- It is against our principles.
- We are too small for this.
- There is something else behind this.
- I know it is not going to work.
- Think about it if you must, but I like the way things are going now and will continue on this path.

Generally, we hear these reactions in organizations that are non-learning organizations. They are expressions that should be unlearned. Some examples of expressions of people who accept change include:

- When are we going to start?
- How can we learn more about that?
- We can also handle it in another way.
- What have we forgotten?
- How can we measure the results?
- Let me see if there are any alternatives.

According to James O'Toole (1996), there are many reasons for people to resist change. These are described in the following boxed text.

James O'Toole's Thirty-Three Hypotheses on Why People Resist Change

1. Homeostasis—Change is not a natural condition.
2. Stare decisis—Presumption is given to the status quo; the burden of proof is on change.
3. Inertia—It takes considerable power to change course.
4. Satisfaction—Most people like things the way they are.
5. Lack of ripeness—The preconditions for change have not been met; the time isn't right.
6. Fear—People fear the unknown.
7. Self-interest—The change may be good for others but not for us.
8. Lack of self-confidence—We are not up to the new challenges.
9. Future shock—Overwhelmed by change, we hunker down and resist it.
10. Futility—We view all change as superficial, cosmetic, and illusory, so why bother?
11. Lack of knowledge—We do not know how to change or what to change to.
12. Human nature—Humans are competitive, aggressive, greedy, selfish, and lack the altruism necessary to change.
13. Cynicism—We suspect the motives of the change agent.
14. Perversity—Change sounds good, but we fear that the unintended consequences will be bad.
15. Individual genius versus group mediocrity—Those of us with mediocre minds cannot see the wisdom of the change.
16. Ego—The powerful refuse to admit that they have been wrong.
17. Short-term thinking—People cannot defer gratification.
18. Myopia—We cannot see that the change is in the broader self-interest.
19. Sleepwalking—Most of us lead unexamined lives.
20. Snow blindness—Groupthink, or social conformity.

21. Collective fantasy—We do not learn from experience, and we view everything in the light of preconceived notions.
22. Chauvinistic conditioning—We are right; they who want us to change are wrong.
23. Fallacy of the exception—The change might work elsewhere, but we are different.
24. Ideology—We have different worldviews and inherently conflicting values.
25. Institutionalism—Individuals may change but groups do not.
26. *Natura no facit saltum*—"Nature does not proceed by leaps."
27. The rectitude of the powerful—Who are we to question the leaders who set us on the current course?
28. "Change has no constituency"—The minority has a greater stake in preserving the status quo than the majority has in changing.
29. Determinism—There is nothing anyone can do to bring about a purposeful change.
30. Scientism—The lessons of history are scientific, and therefore there is nothing to learn from them.
31. Habit.
32. The despotism of custom—The ideas of change agents are seen as a reproach to society.
33. Human mindlessness.

Source: Used with permission from Joseph Boyett and Jimmy Boyett. *The Guru Guide.* New York: John Wiley & Sons, 1998, p. 51.

These reactions of resistance can frustrate the change process completely if there is no adequate response. Resistance to change, and expressions of negative reaction to it, often occur in the following six phases:

1. *Passivity.* People are informed about the new plans and react reserved and with uncertainty.
2. *Denial.* People are skeptical and deny the appropriateness of the suggested improvement plans. This is often expressed in comments such as: "What a backward idea; who thought this up? This is certainly not going to work here."
3. *Anger.* If the plans continue, people react angrily and withdraw.
4. *Negotiation.* They try to reach a compromise (through negotiation) by minimizing proposals and partially accepting the plans.
5. *Depression.* Because the complete plan proposal must be implemented, without any unfinished work, people have to accept the change. This results in passive behavior, which eventually leads to depression.

6. *Acceptance*. Changes are now part of the work process. Now what is often heard is: "Yes, it works! We should have started this earlier."

These different phases must be acknowledged in time to take the proper measures. During the passivity phase and depression phase, management should adopt an understanding attitude and be open to hearing negative reactions. During the phases of denial, anger, and negotiation, a firmer attitude on the part of management is required. The different phases in the responses of employees must be recognized early and should be moved through to the phase of acceptance as soon as possible. That is why those who completely accept the changes should be involved in change projects. John Kotter (1998) explains that before most people can understand and accept a proposed change they seek answers to a lot of questions, such as:

- What will this mean to me?
- What will it mean to my friends?
- What will it mean to the organization?
- What other alternatives are there?
- Are there better options?
- If I'm going to operate differently, can I do it?
- How will I learn the new skills I need?
- Will I have to make sacrifices? What will they be? How do I feel about having to make them?
- Do I really believe this change is necessary?
- Do I really believe what I'm hearing about the direction for the future?
- Is this the right direction for us to take?
- Are others playing some game, perhaps to improve their position at my expense?

"Not understanding" is, according to McCall (1997), one of the most common reasons why people do not change. The following boxed text presents McCall's summary of the answers he received from managers in his workshops whom he had asked the following question: Why didn't you change what you knew needed to change? This summary shows how an inadequate or inaccurate flow of information severely hampers the learning process. According to McCall, many of these obstacles have to do with the person in question, who does not want to listen, is defensive, or refuses to accept feedback.

Reasons Why People Do Not Change

- Mutilated feedback
- Confused announcements
- No feedback
- Do not understand
- Do not listen
- Do not believe
- Do not accept
- Makes me have to admit mistakes or shortcomings
- Does not fit with my self-image
- Take it personally
- Inclined to overreact
- Do not take criticism well
- Distrust the motives of others
- Untrustworthy source
- Others do not know the real me
- Fear that unpleasant facts may be true
- Distrust people who give feedback
- It hurts to hear negative things
- Negative feedback angers me
- Feeling that it is not correct
- Feeling of being put in a corner like a child
- Too much pride
- No support
- No stimulation to change

- Rewarded to remain the same
- The cost in time and energy
- The benefits do not outweigh the costs
- The benefits are unclear
- Imposed on me from the outside
- No personal involvement with change
- Do not know what is really important
- Not clear what should change
- Not clear what the result of change will be
- Do not know what is really important
- Requires giving up something worthwhile
- Do not know how to change
- No possibility to practice
- No role models
- I function well the way I am now
- I feel fine now
- Do not want to change
- Cannot change
- It would be ridiculous
- Feeling of incompetence

- The context has not been changed
- Too busy
- Busy with other things
- Other people do not change
- Other people do not see the changes
- Other people do not allow the change
- Painful, demeaning
- Afraid of manipulation
- Fear of the unknown
- Arrogance
- Afraid to make mistakes
- Vulnerable during change efforts
- Fear of failure
- Fear that I won't be good enough
- Earlier failed effort to change
- Too lazy
- Afraid to take up a vulnerable position
- Convinced of own right not to change
- Need to be thought of as nice by others
- Undermines self-trust
- Threatens self-image
- Deforms self-image
- Intimidated by others

Source: Used with permission from M. W. McCall. *High Flyers: Developing the Next Generation of Leaders*. Boston: Harvard Business School Press, 1998.

Based on my own experiences with improvement processes, I have formulated ten "rules of thumb" that *increase* the resistance to change (Rampersad, 2002). (See the following boxed text.) I use these so-called rules to teach managers and employees the behavior patterns they need to "unlearn." They completely conflict with the Total Performance Scorecard philosophy.

Behavioral Model for Creating Resistance to Change

1. Ignore top management and important key persons when making decisions on drastic changes. Secretly prepare decisions to change and announce them grandly as a surprise.
2. Give misleading information on the what, why, how, and consequences of change, or preferably withhold this information and make sure that it is not readily spread to others. Be completely silent and vague. Do not communicate at all with those involved about the necessity, use, and benefits of the change, and make sure that they do not see it as crucial.
3. Create an atmosphere of organizational fear and distrust; stimulate an "I-feeling" and continue working according to the old customs, norms, and methods.
4. You know everything better and should keep it that way. Knowledge is power, isn't it? Therefore, make sure others do not know more than you. That means, do not share your knowledge with others, and make sure that your employees do not do so either. Stimulate them to "reinvent the wheel again and again" and facilitate this process. Use the principle of "divide and conquer."
5. Pay no attention to the development of newly required skills among your employees. Leave them to fend for themselves; they'll have to find their own way. Make sure your employees do not know how the organization functions, or how to satisfy customer wishes and expectations, and definitely do not give them authority over the processes for which they are themselves responsible.
6. Punish and discourage people with good ideas. Allow employees to criticize each other's suggestions thoroughly. Give mostly negative feedback, and especially do not give compliments.
7. Do not be soft; and do not consider the personal ambition of individual employees during the change. Their preferences and interests do not count. They'll have to take care of themselves.
8. Do not allow mistakes, however small. Treat people who make mistakes harshly and insult them before others. Make it clear that mistakes may lead to discharge, transfer, or other painful decisions.
9. Ignore people who resist change or criticize it. Push through your suggestions, even if there is a lot of resistance to it.
10. From the beginning, tackle the change process on a large scale and begin with the most complex part.

Source: Rampersad, 2002.

There are important methods to handle resistance to change in a positive way, however. These included the following, among others:

- Create inner peace and involvement, self-confidence and commitment in your employees, and change their mindsets by empowering them to formulate their own personal ambitions and then balance these with both their personal behavior and the shared organizational ambition.

- Communicate with employees face-to-face and supply them with information about the context of the Organizational Balanced Scorecard and related organizational changes; in addition, be honest about the actual situation. State clearly how long the change will last and what the consequences will be. Provide timely information to personnel. Silence creates doubt and usually causes rumors to spread, which undermines trust in management. Do not provide too much information at once, because employees need time to absorb the information.

- Support the proposals with clear arguments.

- Inform employees about the advantages of change and how the gap between present and future situations will be closed.

- Have meetings with those people who resist change and give a detailed reaction to all their objections.

- Involve employees in the development and implementation of the scorecards and create transparency in responsibilities and authorities.

- Involve key-persons in the decision-making process; when stakeholders are included in a decision, acceptance will greatly increase, and therefore also the effect of the implementation.

- Put the project on hold if there is too much resistance and you are not able to count on the support of the majority.

- Drive out organizational fear and distrust. These inhibit the ability to learn. According to Pfeffer and Sutton (2002), fear and distrust can be driven out by:

  - *Predictability.* As much as possible, give people information on what will happen to them and when.

  - *Understanding.* Explain in detail why certain actions were taken, especially those that alarm and hurt.

  - *Control.* As much as possible, give people influence over what is happening, when it happens, and how it happens; allow them to decide their own future.

- *Compassion.* Show sympathy and concern about the disruption, emotional needs, and financial burdens confronting employees.

There are also other methods to motivate and stimulate change, such as the following:

1. Probe continuously to determine whether or not people are ready for change.
2. Discuss the Total Performance Scorecard concept and related new ways of working with employees in a series of meetings; articulate this actively. Inform employees directly, honestly, clearly, and consistently (i.e., uniformly throughout the entire organization). Clearly indicate what can be discussed and what cannot. Communicate this both internally and externally and orally as well as in writing. Use brochures, newsletters, and other documents. Keep your communications simple, and use analogies and case studies. Williams Pasmore (1994) states that much of your communication effort may involve educating your employees about the business and competitive environment, such as the points listed in the following boxed text.

What Employees Need to Know about Their Company

- Employees need to know what managers know, including how to read an income statement and a balance sheet, what makes the number on each get larger or smaller, what the numbers really mean, and where the company stands today as compared to where it was before, and how it stands versus the competition.
- Employees need to know the threats to the organization and the plans about how to deal with them, including the rationale for these plans and what alternatives were considered before deciding on this course of action.
- Employees need to understand decision-making processes and criteria and how much risk is acceptable.
- Employees need to understand the consequences of poor decision making and what to do when the unexpected happens.
- Employees need to understand customers' expectations and how to better meet them.
- Employees need to be introduced to global economics.

- Employees need to know about health-care costs and workers' compensation, about the costs of carrying inventory and liability insurance.
- Employees need to understand the technical system used to produce goods or services, how it functions, and why it was designed the way it was designed.
- Employees need to understand what technical alternatives are possible and what will be involved in applying them.
- Employees need to develop the social skills that allow them to take part in participative activities, including speaking in front of others, confronting differences, understanding how to reach a consensus, facilitating the participation of others, and listening.

Source: Used with permission from Joseph Boyett and Jimmy Boyett. *The Guru Guide*. New York: John Wiley & Sons, 1998, p. 64.

3. Indicate why there is a need for change; the organization must be convinced of the need for this change. A popular way to do this is to compare the organization to more successful competitors. Another way is to map customer dissatisfaction and use it to illustrate decreasing performance. Under extreme conditions, make it clear that the long-term survival of the organization is at stake. In such cases the present situation must be perceived as negative. Making people acknowledge how poorly the organization is doing creates dissatisfaction with the present situation. This helps to convince even skeptics of the need to change. This necessity can be illustrated with the help of the following formula (adapted from Jacobs, 1994):

$C = A \times B \times D$

Where:

A = Dissatisfaction with the status quo
B = A clear statement regarding the change objectives
C = The probability of the change being successful
D = Concrete first steps toward the objectives

The formula demonstrates the following: to be able to change successfully it is essential to (A) convince people of the necessity for change, (B) articulate a vision that clearly and distinctly expresses that they will become better if they change, and (D) demonstrate your purposiveness and give a presentation of the first change results.

John Kotter (1996) believes that bold actions, such as those listed in the following boxed text, must be taken to convince employees of needed change. The first two actions in this overview conflict with the Total Performance Scorecard philosophy.

Bold Ways to Convince Employees of a Needed Change

According to Kotter, being bold means doing things like:

- Cleaning up the balance sheet and creating a huge loss for the quarter.
- Selling corporate headquarters and moving into a building that looks like a battle command center.
- Telling all your businesses that they have twenty-four months to become first or second in their markets, with the penalty for failure being divestiture or closure.
- Making 50% of the top pay for the top ten officers based on tough product-quality targets for the whole organization.
- Exposing managers to a major weakness vis-à-vis competitors.
- Allowing errors to blow up instead of being corrected at the last minute.
- Eliminating obvious examples of excess (e.g., company-owned country-club facilities, a large air force, gourmet executive dining rooms, etc.).
- Insisting that more people at lower levels be held accountable for broad measures of business performance.
- Sending more data about customer satisfaction and financial performance to more employees, especially information that demonstrates weaknesses vis-à-vis the competition.
- Insisting that people talk regularly to dissatisfied customers, unhappy suppliers, and disgruntled stakeholders.
- Putting more honest discussions of the firm's problems in company newspapers and senior management speeches.

Source: Used with permission from Joseph Boyett and Jimmy Boyett. *The Guru Guide.* New York: John Wiley & Sons, 1998, p. 59.

---

4. Base the important proposals on solid facts and promise employees clear result improvements; a distinct solution must be presented.
5. Illustrate clearly how the change will be realized, based on a solid implementation plan in which the steps to be taken are explained. During the implementation of the change, inform employees regularly with trustworthy information.

6. Introduce new training to develop new skills such as interpersonal skills, customer orientation, teamwork, leadership, and others.

7. Involve employees in the planning and introduction of the change; acceptance by and involvement of the employees is essential for implementing change successfully. Without the continuous involvement of people, every project is doomed to fail. After all, the effectiveness of a strategy is not only dependent on its quality but on the acceptance of it by the employees as well. I am referring to the well-known formula:

Effectiveness = Quality × Acceptance

The importance of this involvement is illustrated with the following example, which is based on Kamp (1999):

> A business unit of a financial organization wanted to carry out important changes in their working practices. The business unit leader came up with the basic idea for this change but wanted to involve his employees in its further execution. They were asked to attend workshops where the results would be discussed and proposals could be made regarding the way in which the new system would be implemented. Nearly 40% of the employees participated, and their feedback was used to formulate the implementation plan. They reported that this process made them feel like active participants in the change, which made them consider the change more positively. In terms of useful ideas and employee morale the results were astounding. The rest of the employees then asked if they could attend a session as well, because they saw how much it had benefited the others.

8. Reward those who produce results; intrinsic rewards (such as acknowledgment and recognition) are preferred over extrinsic rewards (such as money). Julie Bick (1997), referring to her experiences at Microsoft, says the following concerning this subject: " 'Good work!' can accomplish a lot. And it is cheaper and easier than giving a raise or promotion. Giving credit raises morale and ensures that your team works harder; this is because they know they are appreciated."

There are different forms of intrinsic reward. In the following boxed text Kouzes and Posner (1999) give an overview of the possible ways to say "thank you" and encourage the heart. (Their points are based on a memo by John Schallau of Centigram Communications Corporation).

Ways to Encourage the Heart

Individual rewards:

- Tickets for events
- Weekend trips
- Attending a company event
- Dinner or a night out
- Visit to a health spa or weekend resort
- Attending an outside seminar
- Magazine subscription

Acknowledgement for group milestones reached:

- Office party with award presentation
- Lunch with personnel and partners at a nice restaurant
- Football match
- Afternoon at the beach

Theme days to encourage fellowship:

- T-shirt day
- Ugly-ties day
- Hawaiian-shirt day
- Costumes during Halloween

Symbolic articles to give away as rewards:

- T-shirts with company logo
- Sport bags
- Coffee mugs
- Beer mugs or wine glasses
- Pen and pencil sets

Food (for special events):

- Sandwiches
- Special lunches
- Pizza
- Catered breaks
- Donuts

Source: J. M. Kouzes and B. Z. Posner. *Een hart onder de riem: hoe kan ik anderen erkenning geven en belonen?* Schiedam, The Netherlands: Scriptum Management, 1999.

9. Provide the reorganization project with a strong identity; give it an ambitious name so that employees can feel they have a real objective to accomplish and a dream to realize.
10. Start cautiously with a pilot project and practice with it. Start with the easiest part of the project, one that can produce quick results.
11. With the Total Performance Scorecard philosophy in mind, create buy-in at the higher echelons of the organization. Top management must take the lead in the introduction of this concept to achieve change. Place this subject on the agenda of monthly management team meetings. In this context, keep in mind the following statements (Senge, 1990):
    - Substantial change is hardly possible if it is only directed from top management.
    - Cynicism is mainly cultivated when there are elaborate announcements from the CEO and programs rolled out by headquarters that distract everyone from the actual change activities.
    - Support of top management does not measure up to the real commitment and learning capacities at all levels of the organization. When management authority is used unwisely, it diminishes the chances that commitment and learning capacity will develop.
12. Start the process of continuous improvement, learning, and development at the top management level, and use a layered implementation approach to reach lower levels (see Figure 4.2).
13. Eliminate those elements that have a negative effect on people's morale and motivation within the organization. In practice, opponents of change seem to slow down, boycott, and sabotage things; use old rules and hidden agendas; supply wrong information; evade new tasks; and play the victim. Those who block and oppose change must be guided to improve their attitude. If this does not succeed, they will have to be put on a sidetrack elsewhere in the organization or even removed, if possible. Dare to take these measures, because my experience has shown that "rotten apples" in the organization can completely disrupt and frustrate a change project. Therefore, do not hold off taking the appropriate measures!
14. Give leaders and teams authority and "ownership" over the processes for which they are responsible.
15. Make employees shareholders so that they will behave as owners.

Before you implement the change, verify if the circumstances for implementation are favorable. Insight into the problems that may occur during execution will be needed. In Table 10.1 I introduce a checklist that can be used to create insight into the introductory circumstances of change projects (Rampersad, 2002). The implementation of the change project will be unfavorable if there are too many questions answered with "no." Such questions should receive extra attention beforehand.

At Business Jet the top management completed this checklist (see Xs in Table 10.1) in order to gain insight into the circumstances surrounding the implementation of the Total Performance Scorecard concept. From this checklist it is evident that Business Jet is not yet ready to execute most of the improvement actions discussed in Chapter 3 (see Table 3.8). More attention should be given to obtaining buy-in for these initiatives. Communicating the necessity for and benefits of improvement actions, involving certain key-persons, and articulating the consequences for the employees also deserves more attention prior to the implementation of these initiatives.

As I mentioned early in this book, traditional change management concepts do not result into a durable change. These are often counterproductive and mostly cosmetic in nature. For this reason I now introduce, as part of the TPS concept, an integral model that provides a stable basis for sustainable organizational change (Rampersad, 2002). This model is presented in Table 10.2. It also includes a summary of

Table 10.1

Checklist Implementation Circumstances, Used on Business Jet			
Areas of Attention	**Yes**	**Somewhat**	**No**
Is there commitment in top management to implement the change?	X		
Have those involved formulated their personal ambitions and aligned them with the shared organizational ambition?			X
Do those involved consider the change crucial to the company's survival, and do they realize the usefulness of it?			X
Has attention been paid to the involvement of all key-persons in the decision-making process?		X	
Has a competent change manager been appointed to coach and facilitate the change processes?	X		
Can managers handle the change?	X		
Has special attention been given to developing the new skills that employees will need?		X	

Table 10.1 *continued*

Checklist Implementation Circumstances, Used on Business Jet			
Areas of Attention	**Yes**	**Somewhat**	**No**
Have the most important obstacles and barriers to the use and exchange of knowledge been removed?			X
Has the change been aligned to both individual and organizational values?	X		
Has a cultural diagnosis been conducted and the results communicated to the employees?	X		
Has the information regarding the introduced change been clear?	X		
Can the idea behind the change be made understandable to all involved?	X		
Can adequate information be given about the what, why, how, and consequences of the change?	X		
Is there sufficient necessity for the introduction of the change?	X		
Is the necessity for and advantage of the change been clearly communicated to all those involved?			X
Have the advantages of change been carefully weighed against the disadvantages?	X		
Do the employees know what has to be changed?		X	
Does a plan exist in which the steps of the change to be implemented are clearly defined?		X	
Has special attention been given to those who feel they will become victims of the change?			X
Have you listened effectively to the people who resist change, and have you studied their situation?			X
Have the problems that accompanied previous changes been solved?		X	
Has there been benchmarking regarding the change?	X		
Has there been fear and distrust among the employees regarding the change?		X	
What possibilities could diminish the chances of success of the change?		X	
Will enough people change?			X
Source: Rampersad, 2002.			

Table 10.2

Model for Sustainable Organizational Change

Plan			Do	Check	Act
Define the Change	**Formulate Change Actions**	**Create Buy-in for the Change**	**Implement the Change on a Limited Scale**	**Check If the Change Works**	**Introduce the Proven Change Definitely**
• Formulate one or more change teams and appoint a change manager. • Describe and specify the necessary change. • Make an inventory of and test possible root causes of the problem. • Formulate the change objectives, related performance measures, and targets. • Give the change route a strong identity (an ambitious name).	• Indicate how you want to realize the change. • Think of solutions to the problem. • Determine which solution will solve the problem and change the organization successfully. • Develop these solutions. • Define the effects, limiting conditions, and control factors (time, money, quality, information, and communication).	• Create inner peace, personal involvement, self-confidence, and commitment with the employees, by stimulating the formulation of their PBSC. • Allow top management to communicate the change to employees honestly, clearly, actively, and face-to-face in a timely way that reveals consequences and shows them that they support it completely. • Communicate the necessity and the advantages of the change to all involved. Base change proposals on clear arguments. • Check who resists change and why. Listen carefully to them and reflect upon their situation. • Eliminate the elements that influence the morale of the employees unfavorably. Pay	• Start carefully with a pilot project. • Practice with the simplest part of the project. • Test the change and conduct possible experiments. • Give feedback. • Develop new training to obtain the needed skills, such as teamwork, coaching, etc. • Train all those involved in the new skills required. • Describe the processes related to the change. • Create transparency about tasks,	• Verify if the problem has disappeared or if the change works. • Review the test project. • Check if the change objectives have been realized. • Compare the results with the formulated targets. • Give feedback • Start again if necessary.	• Implement the proven change on a large scale. • Train all those involved. • Review the results. • Reward those who produce results, preferably with intrinsic rewards. • Make the employees shareholders so that they will behave as owners. • Standardize process modifications. • Monitor the

attention also to those who , delay boycott, and sabotage the change. • Involve all key-persons in the decision making. • Conduct a culture diagnosis and communicate the results to all involved. • Complete the presented checklist "introduction circumstances" collectively and discuss the results with all involved. • Are the introductory circumstances favorable? Is the timing for change good?	responsibilities, and authorities. • Give people the authority and ownership over the processes for which they are responsible. • Involve the employees with the implementation of the change.	change continuously. • Document the lessons learned. • Give feedback. • Go back to the start of this change model.

Source: Rampersad, 2002.

the points in this chapter. In conclusion, I state here the following important thesis in the form of a formula:

no individual learning + no collective learning + no necessity + no buy-in + no perspectives + no communication + no inner peace + no inner involvement + no commitment + no trust + no enjoyment + no mindset change = no sustainable organizational change

Organizational Culture

11

Organization-wide learning involves change in culture and change in the most basic managerial practices, not just within a company, but within a whole system of management. . . . I guarantee that when you start to create a learning environment, people will not feel as though they are in control.

Peter Senge

Morality is of the highest importance—but for us, not for God.
Albert Einstein

The successful implementation of the Total Performance Scorecard approach is closely related to the review and change of the existing organizational culture. Organizational culture, a concept without a clear definition, is difficult to describe. It is also a fashionable subject, one about which numerous authors have been eager to express their opinions during the past ten years. The most important guru in this area is Edgar Schein (1992). According to Schein organizational culture includes a collection of consciously or unconsciously shared ideas, assumptions, and convictions regarding those aspects of reality that are relevant to the organization. He rightly considers the organizational culture to elicit a learning process that gives direction to employee behavior. The organizational culture prescribes which behavior is acceptable, correct, or preferable. It includes what is visible from the outside (explicit culture) and the values behind it (implicit culture). Organizational culture also involves the shared behavior of employees with regard to the job, organization, and relationship with, for instance, customers, suppliers, and colleagues. It can be described as the total of shared opinions, ideas, fundamental values, rules, customs, traditions, manners, behavioral patterns, and norms of the people in the organization. This definition corresponds with that of Hofstede (1991), who states that organizational culture is the collective mental programming of the company's stakeholders. Thus, organizational culture has to do with organizational learning (see Chapter 7).

When working according to the principles of Total Performance Scorecard, systematic attention to the organizational culture is inevitable. In the TPS approach, attending to organizational culture assists in fulfilling the following important functions (Schein 1992; Dooreward and de Nijs, 1999):

1. Internal integration:
   - Alignment and coordination of internal processes.
   - Streamlining and focusing the manner of cooperation.
   - Giving meaning and justification for one's own behavior.
   - Strengthening the we-feeling.
   - Reducing individual insecurity and fear.
   - Providing stability, certainty, and security.
   - Utilizing mutual competition.
2. External adjustment:
   - Aligning, sensing, and anticipating surrounding developments.
   - Identifying with organization goals.
   - Providing continuity by emphasizing the norms and values that make the organization prepared for survival.

Besides the functions mentioned before, organizational culture also influences motivation, self-guidance, and commitment. It plays an important role in the organization's development because it influences human action within an organization. The organizational culture is expressed in, for instance: the nature of people (good, bad, active, passive, how knowledge is interpreted, customer orientation, respect for the individual, performance focus); the nature of personal relations (teamwork, solidarity, dispute, competition); management style (task-oriented, dominant, human-oriented); formal statements (such as mission and vision statements); organizational structure (bureaucratic or self-guiding teams); HRM policy (such as coaching, appraisal, competence development); communication system (formal, informal, open communication); specific regulations (rules, guidelines, procedures); and organizational traditions. People's mindsets are also closely related to organizational culture; as we have seen mindsets are the preconceived ideas we have about reality that color our observations of the world, which in turn influence our creativity. Our mindsets consist of our opinions, assumptions, and prejudices. Some examples of mindsets are: *all politicians are corrupt; a good education is important for the future;* and *men with long beards are dangerous Taliban who have something to hide.*

The organizational culture determines, among other things, if employees are motivated to learn and if they are willing to develop their competences. In practice, available knowledge is difficult to absorb and share if it conflicts with cultural norms and values. The successful introduction of Total Performance Scorecard usually requires a cultural change; this above all requires a fundamental behavioral adjustment in the people in the organization. This behavior is strongly related to the organization's principles, that is, what the organization considers normal or decent. These principles translate to norms and values. Norms are related to the written and unwritten rules that indicate which behavior is expected of someone, what is permitted, and what forbidden. On the other hand, values are the feelings about what we collectively endeavor and consider. As we saw in Chapter 2, these cultural components are part of the company's organizational vision and core values.

Doorewaard and de Nijs (1999), inspired by Schein (1992) and Hofstede (1991), have roughly divided organizational culture in two layers (see Figure 11.1):

1. *An explicit part* (the cultural practice) includes the visible and difficult to decode behavioral patterns and cultural expressions of people, such as business principles, behavioral codes, jargon, myths, ceremonies, rituals, and beliefs.
2. *An implicit part* (the core) includes the unwritten rules, assumptions, expectations, and invisible patterns of thinking that bring about much resistance to change.

Figure 11.1

Cultural Model

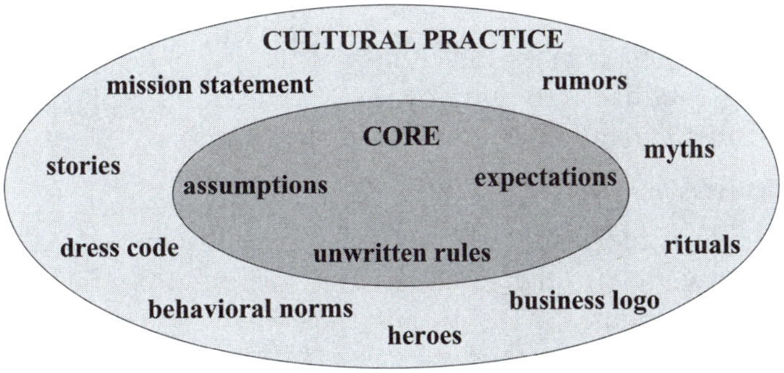

The dichotomy between explicit and implicit culture may be related to Schein's three successive culture levels:

1. *Artifacts*; that which is said and written within the organization and is visible.
2. *The higher level of awareness*; these are familiarized norms (what is allowed or forbidden) and values (what is important) that are open for discussion.
3. *The invisible part of shared underlying values*; principles that function as a starting point and cannot or can hardly be discussed (basic assumptions).

Schein's first two levels correspond to the cultural practice in the cultural model and his third to the core (see Figure 11.1). Successful implementation of the TPS concept requires ample attention to and insight into these cultural components, as well as a business culture characterized by:

- Well-balanced representation of all stakeholders.
- Employees who have a lot in common due to team learning.
- High motivation, active participation, and devotion to realizing the stated objectives.
- Committed involvement of employees and managers in the decision-making process.
- Teamwork, mutual trust, respect, and a we-feeling.
- Clear, recognizable assumptions about the requested behavior.
- Employees who feel that their individual performance contributes to the realization of the organization's objectives.
- Employees and managers who are open to change and are convinced that this will lead to improvement.
- Multifunctional employability, flexibility, and willingness of the employees to change.
- Top-down and bottom-up communication.
- An open way of communicating within the organization.
- Giving feedback to employees, and making information and instruments available.
- A decisive incentive policy.
- Effective leadership; a leader who coaches in such a way that people want to change instead of feeling that they are being forced to change.

- An objective appraisal system linked to an effective talent and career development system.

- Employees who make independent decisions and have a sense of responsibility.

- Employees who regularly experience professional challenges.

The following boxed text summarizes Schein's (1990) recommendations on how an organization can develop its own culture.

Developing an Organizational Culture

Culture can be thought of as the way an organization's members, and particularly its founders, have resolved important issues, such as:

The organization's relationship to its environment
- Does the organization perceive itself to be dominant, submissive, harmonizing, or searching for a niche?

The nature of human activity
- Is the correct way for humans to behave to be dominant/proactive, harmonizing, or passive/fatalistic?

The nature of reality and truth
- How do we define what is true and what is not?
- How is truth ultimately determined, both in the physical and social world—by pragmatic test, reliance on wisdom, or social consensus?

The nature of time
- What is our basic orientation in terms of past, present, and future?
- What kinds of time units are most relevant for the conduct of daily affairs?

The nature of human nature
- Are humans basically good, neutral, or evil?
- Is human nature perfectible or fixed?

The nature of human relationships
- What is the correct way for people to relate to each other to distribute power and affection?
- Is life competitive or cooperative?
- Is the best way to organize society on the basis of individualism or groupism?
- Is the best authority system autocratic/paternalistic or collegial/participative?

Homogeneity versus diversity
- Is the group best off if it is highly diverse or if it is highly homogeneous?
- Should individuals in a group be encouraged to innovate or conform?

Source: Used with permission from Joseph Boyett and Jimmy Boyett. *The Guru Guide*. New York: John Wiley & Sons, 1998, p. 121.

Neglecting these matters leads to the creation of organizational incompetence. The following boxed text presents Gilbert's (1987) behavioral model for dealing with the creation of incompetence. Managers should also unlearn these behavior patterns under the umbrella of Total Performance Scorecard. Indeed, cultural change is an unlearning as well as a learning process.

Behavioral Model for Creating Incompetence

1. *Withhold information.*
   Don't let employees know how well they are performing.
   Give people misleading information about how they are performing.
   Hide from people what is expected from them.
   Give people little or no guidance about how to perform well.
2. *Don't involve people in selecting the instruments of work.*
   Design the tools of work without ever consulting the people who will use them.
   Keep the engineers away from the people who will use these tools.
3. *Don't provide incentives for good performance.*
   Make sure that poor performers get paid as well as good ones.
   See that good performance gets punished in some way.
   Don't make use of nonmonetary incentives.
4. *Don't help people to improve their skills.*
   Leave training to chance.
   Put training in the hands of supervisors who are not trained instructors.
   Make training unnecessarily difficult.
   Make training irrelevant to the employee's purpose.
5. *Ignore the individual's capacity.*
   Schedule performance for times when people are not at their sharpest.
   Select people for tasks that they have intrinsic difficulties performing.
   Do not provide response aids.
6. *Ignore the individual's motives.*
   Design the job so that it has no future.
   Avoid arranging working conditions that employees would find more pleasant.
   Give pep talks rather than incentives to promote performance in punishing situations.

Source: Used with permission from Joseph Boyett and Jimmy Boyett. *The Guru Guide.* New York: John Wiley & Sons, 1998, p. 241.

The following boxed text shows, for the benefit of the unlearning process, the behavioral model for breaking the will. It is based on the techniques used by the secret police of Montevideo (adapted from Landsberg, 1999). These behavior patterns also completely conflict with the Total Performance Scorecard philosophy.

Behavioral Model for Breaking the Will

Destroy all visions and hopes for freedom; disorient (e.g., change things unexpectedly) and administer severe punishments.

Suppress self-confidence; humiliate, come down on someone severely, and depress (e.g., dole out actions that destroy self-confidence with continuously increasing severity).

Take away any prospect of voluntary action; do not allow people to build self-confidence based on the successful implementation of activities they have initiated themselves.

Tell lies; for example, telling people that their health or performance is seriously deteriorating.

Ridicule; especially in the presence of others.

Take away all possible sensorial incentives; solitary labor.

Systematically destroy people's self-image; for instance, by frightening, confusing, and showing them how others in the same position are totally destroyed.

I am now making a transition back to positive recommendations, as opposed to the "unlearning" approaches just outlined. It is useful at this point to consider the ten cultural components outlined by Galpin (1996) in the following boxed text.

Ten Cultural Components of Galpin

1. *Rules and Policies*

Eliminate the rules and policies that will hinder the performance of new methods and procedures. Create new rules and policies that reinforce desired ways of operating. Develop and document new standard operating procedures.

2. *Goals and Measurement*

Develop goals and measurements that reinforce desired changes. Make goals specific to operations. For example, establish procedural goals and measures for employees who are conducting the process that is to be changed, rather than financial goals that are a by-product of changing the process and that employees cannot easily relate to their actions.

(continues)

3. *Customs and Norms*

Eliminate old customs and norms that reinforce the old ways of doing things and replace them with new customs and norms that reinforce the new ways. For example, replace written memos to convey information through the organization with face-to-face weekly meetings of managers and their teams.

4. *Training*

Eliminate training that reinforces the old way of operating and replace it with training that reinforces the new. Deliver training "just-in-time" so people can apply it immediately. Develop experiential training that provides real-time, hands-on experience with new processes and procedures.

5. *Ceremonies and Events*

Establish ceremonies and events that reinforce new ways of doing things, such as awards ceremonies and recognition events for teams and employees who achieve goals or successfully implement changes.

6. *Management Behaviors*

Develop goals and measurements that reinforce the desired behaviors. Provide training that focuses on the new behaviors. Publicly recognize and reward managers who change by linking promotion and pay rewards to the desired behaviors. Penalize managers who do not change behaviors. For example, do not give promotions, pay increases, or bonuses to managers who do not demonstrate desired behaviors.

7. *Rewards and Recognition*

Eliminate rewards and recognition that reinforce old methods and procedures, and replace them with new rewards and recognition that reinforce the desired ways of operating. Make rewards specific to the change goals that have been set.

8. *Communications*

Eliminate communication that reinforces the old way of operating; replace it with communication that reinforces the new. Deliver communication in new ways to show commitment to change. Use multiple channels to deliver consistent messages before, during, and after changes are made. Make communications two-way by soliciting regular feedback from management and employees about the changes being made.

9. *Physical Environment*

Establish a physical environment that reinforces the change. Relocate management and employees who will need to work together to make changes successful. Use "virtual offices" to encourage people to work outside the office with customers, and telecommunications to connect people who need to interact from a distance.

10. *Organizational Structure*

Establish an organizational structure that will reinforce operational changes. For example, set up client service teams, eliminate management layers, centralize or decentralize work as needed, and combine overlapping divisions.

Source: Used with permission from Joseph Boyett and Jimmy Boyett. *The Guru Guide*. New York: John Wiley & Sons, 1998, p. 68.

Table 11.1

Actions Related to Culture	
Actions That May Indirectly Influence Organizational Culture	**Actions That Hardly Influence Organizational Culture**
• Rotation of employees between business units. • Other new ways of recruiting, selecting, and hiring personnel. • Creating new heroes and role models by, for instance, using an altered promotion policy. • Creating a large-scale socialization program consisting of a combination of working conferences, game simulations, training, etc. • Stimulating active participation and linking appraisal and reward systems partially to the core values and desired behavior. • Centralizing, or decentralizing, management. • Moving to another building or doing a rigorous internal move. • Supporting the cultural change with internal publicity stunts, happenings, an action name for the cultural change, and a newsletter related to this.	• Changing the house style and the function name (market coordinator becomes account manager). • Creating slogans and posters. • Changing the formal organizational structure. • Letting external consultants draft advice reports. • Announcing loudly that everything has to change, that the culture has to be "different." • Threatening with sanctions.
Source: Weggeman, 1997.	

The preceding boxed text describes some basic conditions that may be used to influence organizational culture. In practice, however, the actions used for this purpose are not equally successful (see Table 11.1).

Introducing the Total Performance Scorecard philosophy into an organization results in cultural change. Indeed, in this management concept one starts by developing self-knowledge, changing mindsets, and creating inner peace, inner involvement, self-confidence, and employee commitment. This happens through stimulating employees to formulate their personal ambition and balance it with their personal behavior and the shared organizational ambition. Finding such a balance begins to create the conditions whereby employees shift from individual learning to collective learning. Individual behavioral change can then be converted into collective behavioral change, or organizational change. In general this change also requires an analysis of the

Table 11.2

<table>
<tr><th colspan="3">Culture Diagnoses According to Hofstede (1991), Used on Business Jet</th></tr>
<tr><td>1 PROCESS-ORIENTED
• Avoiding risks
• As little exertion as possible
• Every day is the same</td><td rowspan="6">1 2 3 4 5
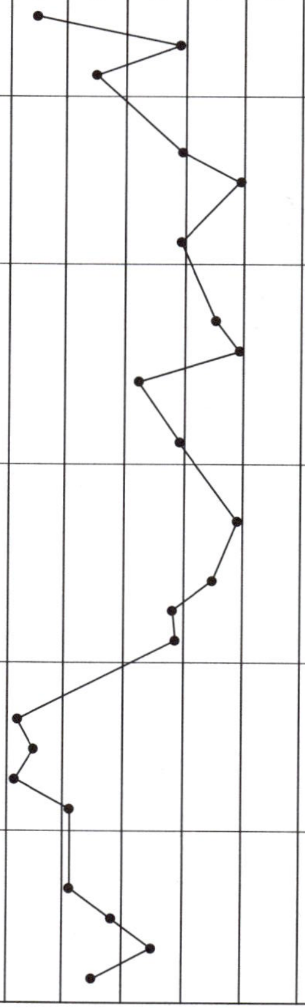</td><td>RESULT-ORIENTED
• At ease in situations full of risks
• Purposefully doing your utmost
• Every day a new challenge</td></tr>
<tr><td>2 PERSONAL-ORIENTED
• Considering personal problems
• Taking responsibility for the well-being of the employees
• Decisions are taken by groups</td><td>JOB-ORIENTED
• A lot of pressure to finish the job
• Performances are more important than the well-being of the employees
• Decisions are taken by individuals</td></tr>
<tr><td>3 ORGANIZATIONALLY LINKED
• Employees identify themselves with their organization
• Employees do not look far ahead
• Hiring people from the right family, social class, and educational background
• Norms from work also count at home</td><td>PROFESSIONAL
• Employees identify with their profession
• Employees look far ahead
• Hiring people because of their work ability
• Private life is everyone's own business</td></tr>
<tr><td>4 OPEN
• Openness towards newcomers and outsiders
• Nearly everyone fits into the organization
• New employees feel quickly at home
• New ideas are accepted</td><td>CLOSED
• Closeness through mysteriousness, even for their own employees
• Only special people fit in the organization
• New employees don't feel at home
• New ideas are rejected</td></tr>
<tr><td>5 TIGHT CONTROL
• Are aware of costs
• Strictly sticking to meeting times
• Seriously talking about work and the organization
• There are strict codes for correct behavior</td><td>EASY CONTROL
• Are not aware of costs
• Approximately abiding by meeting times
• Joking about the company and work
• There are no strict conduct rules</td></tr>
<tr><td>6 PRAGMATIC
• Meeting the demands of the customer
• Is guided by the market
• Results are more important than procedures
• Pragmatic ethical attitudes</td><td>NORMATIVE
• Correct use of procedures
• Is guided by the appointed task
• Procedures are more important than results
• High ethical norms</td></tr>
</table>

existing organizational culture in order to create insight into what employees do, what they say, what they want to do, and what kind of resistance to the implementation may be expected. In the business literature there are several approaches to cultural diagnosis that are somewhat superficial and mostly subjective (e.g., questionnaires); nevertheless, they deliver a valuable contribution to organizational analysis. The best known is Hofstede's (1991) diagnostic system, which aims at taking an organizational snapshot. Another diagnostic system that is used frequently by consultants is Handy's (1988).

For the purposes of our discussion, I here present Hofstede's system as illustrated by the Business Jet case. In this system the organizational culture is characterized according to the following six dimensions:

1. Process-oriented versus result-oriented.
2. Personal-oriented versus job-oriented.
3. Organizationally linked versus professional.
4. Open versus closed.
5. Tight control versus easy control.
6. Pragmatic versus normative.

These dimensions are shown in Table 11.2. The organizational culture of Business Jet was analyzed by judging each dimension on a scale of 1 to 5. The results of this analysis are shown in Table 11.2. This diagnosis suggests that the organization is not personal-oriented enough, that the employees identify themselves insufficiently with the company, that the organization can be classified as closed, and that, as a result of the tight control, creativity in Business Jet is influenced unfavorably. In addition, the closed character of the organizational culture has a negative effect on the buy-in for the formulated improvement actions. The results of this culture scan thus corresponds to the leadership style of Frank Jansen, the acting manager of Business Jet (see Figure 8.7), as well as to the quick scan of the implementation circumstances (see Table 10.1).

Epilogue

Organizations whose leaders regard the provision of guided experience as essential, and development of people as one of the primary responsibilities of all managers—one for which they are held accountable in job evaluations—have a competitive advantage.

Dorothy A. Leonard

Learn from yesterday, live for today, hope for tomorrow. The important thing is not to stop questioning.

Albert Einstein

I wrote this book, on the one hand, because I wanted both to understand and to tell others why so many organizational development and change routes fail, and, on the other hand, because I wanted to provide managers with a new holistic management concept and some practical methods, and techniques that might lead to sustainable organizational development and ethical behavior. Most methods of organizational change fail because they do not start at the very beginning, that is, with the core of personal identity itself. Their failure is also related to the limited action orientation of numerous managers. Managers, despite the wealth of expensive management training programs and organizational advice, as well as many new management books, often neglect to do something with what they already know, and omit to convert their new knowledge into action.

In the United States more than 1000 business management books are published yearly and more than \$60 billion are spent on management training programs (see also Pfeffer and Sutton, 2002). Most of these books and training programs include concepts, ideas, and analyses that are advertised as new, when in fact they were formulated decades ago and are simply dressed in new clothing each year. Many of these so-called "new" books and training programs lack some essential management elements. Nevertheless these books sell well, while training programs become more and more expensive every year.

As I have mentioned in the Preface and Introduction, this book differs in a number of essential points from most other management books in the field. It is up to you, the reader, to judge whether this is true. I gladly welcome any reactions and suggestions from you regarding this book. Please send your feedback by e-mail to Hubert.Rampersad@Total-Performance-Scorecard.com. The development of the Total Performance Scorecard concept and the writing of this book has been a continuous learning process. If you want to keep track of the new developments in this field, visit the website www.Total-Performance-Scorecard.com.

For more information about the Total Performance Scorecard concept, the international office closest to you, or for a free catalog of TPS products and programs, call or write:

Quality Management Consulting
Riet Blom-Mouritsstraat 27
3066 GL Rotterdam, The Netherlands

Phone: 31-10-2096564
Fax: 31-10-2097189
Mobile: 31-6-53831159
E-mail: info@qmconsulting.nl
Website: www.Total-Performance-Scorecard.com and www.qmconsulting.nl

Appendix A

Appraisal Forms for Business Jet

Result Areas	Essential areas, based on the balanced scorecards and the individual performance plan, on which the employee has to focus in order to achieve results.
	Result Area 1: FINANCIAL
	Result Area 2: CUSTOMERS
	Result Area 3: INTERNAL PROCESSES
	Result Area 4: KNOWLEDGE and LEARNING
COMPETENCE PROFILE	Collection of knowledge, experience, skills, attitudes, values and norms, and behavior essential to effective job fulfillment and achievement of related result areas.
Job-Oriented Competences	1. Learning Ability 2. Problem Solving 3. Stress Proof 4. Coaching 5. Customer-Oriented Behavior 6. Listening 7. Persuasiveness 8. Vision
Development Actions	Actions to Develop Competences • On-the-job training of failure cost analyses, project management, learning to learn, how to deal with resistance against change, conflict handling, and constructive negotiation. • Following a course in knowledge and time management. • Creating practice situations. • Individual guidance and coaching (once a month) in the area of giving constructive feedback and managing stress. • Accompanying experienced colleagues in order to improve skills in the area of persuasion. • 360°-feedback meetings with customers to improve customer orientation. • Benchmarking in the area of safety. • Traineeship: going through a training period of one month at Business Jet at New York and London airports. • Developing and executing a talent developing program.

General Information	Employee Name: John van Dam Manager Name: Steve Daniel	Job: Team Leader Position: Business Unit Manager
	Business Unit: Safety	Team: Security Schiphol Airport	Review Period: Jan.–Dec. 2002

Review Meeting

Review Date: January 15, 2002

Approval Signature Manager:

Endorsement Signature Employee:

Coaching Meeting

Review Date	Approval Signature Manager	Endorsement Signature Employee
4-19-2002		
8-15-2002		

Appraisal Meeting

Review Date: December 6, 2002

Approval Signature Manager:

Endorsement Signature Employee:

Outcome

Outcome regarding different result agreements and job-oriented competences. Base the final opinion on these two Outcomes.

	Outcome Result Agreements	Outcome Job-Oriented Competences	Final Outcome
1. Above stated requirements	1 ☐	1 ☐	1 ☐
2. According to stated requirements	2 ☑	2 ☐	2 ☐
3. Not completely according to stated requirements	3 ☐	3 ☑	3 ☑
4. Below stated requirements	4 ☐	4 ☐	4 ☐

Result Agreements	Documenting the result agreements in terms of clearly defined objectives, related performance measures, and targets (derived from the individual performance plan).
Result Agreement 1	Result Area: **Financial** Relative Importance: Low ☐ ☐ ☑ High
Planning Meeting	Objective 1: Working more Cost Consciously Performance Measure 1: Efficiency Target 1: Increase of 10% in 2002 Objective 2: Implemented Cost-Saving Measures Performance Measure 2: Number of Implemented Measures Target 2: At least two per quarter Objective 3: Contribution to Failure Cost Study Performance Measure 3: Number of developed improvement proposals Target 3: Increase of 30% in 2002 Support/Guidance by manager with the achievement of the agreed upon result: • Training in failure cost analyses • Making information about failure costs available • Helping create buy-in with the implementation of cost-saving measures
Coaching Meeting	Interim Review: ☑ Below Par ☐ At Par With ☐ Above Par Situational factors that influenced the functioning: • Conflicts within the Security team • A lot of resistance from the employees about the implementation of improvement proposals • Limited knowledge and experience in the area of failure cost analyses Agreements/Recommendations in the period prior to the appraisal: • Good communication of improvement proposals beforehand to all employees and colleagues. • Better planning of the implementation. • Improvement proposals concerning the reduction of failure costs must be worked out integrally.
Appraisal Meeting	Conclusions regarding the results: • Objective 1 partially realized; increase of 4% on December 6, 2002 • Objective 2 not realized according to the agreement; not to be blamed on his own effort • Objective 3 partially realized; increase of 20% on December 6, 2002 Outcome 1. Above stated requirements ☐ 2. According to stated requirements ☐ 3. Not completely according to stated requirements ☐ 4. Below stated requirements ☑ Clarification of the Outcome: Improving the functioning in this area. For this purpose: • Coaching is needed with the development and implementation of improvement proposals • On-the-job training is required: failure costs analysis, how to deal with resistance against change, and handling conflicts • Following time management courses

Result Agreements	Documenting the result agreements in terms of clearly defined objectives, related performance measures, and targets (derived from the individual performance plan).
Result Agreement 2	Result Area: **Customers** Relative Importance: Low ☐ ☐ ☑ High
Planning Meeting	Objective: Customer-friendly behavior while executing security tasks Performance Measure: Number of passenger complaints Target: Reducing complaints by at least 50% this year Support/Guidance by manager for the achievement of the agreed upon result: • Giving training in customer orientation • Giving instructions on how to prepare evaluation survey forms to be used at customer orientation
Coaching Meeting	Interim Review: ☑ Below Par ☐ At Par With ☐ Above Par Situational factors that influenced the appraisal: • Time Pressure • Terrorist attacks on September 11, 2001 in the United States have resulted in more rigorous safety measures, in certain cases at the cost of customer satisfaction Agreements/Recommendations during the period prior to the review: • 360° feedback in the area of customer orientation • Executing customer orientation audit • Preparing a procedure dealing with customer complaints • Having routine passenger surveys • Systematically registering and analyzing passenger complaints • Continuously benchmarking customer satisfaction against competitors
Appraisal Meeting	Conclusions regarding the results: Objective has not been realized completely according to agreement; the number of complaints from passengers has only been reduced by 15%. His own effort should increase. Outcome 1. Above stated requirements ☐ 2. According to stated requirements ☐ 3. Not completely according to stated requirements ☐ 4. Below stated requirements ☑ Clarification of the Outcome: Improving operations in this area. Systematically paying attention to customer satisfaction (see recommendations).

Result Agreements

Documenting the result agreements in terms of clearly defined objectives, related performance measures, and targets (derived from the individual performance plan).

Result Agreement 4

Result Area: **Knowledge and learning**   Relative Importance: Low ☐ ☑ ☐ High

Planning Meeting

Objective 1: Improved Competences in Safety Area
Performance Measure 1: Safety Certificate
Target 1: Obtaining 30% partial certificates in 2002

Objective 2: Openness and honesty in knowledge exchange among colleagues
Performance Measure 2: Experience level of colleagues regarding knowledge exchange
Target 2: 75% by the end of 2002

Support/Guidance by manager for the achievement of the agreed upon result:
- Making relevant literature available regarding airline industry safety
- Encourage Internet use
- Drawing up and making available a behavioral code regarding knowledge exchange

Coaching Meeting

Interim review: ☐ Below Par ☑ At Par With ☐ Above Par

Situational factors that influenced the functioning:
Very motivated to finish the safety study. Due to this may become eligible for promotion. Is helpful and enjoys sharing his knowledge with others.

Agreements/Recommendations during period prior to appraisal:
None

Appraisal Meeting

Conclusions regarding the results:
Objective 1 realized on November 22, 2002.
Objective 2 realized on December 6 according to the agreement.

	Outcome
1. Above stated requirements	☐
2. According to stated requirements	☑
3. Not completely according to stated requirements	☐
4. Below stated requirements	☐

Clarification of the Outcome:
Very good.

Result Agreements

Documenting the result agreements in terms of clearly defined objectives, related performance measures, and targets (derived from the individual performance plan).

Result Agreement 3

Result area: **Internal Processes**   Relative Importance: Low ☐ ☐ ☑ High

Planning Meeting

Objective 1: Developed Safety Procedures
Performance Measure 1: Number of Developed/Updated Procedures
Target 1: 8 procedures in 2002

Objective 2: Physical and Mental Health
Performance Measure 2a: % Sick Leave
Performance Measure 2b: % Stress
Target 2a: At the latest by November 2002, reduce sick leave to less than 2%
Target 2b: Decrease stress levels by at least 30% by the end of 2002

Support/Guidance by manager for the achievement of the agreed upon result:
- Make literature available in the area of safety procedures
- Give positive feedback
- Give more support and advice with regard to stress

Coaching Meeting

Interim Review: ☑ Below Par ☐ At Par With ☐ Above Par

Situational factors that influenced the functioning:
- Personal setbacks
- High blood pressure, depression; because of this, sick leave has not been reduced

Agreements/Recommendations during period prior to the appraisal:
- Regular physical exercise
- Doing stress exercises more often
- Visiting the family doctor, positive thinking, vacations

Appraisal Meeting

Conclusions regarding the results:
Objective 1 realized on November 25, 2002 according to agreement.
Objective 2 not realized because of indicated problems.
Sick leave is 5% due to instances of stress.

	Outcome
1. Above stated requirements	☐
2. According to stated requirements	☐
3. Not completely according to stated requirements	☐
4. Below stated requirements	☑

Clarification of the Outcome:

Stress reduction recommendations not adhered to completely; this had an adverse effect on sick leave percentages. Due to personal problems no changes in the situation are to be expected within a half year.

Result Agreements 5

Result Agreements	Documenting the result agreements in terms of clearly defined objectives, related performance measures, and targets (derived from the individual performance plan).
Result-Agreements 5	Result Area: **Knowledge and Learning** Relative importance: Low ☐ ☑ ☐ High
Planning Meeting	Objective 1: Active participation in improvement teams Performance Measures 1: Number of solved safety problems Target 1: Increase of 30% by the end of 2002 Objective 2: Colleagues trained in "frisking of and dealing with aggressive passengers" Performance Measure 2: Number of Trained Colleagues Target 2: 25 colleagues in 2002 Support/Guidance by manager for the achievement of the agreed upon level: • Giving instructions regarding frisking of passengers • Functioning once in a while as a visiting lecturer • Assisting with the development of course materials
Coaching Meeting	Interim Review: ☑ Below Par ☐ At Par With ☐ Above Par Situational Factors that influenced the functioning: Terrorist attacks on September 11, 2001 in the United States resulted in more rigorous and extensive safety measures. Due to this the course has been strongly adjusted; there is an increase to 40 colleagues to be trained in 2002. Agreements/Recommendations during period prior to the appraisal: • Systematically registering and analyzing safety incidents at Schiphol Airport related to Business Jet • Continuous benchmarking of safety activities in relation to competitors
Appraisal Meeting	Conclusions regarding the results: Objective 1 Realized on November 29, 2002 according to agreement Objective 2 Realized to an important degree; 23 colleagues trained. |	Outcome | 1. Above stated requirements ☐ 2. According to stated requirements ☑ 3. Not completely according to stated requirements ☐ 4. Below stated requirements ☐ Clarification of the Outcome: On schedule, despite expansion of safety activities at Schiphol Airport. This competence is of essential importance due to current developments. It seems that operations in this area will continue to improve.

Result Agreements 6

Result Agreements	Documenting the result agreements in terms of clearly defined objectives, related performance measures, and targets (derived from individual performance plan).
Result-Agreement 6	Result Area: **Knowledge and Learning** Relative Importance: Low ☐ ☑ ☐ High
Planning Meeting	Objective: Improved Coaching Skills Performance Measure: Degree of Satisfaction of Team Members regarding way of coaching Target: At least 75% in 2002 Support/Guidance by manager for the achievement of the agreed upon level: • Developing self-knowledge regarding his own team roles • Executing Belbin's team role test. • Discovering his own learning style, executing learning style test. • Based on this, learning how to coach the four learning styles.
Coaching Meeting	Interim Review: ☐ Below Par ☑ At Par With ☐ Above Par Situational factors that influenced the functioning None Agreements/Recommendations during period prior to the appraisal: • Executing aforementioned tests • Reviewing teamwork process more frequently • Systematically applying interpersonal skills
Appraisal Meeting	Conclusions regarding the results: On December 6, 2002, objective was realized according to agreement. |	Outcome | 1. Above stated requirements ☐ 2. According to stated requirements ☑ 3. Not completely according to stated requirements ☐ 4. Below stated requirements ☐ Clarification of the Outcome: *Is reasonably good, but could be improved if recommendations are followed.*

Planning Meeting	Agreement regarding expected behavior in the coming assessment period: Follow through levels 1 to 5 in stages. Reach level 5 by the end of this year.
	Support/Guidance by manager for the application of the agreed upon competencies: • Sharing knowledge with John and making relevant information available • Stimulating Internet use • Giving instructions regarding mapping out of his own learning style • Learning to learn effectively
Coaching Meeting	Interim Review: ☑ Below Par ☐ At Par With ☐ Above Par
	Situational factors that influenced the functioning: • Limited skills in the area of knowledge management. • Insufficient awareness of the necessity and importance of this.
	Agreements/Recommendations in the period prior to the appraisal: • Executing learning style test; discovering his own favorite learning style • Emphasis on continuous learning based on experiences • Emphasis on doing things right the first time and "preventing instead of correcting" • Applying 360° feedback
Appraisal Meeting	Outcome 1. Above stated requirements ☐ 2. According to stated requirements ☐ 3. Not completely according to stated requirements ☑ 4. Below stated requirements ☐ Clarification of the Outcome: • Got bogged down in level 2. • Not yet fully aware of the necessity of continuous learning. • Does not make sufficient efforts to increase his learning ability. • Limited insight in the area of knowledge management. • Needs training session in "learning how to learn."

Job-Oriented Competence

Competence 1: Learning Ability

Relative Importance: Low ☐ ☐ ☑ High

Definition:
Continuously making an inventory of, reviewing, absorbing, and implementing new and relevant knowledge.

Levels:

1. **Asks Questions:** Asks open questions, consults available sources of information and databases, uses available information.

2. **Applies Knowledge:** Goes out to gather knowledge, is willing to reflect on problems, integrates new knowledge into existing knowledge. Absorbs new facts quickly and applies them correctly.

3. **Digs Deeper:** Asks questions to reach the core of the problem and searches for possible solutions. Generates alternative solutions based on clear problem definition. Is curious and eager to learn.

4. **Continuously Updates and Mobilizes Knowledge:** Knowledge and learning is the most important result area in his/her Personal Balanced Scorecard. Makes an inventory, develops, implements, reviews, and mobilizes knowledge continuously. Learns from his/her own mistakes, improves his/her own skills, and learns new ones.

5. **Stimulates Team Learning:** Knows which knowledge is essential, who has it, how that knowledge can be used adequately, how this provides value added, how this can be maintained, and how the knowledge can be shared with others. Knows his/her own favorite learning style and that of other team members. Identifies any team shared problems and resolves them, creates a learning environment in which there is positive thinking, creativity, responsibility for business performances, and team members who are motivated to learn individually as well as collectively.

Job-Oriented Competence

Competence 2: Problem Solving

Relative Importance: Low ❑ ☑ ❑ High

Definition:
Systematically resolving problems based on the Problem-Solving Cycle.

Levels:

1. **Distinguishes subproblems within complex problems:** Divides complex problems into sub-problems. Gives a description of problems and determines delineation of the problem area.

2. **Gathers information in a systematic manner:** Tries as much as possible to gather concrete information about the problem. Consults several sources of information, such as survey results among customers, customer complaints, information regarding process performances, and meetings with internal customers. Gathers all this information and analyzes it.

3. **Clearly defines problems:** Determines the problem definition as concretely as possible and formulates the requested end situation in order to find the correct cause of it. Based on this tries to generate creative solutions. Clearly indicates characteristics of the problem; determines its effect, focuses on the difference between how it is and how it should be, includes a global measurement of the problem (how often, how much, when). By means of this, also knows where the problem occurs and which aspects are playing a part in it.

4. **Visualizes processes to identify problems:** Visualizes business processes with the aid of flow-charts and also consults colleagues directly involved in the process. Takes measurements at several points in the process and continuously registers the number of customer complaints, in order to understand the details of the problem and translate customer needs into measurable and concrete specifications.

5. **Uses problem-solving techniques to systematically generate creative solutions:** Uses the problem-solving cycle and brainstorming techniques effectively to define problems from all angles; based on this, comes up with creative solutions. Systematically applies the five Ws (when, where, what, who and why) in order to be convinced that all relevant questions regarding the problem have been asked. Thus: When does the problem occur? When did it occur for the first time? Where does it occur? Where is the need for a solution the biggest? What is the problem? What are the consequences? What are the limitations? Who causes it? Who is presently struggling with this problem? Who has caused it? Who is responsible for finding a solution? Why does it occur? Why must it be solved? By doing this, he/she obtains a clear specification of the problem.

Planning Meeting	Agreement regarding expected behavior during coming review period: Follow levels 1 to 5 in stages. Reach level 5 by the end of this year. Apply problem-solving cycle more frequently during execution of risk analyses and improvement actions. Use this as an integral part of brainstorming sessions.
	Support/Guidance by manager for the application of the agreed upon competences: • Giving training in area of systematic problem solving • Give instructions regarding effective use of the problem-solving cycle • Giving feedback more frequently in this area
Coaching Meeting	Interim Review: ❑ Below Par ☑ At Par With ❑ Above Par
	Situational factors that influenced the functioning: Increasing pressure from management to deal more adequately with safety problems. Performance rewards are linked to it. Problem solving is part of the safety education John is presently following.
	Agreements/Recommendations during the period prior to the appraisal: Developing problem-solving form and related procedures and systematically applying them.
Appraisal Meeting	Outcome 1. Above stated requirements ❑ 2. According to stated requirements ☑ 3. Not completely according to stated requirements ❑ 4. Below stated requirements ❑
	Clarification of the Outcome: Has reached level 4. In view of the present situation, further development of this competence will be inevitable.

Planning Meeting	Agreement regarding expected behavior during the coming review period: Follow through levels 1 to 5 in stages. Reach level 5 by the end of this year. See Result Agreement 3.
	Support/Guidance by manager for the application of the agreed upon competences: • Creating practice situations • Giving tips and instructions for better stress control
Coaching Meeting	Interim Review: ☑ Below Par ☐ At Par With ☐ Above Par
	Situational factors that influenced the functioning: • Setbacks in personal environment. • High blood pressure, depression, headache. Due to this, he sometimes becomes aggressive.
	Agreements/Recommendations during period prior to the appraisal: • Doing stress exercises more often • Regular physical fitness • Visiting the family doctor, vacations, positive thinking • Take the course "How to deal with fear of failure"
Appraisal Meeting	Outcome 1. Above stated requirements ☐ 2. According to stated requirements ☐ 3. Not completely according to stated requirements ☑ 4. Below stated requirements ☐ Clarification of the Outcome: • Got bogged down in level 1. • Lack of concentration as a result of stress. Sick leave is relatively high due to this. Individual guidance is needed in this area.

Job-Oriented Competence

Competence 3: Stress Proof

Relative Importance: Low ☐ ☐ ☑ High

Definition:
Continue to function effectively during emotions, tensions, conflicts, in times of setbacks, and under time pressure.

Levels:

1. **Keeps emotions under control:** Keeps his/her emotions barely under control during stressful situations. Under these circumstances he/she has some difficulties in continuing to function effectively.

2. **Stays in control:** Recognizes his/her own emotions and irritations and takes distance. Promptly calls in others when it gets to be too much. Keeps reacting in a controlled manner under time pressure, during tensions and emotions. Is not distracted by stress, difficulties at home, etc. too much. Is very capable of finishing what he/she started.

3. **Handles stress effectively:** Keeps on looking for possible alternative solutions during severe emotions and under time pressure. In spite of this he/she keeps on working adequately. Continues to perform the same under pressure.

4. **Handles stress proactively:** Acknowledges increasing tension and emotions within him/herself and with others in a timely manner and takes actions to reduce these. Reflects beforehand on how to deal with unexpected problems, tensions, conflicts, setbacks, and severe emotions.

5. **Radiates tranquility:** Under all circumstances radiates tranquility, which has a positive effect on team performances. By doing this, he/she maintains organizational tranquility.

Job-Oriented Competence

Competence 4: Coaching

Relative Importance: Low ☐ ☐ ☑ High

Definition:
Helping team members develop themselves and perform optimally as a team.

Levels:

1. **Offers help to team members:** Offers help to team members if they ask for it. Provides them with relevant information. Helps them distinguish the main issues from the side issues.

2. **Encourages team members and creates involvement:** Encourages team members regarding their strong points and supports them with shortcomings. Inspires them, showing them appreciation; involves them and listens to their problems.

3. **Creates conditions for effective teamwork:** Based on trust, creates respect and open communication. Provides a nonthreatening atmosphere. Is focused on personal goals, review of progress made, feedback about behavior, and increase of insights in the job. Offers the support needed to ensure that team members are willing to accept the responsibility for delegated tasks.

4. **Understands which types of behavior are present in his/her team and knows how to coach these successfully:** Has mapped the four types of behavior (dominant-directive type, social-interactive type, gradual-stable type, and thoughtful type) of all team members and knows how to coach each one of them successfully. Has the ability to adequately balance the role of coach and mentor with the other leadership roles and mix these optimally. He/she knows his/her own team role and learning styles as well as those of other team members. He/she stimulates and inspires them to take initiatives, determine concrete objectives, and realize them successfully.

5. **Provides team spirit and a climate for team learning:** Creates an environment of enjoyment, passion, devotion, and enthusiasm. Gives form and direction to the effort of the team and creates an environment in which team members trust, help, accept, and appreciate each other and are strongly motivated. Is continuously focused on the development and mobilization of knowledge of team members. Keeps team moral high.

Planning Meeting	Agreement regarding expected behavior during coming review period: Follow levels 1 to 5 in stages. Reach level 5 by the end of this year. See result area 6.
	Support/Guidance by manager for the application of the agreed upon competences: • Develop self-knowledge about his own role in team, core qualities, and learning style • Give instructions regarding the effective coaching of the four learning styles
Coaching Meeting	Interim Review: ☐ Below Par ☑ At Par With ☐ Above Par
	Situational factors that influenced the functioning: N/A
	Agreements/Recommendations during period prior to the appraisal: • Execute Belbin's test and learning style test • Review teamwork process more frequently • Apply 360° feedback with regard to coaching
Appraisal Meeting	Outcome 1. Above stated requirements ☐ 2. According to stated requirements ☑ 3. Not completely according to stated requirements ☐ 4. Below stated requirements ☐ Clarification of the Outcome: Reasonably good. Lies between levels 3 and 4. Because of the responsibilities within John's function, this competency should be developed further.

Planning Meeting	Agreement regarding expected behavior during upcoming review period: Follow levels 1 to 5 in stages. Reach level 5 by the end of this year. See result area 2. Support/Guidance by manager for the application of the agreed upon competences: • Provide customer-orientation training • Give instructions regarding development of survey form to be used for review of customer orientation
Coaching Meeting	Interim Review: ☑ Below Par ☐ At Par With ☐ Above Par Situational factors that influenced the functioning: • Terrorist attacks in the U.S. on September 11, 2001 have resulted in more rigorous safety measures. In certain cases this was at the cost of customer orientation. Agreements/Recommendations during period prior to the appraisal: • Arranging 360°-feedback meetings with customers to improve customer orientation • Benchmarking in the area of customer orientation • Conduct customer-orientation audit • Drafting and executing procedures for handling customer complaints • Conducting routine passenger surveys • Systematically registering and analyzing passenger complaints
Appraisal Meeting	Outcome 1. Above stated requirements ☐ 2. According to stated requirements ☐ 3. Not completely according to stated requirements ☑ 4. Below stated requirements ☐ Clarification of the Outcome: • Got bogged down in level 1. • Did not stick to the agreement and did not follow recommendations completely! • Does not systematically deal with customer orientation. Needs guidance in this area.

Job-Oriented Competence

Competence 5: Customer-Oriented Behavior

Relative Importance: Low ☐ ☐ ☑ High

Definition:
Continuously satisfying customer wishes and needs.

Levels:

1. **Reacts to complaints:** Reacts to customer complaints in a timely fashion. Keeps customer informed about how the handling of the complaint is progressing.

2. **Maintains relationships and expands these:** Recognizes customer needs and recognizes ways to keep customers. Is service oriented, listens to customers, and asks them if they are satisfied. In order to achieve this, he/she regularly conducts surveys. From time to time he/she executes the customer-oriented audit.

3. **Builds up relationships and broadens them:** Puts him/herself in the shoes of the customer. Develops a relationship with the customer and continuously takes actions to increase customer satisfaction.

4. **Acts as a partner:** Understands customer situation and provides suitable solutions. Customers consider him/her as a partner. Takes personal responsibility for correcting customer problems.

5. **Performs unsolicited additional actions:** Translates customer needs to product and process improvements including new products and services to be developed. As a partner he/she performs additional actions and services unsolicited (in consultation with the customer).

Job-Oriented Competence

Competence 6: Listening

Relative Importance: Low ☐ ☑ ☐ High

Definition:
Actively registering and processing of words in the brain, and then acting on it; listens, understands, remembers, and does something with it.

Levels:

1. **Listens selectively:** Listens to facts only. Drops out when something is tedious or not interesting; does not always pay attention, listens until he/she has something to say, and likes to hear what he/she expects.

2. **Listens actively:** Keeps quiet when others are expressing their opinion, tries to understand what the other means, and follows up on it. Returns to what was said previously. Picks up on subtle statements or signals regarding the feelings and intentions of others. Asks open questions in order to figure out if he/she understood correctly what the other meant. Summarizes the message of the other correctly.

3. **Makes a correct assessment of what is said:** Keeps his/her opinions to him/herself and does not jump to conclusions before the other has finished speaking. Understands the content as well as the underlying aspects of a message. Places him/herself in the position of the other and by doing this can make a correct assessment of what is said. Lets others keep their self-esteem and builds on it. Understands the situation of the other and follows up on it effectively.

4. **Concentrates on the contents:** Is not distracted by external disturbances and manner of presentation. Concentrates on the contents and not the packaging. Uses knowledge and understanding of others to anticipate their reactions. Understands the effects of the statements of others.

5. **Understands underlying thoughts and feelings:** Prepares him/herself mentally to listen. Listens critically and intently to the entire message; listens to ideas, feelings, intentions, and facts, and summarizes the most important themes. By doing this, he/she understands the underlying reasons for the feelings, thoughts, and concerns of others.

Planning Meeting	Agreements/Recommendations during period prior review: Follow levels 1 to 5 in stages. Reach level 5 by the end of this year. Support/Guidance by manager for the application of the agreed upon competences: • Provide training in "Effective Listening." • Give feedback in this area.
Coaching Meeting	Interim Review: ☑ Below Par ☐ At Par With ☐ Above Par Situational factors that influenced the functioning: Insufficient awareness of his limited listening skills.
Appraisal Meeting	Agreements/Recommendations during period prior to the appraisal: • Practice listening effectively more often. • Request feedback regularly from team members and colleagues. • Review teamwork process frequently. Outcome 1. Above stated requirements ☐ 2. According to stated requirements ☐ 3. Not completely according to stated requirements ☑ 4. Below the stated requirements ☐ Clarification of the Outcome: • Has reached level 4. • Follow recommendations to improve behavior further.

Job-Oriented Competence

Competence 7: Persuasiveness

Relative Importance: Low ☐ ☐ ☑ High

Definition:
Convincing others effectively of a certain point of view, aimed at obtaining approval and the creation of buy-in and commitment.

Levels:

1. **Undertakes a single act to convince:** Uses concrete examples, facts, and arguments to convince others in a discussion. Does not make sufficient efforts to show interest in the ideas of others.

2. **Undertakes coordinated action to convince:** Undertakes several steps to convince. Directs information regarding the struggle with organizational problems. Substantiates suggestions well and promises clear result improvements. Indicates how things will be realized. Enjoys convincing others of his/her opinions.

3. **Uses indirect influence:** Also uses subject matter experts or other colleagues to influence others. Presents his/her arguments and opinions at the right moment.

4. **Uses influencing strategies:** Builds coalitions and creates "behind the scenes" support for ideas. Uses information intentionally to achieve results. Makes it clear that in extreme cases, long-term survival is at stake.

5. **Uses bold ways to convince:** Allows mistakes to be made instead of correcting them at the last minute. Sends out information that brings out his/her own weaknesses. Insists that employees regularly communicate with unsatisfied customers and are responsible for team results. Sees to it that the present situation is experienced as negative and, by doing this, creates dissatisfaction about it. Through this, tries to convince skeptics of the necessity to improve and change. Explains to associates the consequences of not achieving agreed upon results.

Planning Meeting	Agreements/Recommendations during period prior to review: Follow levels 1 to 5 in stages. Reach level 5 by the end of this year. Because of actual developments, perform with more conviction, in order to successfully implement the team scorecard.
	Support/Guidance by manager for the application of the agreed upon competencies: • Help John handle his work/job with more conviction and assertiveness. • Give him feedback more often in this area.
Coaching Meeting	Interim Review: ☑ Below Par ☐ At Par With ☐ Above Par
	Situational Factors that influenced the functioning: Insufficient experience as a team leader. Needs more time to master skills.
	Agreements/Recommendations during period prior to the appraisal: • Accompany experienced colleagues in order to improve skills in area of persuasiveness. • Request feedback regularly from team members and colleagues.
Appraisal Meeting	Outcome 1. Above stated requirements ☐ 2. According to stated requirements ☐ 3. Not completely according to stated requirements ☐ 4. Below stated requirements ☑ Clarification of the Outcome: • Got bogged down in level 1. • Did not keep to the agreement! • Has to be mentored by experienced colleagues.

Job-Oriented Competence

Competence 8: Vision

Relative Importance: Low ☐ ☐ ☑ High

Definition:
A long-term dream of the future and the change routes needed to reach it; knows where he/she wants to go with the organization, which values and principles guide him/her, what he/she stands for, what he/she wants to help realize, and what his/her ideals are.

Levels:

1. **Has formulated his/her personal ambition:** Uses this as an instrument for continuous personal improvement.

2. **Thinks strategically:** Participates actively with the formulation of the Organizational Balanced Scorecard. Acts completely in accordance to this. Through this, also sees long-term chances and opportunities and knows the way to achieve them.

3. **Aligns his/her personal ambition with the shared organizational ambition:** Has identified him/herself with the shared organizational ambition. His/her personal ambition can be found in the corporate, business unit, and team scorecard.

4. **Translates the organizational mission and vision into operational objectives and concrete tasks:** Prioritizes, based on the correct long- and short-term balance. Translates organizational vision into operational objectives and activities and vice versa. Translates external and internal developments into objectives and improvement actions. Based on this, he/she evaluates and updates the scorecards frequently. Develops new strategies to realize the shared organizational ambition.

5. **Shows vision, propagates this decisively, and can foresee the unforeseeable:** Has the ability to determine which directions his/her team/business unit/organization should go. Has the talent for recognizing striking trends and anticipating them in a timely manner. Makes the distinction between pipe dreams and hard facts. Can convince employees that the chosen path is the right one, and shows them how their activities may contribute to the greater whole. Assertively articulates the shared organizational ambition, so that a company feeling is created.

Planning Meeting

Agreements/Recommendations during period prior to review:
Follow levels 1 to 5 in stages. Reach level 5 by the end of this year.
Clear vision required of his own future and that of Business Jet, as well as the translation of this into operational activities and into the assertive articulation to his own team members.

Support/Guidance by manager for the application of the agreed upon competences:
• Help with the translation of business unit scorecard into team scorecard.
• Provide support with development and articulation of the team vision.

Coaching Meeting

Interim Review: ☑ Below Par ☐ At Par With ☐ Above Par

Situational factors that influenced the functioning:
• Sudden increase of the Security team's activities

Agreements/Recommendations during period prior to the appraisal:
• Finish Personal Balanced Scorecard and align it further to the shared team scorecard.
• Stimulate his own team members to do the same.
• Display and communicate the team vision.

Appraisal Meeting

	Outcome
1. Above stated requirements	☐
2. According to stated requirements	☑
3. Not completely according to stated requirements	☐
4. Below stated requirements	☐

Clarification of the Outcome:
• Is at the beginning of level 4.
• Follow recommendations to improve this competence.

Appendix B

360° Feedback for Business Jet

360° Feedback	
Organization: Business Jet Employee Name: John van Dam Manager Name: Steve Daniel Business Unit: Security	Review Period: Jan. 2002–Dec. 2002 Position: Team Leader Position: Business Unit Manager Team: Security Schiphol Airport

Feedback Regarding Job-Oriented Competences:

- Customer-Oriented Actions
- Coaching
- Knowledge Application

Feedback Providers:

Name	Position	Relationship
1. Steve Daniel	Business Unit Manager	Manager
2. Rita Reeves	Team Leader HRM	Colleague other Bus. Unit
3. Rodney Johnson	Team Leader Maintenance	Colleague other Bus. Unit
4. Warren Jackson	Security Employee	Business Unit Associate
5. Robert Dean	Security Employee	Business Unit Associate
6. Danny Job	Security Employee	Business Unit Associate
7. James Kean	N/A	Regular BJ passenger who flies weekly between Amsterdam and London (gives feedback regarding customer orientation)

360° Feedback						
Job-Oriented Competence: **Customer-Oriented Actions**						
Definition: **Complying continuously with customer wishes and needs**						
Relative Importance: Low ❏ ❏ ☑ High						
Possible Answers **Competence Postulations**		Completely agrees with	Agrees with	Somewhat agrees with	Disagrees with	Completely disagrees with
Listens to customers and inquires whether they are satisfied.	John	X				
	Steve		X			
	Rita			X		
	Rodney				X	
	Warren			X		
	Robert	X				
	Danny		X			
	James		X			
Knows customer needs and identifies ways to keep customers.	John	X				
	Steve			X		
	Rita				X	
	Rodney					X
	Warren				X	
	Robert			X		
	Danny		X			
	James			X		
Concentrates on customer situation and focuses on improvement of customer relationship.	John	X				
	Steve				X	
	Rita				X	
	Rodney					X
	Warren			X		
	Robert				X	
	Danny			X		
	James				X	
Takes action to continuously improve customer satisfaction.	John		X			
	Steve			X		
	Rita					X
	Rodney					X
	Warren				X	
	Robert			X		
	Danny				X	
	James				X	
Behaves as a partner and offers unsolicited additional services.	John			X		
	Steve					X
	Rita					X
	Rodney					X
	Warren				X	
	Robert					X
	Danny				X	
	James					X

360° Feedback

Job-Oriented Competence: **Coaching**

Definition: **Helping team members to develop themselves and to perform optimally as a team.**

Relative importance: Low ❑ ❑ ☑ High

Competence Postulations	Possible Answers	Completely agrees with	Agrees with	Somewhat agrees with	Disagrees with	Completely disagrees with
Has an open-door policy for all team members, helps them, shows concern, and coordinates team activities.	John	X				
	Steve		X			
	Rita			X		
	Rodney				X	
	Warren			X		
	Robert		X			
	Danny		X			
Promotes teamwork, encourages team members, creates participation, listens to them, and appreciates contributions of others.	John	X				
	Steve			X		
	Rita					X
	Rodney				X	
	Warren		X			
	Robert			X		
	Danny			X		
Gives constructive feedback, maintains sympathetic relationships with team members, stimulates them to take initiatives, and clearly shows them where they can independently make decisions.	John	X				
	Steve		X			
	Rita				X	
	Rodney		X			
	Warren	X				
	Robert		X			
	Danny			X		
Inspires team members to formulate objectives and realize them. Displays a vision and articulates it decisively.	John	X				
	Steve			X		
	Rita		X			
	Rodney				X	
	Warren			X		
	Robert				X	
	Danny			X		
Gives form and direction to the team effort and creates an environment where team members are motivated and trust, help, accept, and appreciate each other.	John		X			
	Steve				X	
	Rita				X	
	Rodney				X	
	Warren			X		
	Robert			X		
	Danny				X	

360° Feedback

Job-Oriented Competence: **Knowledge Application**

Definition: **The degree of expertise shown during the execution of tasks**

Relative importance: Low ❏ ❏ ☑ High

Competence Postulations / Possible Answers		Completely agrees with	Agrees with	Somewhat agrees with	Disagrees with	Completely disagrees with
He/she more often needs professional assistance during routine activities.	John	X				
	Steve			X		
	Rita			X		
	Rodney		X			
	Warren			X		
	Robert		X			
	Danny			X		
Has complete command of routine activities. Only needs assistance with complex matters.	John	X				
	Steve				X	
	Rita			X		
	Rodney		X			
	Warren				X	
	Robert			X		
	Danny				X	
He/she performs all tasks satisfactorily. Has sufficient knowledge to complete these tasks.	John		X			
	Steve				X	
	Rita					X
	Rodney				X	
	Warren			X		
	Robert				X	
	Danny				X	
Comprehends things quickly. Therefore picks up new tasks quickly.	John		X			
	Steve				X	
	Rita				X	
	Rodney			X		
	Warren				X	
	Robert				X	
	Danny			X		
Keeps informed about new developments in his/her field. Others always ask him/her for advice.	John		X			
	Steve			X		
	Rita				X	
	Rodney			X		
	Warren				X	
	Robert			X		
	Danny		X			

Actions/Agreements in the Scope of 360° Feedback					
	Competence	**Action/Agreement**	**Action by**	**Action date**	**Realization**
Actions/ Agreements regarding tasks to complete next year	Customer-Oriented Actions	Conducting Passenger Surveys	Employee	March and July	—
		Conducting customer-orientation audit	Employee	February	
		Benchmarking customer satisfaction	Employee	February	April
		Giving instructions regarding drafting and application of a customer complaints procedure	Manager	March	—
		Drafting a customer complaints procedure	Employee	March	April
		Systematically registering and analyzing passenger complaints	Employee	March and July	—
	Coaching	Evaluating teamwork process more often	Employee	Weekly	—
		Systematically applying interpersonal skills	Employee	Constantly	—
		Developing self-knowledge about his own team role; executing Belbin's team role test	Employee	January	January
	Knowledge Application	Making relevant literature available and giving instructions	Manager	—	—
		Drafting behavioral code concerning knowledge exchange and making it available	Manager and HRM advisor	June	July
		Executing learning style test; discovering own favorite learning style	Employee	January	January
		Continuous learning based on previous experience	Employee	Constantly	Constantly
		Using the Internet more extensively	Employee	—	—
		Sharing knowledge with John	Manager	Constantly	Constantly

Actions/Agreements in the Scope of 360° Feedback					
	Competence	Action/Agreement	Action by	Action date	Realization
Actions/ Agreements regarding further employee development	Customer-Oriented Actions	Being in charge of customer-orientation training	Manager	April	April
		Feedback meetings with BJ-passengers to improve customer orientation	Employee	August	August
		Traineeship at Business Jet in New York and London	Employee	May	May
	Coaching	Accompanying experienced colleagues at Business Jet in Boston	Employee	September	September
		Creating situations for practice	Manager	June	June
		Following "effective coaching" training	Employee	March	March
	Knowledge Application	Following course knowledge management and "learning to learn"	Employee	April	April
		Providing individual guidance and coaching	Manager and HRM advisor	Once a month	—
		On-the-job training in failure costs analyses	Employee	October	October
		Developing and executing talent development program	Employee, Manager, and HRM advisor	March	December

Appendix C

Total Performance Scorecard Quick Scans

Quick Scan Customer Orientation	Yes	Somewhat	No
I. General			
1. Do you know who your customers are and how many there are?			
2. Do you listen effectively to all your customers, and do you familiarize yourself with their situation?			
3. Do you routinely conduct surveys among your customers about your products and services?			
4. Do all your employees know about the results of these surveys?			
5. Did you segment your customers based on their needs?			
6. Are more than 75% of your customers satisfied?			
7. Do you anticipate customer needs?			
8. Do you consider each customer a unique partner?			
9. Are complaints addressed within two business days and resolved within one week?			
10. Do you encourage dissatisfied customers to notify you of their complaints?			
11. Do you undertake unsolicited additional actions, and do you provide additional unsolicited services to satisfy your customers?			
12. Do you have a customer helpdesk or a call center?			
13. Do you know the percentage of customers who terminate their relationship with your organization because of dissatisfaction?			
14. Are complaints systematically registered and analyzed in your organization?			
15. Have you established procedures for handling complaints, and are these routinely used in your organization?			
16. Do you measure the degree of customer loyalty?			

Quick Scan Customer Orientation	Yes	Somewhat	No
17. Do you regularly advise customers about your products/services that best fit their needs?			
18. Do you know what the costs are when you lose a customer?			
19. Do you know what the costs are to gain a new customer?			
20. Do you know how much in sales you lose due to dissatisfied customers?			
21. Do you maintain relationships with your customers and do you expand these relationships?			
22. Do you regularly organize meetings with customer groups to learn about their needs, wants, ideas, and complaints?			
II. Leadership Style			
23. Is there commitment in top management to customer orientation?			
24. As a manager, do you know how many complaints are received yearly?			
25. Is management convinced of the importance of satisfied customers, and do they act accordingly?			
26. Have you integrated customer satisfaction into your organization's vision?			
27. Has this vision been clearly communicated to all your employees and customers?			
28. Does management recognize notable trends, and do they anticipate these in a timely manner?			
29. Does management set a good example regarding customer-friendly behavior?			
30. Is management open to suggestions and ideas from customers?			
31. Does management personally reward those employees who deliver a valuable contribution to increased customer satisfaction?			
32. Are relationships between management and customers supported and eagerly encouraged?			
33. Is management at all times available to the customer?			
34. Do all managers have regular personal contact with customers?			
35. Does customer satisfaction also belong to the evaluation criteria of management?			
36. Are the customer's wishes continuously taken into consideration when making decisions?			
37. Does top management also personally handle complaints of customers?			
III. Strategic Vision			
38. Are there at least 5 customer-orientation objectives and related performance measures formulated in the corporate, business unit, and team scorecard?			
39. Have all managers formulated at least 3 customer-related personal objectives and performance measures in their Personal Balanced Scorecard?			
40. Have you developed e-business strategies for the coming years to increase customer satisfaction?			
41. Is the strategy regarding customer orientation continuously communicated to all employees?			

Quick Scan Customer Orientation	Yes	Somewhat	No
42. Do you have a partnership relation with all your customers based on mutual respect and trust?			
43. Do you guarantee your customers a minimal service level and/or complete satisfaction?			
44. Do you continuously benchmark with regard to customer satisfaction?			
45. Do you involve your customers with the execution of improvement processes?			
46. Are all of your employees involved with the improvement of customer orientation?			
47. Do you have guidelines regarding optimal satisfaction of the customer?			
48. Do you consider customer information a strategic asset?			
49. Do you have an up-to-date databank in which all customer characteristics are registered?			
IV. Internal Processes			
50. Did you appoint process owners for controlling business processes?			
51. Are products/services delivered within the period expected by the customer?			
52. Do your phone, fax, Internet, and other e-business tools match the way your customers prefer to communicate?			
53. Is the phone in your organization answered within 3 rings in more than 80% of the cases?			
54. Is every process in your organization arranged in such a way as to optimally comply with customer expectations?			
55. Do these expectations form the basis for performance measures?			
56. Have you implemented a Customer Relationships Management (CRM) system within your organization?			
57. Do you use measured customer satisfaction as an indicator for process improvement?			
58. Do you involve your customers in the development of new products/services?			
59. Do you also measure the satisfaction of your internal customers?			
60. Are employees personally responsible for solving customer problems?			
61. Do you translate customer needs to product and process improvements and the development of new products and services?			
62. Do supporting departments within your organization guarantee the quality of the work they deliver?			
63. Are your marketing employees free to spend what is necessary to correct a mistake made with a customer?			
V. Human Resources			
64. Does customer orientation belong to the competence profile of all employees?			
65. Do you give extra rewards to employees who continuously perform in a customer-oriented manner?			
66. Do you regularly organize trips to your important customers for your employees?			

Quick Scan Customer Orientation	Yes	Somewhat	No
67. Are your customer service employees free to make decisions in order to satisfy customers?			
68. Are the employees' interest and the interest of your customers related?			
69. Do you encourage your employees to generate ideas regarding the increase of customer satisfaction?			
70. Do you have an introductory program in which new employees are also educated concerning the importance of satisfied customers?			
71. Is training mandatory for each employee in your organization?			
72. Are there customer orientation and continuous improvement criteria for promotion?			
73. Do your marketing employees receive a training of at least two weeks each year in customer orientation?			
Source: © H. Rampersad.			

Knowledge Management Quick Scan				
GENERAL				
1. Making mistakes is allowed; failures are tolerated and not penalized. People learn from each other's mistakes, and errors are openly discussed.	1	2	3	4
2. Employees know where particular knowledge can be found in the organization, and it is transparent to everyone who knows what.	1	2	3	4
3. Employees get the space to think, learn (consciously as well as unconsciously), act, make informal contacts, gain experience, experiment, and take risks.	1	2	3	4
4. Management information systems are integrated and continually updated.	1	2	3	4
5. The necessary knowledge for important decisions is usually readily available and easily accessible.	1	2	3	4
6. There are no barriers to the use and exchange of knowledge.	1	2	3	4
7. Employees have the skills to adequately categorize, use, and maintain knowledge.	1	2	3	4
8. The organization has a network of knowledge workers.	1	2	3	4
9. The organizational structure is simple, has few hierarchical levels, and consists of autonomous units.	1	2	3	4
10. The organization is characterized by diversity (people with different cultural backgrounds and learning styles), a planned as well as intuitive approach, people with different team roles, etc.	1	2	3	4
11. There is an active program for developing ideas. Based on this, new knowledge is continually generated.	1	2	3	4
12. There is no competition between colleagues. Internal competition is not reinforced.	1	2	3	4
13. There does not exist an atmosphere of fear and distrust in the organization.	1	2	3	4
LEADERSHIP STYLE				
14. Top management is committed to enlarging learning ability and creating a learning organization.	1	2	3	4
15. Employees are continually stimulated and encouraged to identify and solve shared problems as a team, to brainstorm to generate creative ideas, and to share these with each other.	1	2	3	4
16. Managers have the knowledge that is important to organizational success.	1	2	3	4
17. Managers fulfill the styles of *coaching, inspiring, and serving leadership* in an optimal mix. They stimulate a fundamental learning attitude, intensive knowledge exchange, and internal entrepreneurship, and promote individual as well as team learning.	1	2	3	4
18. Managers are continually focused on developing and mobilizing the knowledge of employees and regularly give constructive feedback about attempted improvement, development, and learning actions.	1	2	3	4
19. Managers use simple oral and written language, are action oriented, and facilitate the process of "learning by doing."	1	2	3	4
20. Management knows which employees are the carriers of valuable and scarce knowledge. Sources of internal expertise have been mapped out.	1	2	3	4
21. A knowledge manager, one who coaches and facilitates the learning processes, has been appointed. His/her most important skills are: understanding, processing, communicating, and sharing knowledge.	1	2	3	4
STRATEGIC VISION				
22. Knowledge management is a strategic theme that is part of the shared organizational ambition.	1	2	3	4
23. There is continuous collective learning in order to develop the core competences of the organization.	1	2	3	4

Knowledge Management Quick Scan				
24. There are a minimum of 5 knowledge and learning objectives and related performance measures formulated in the corporate scorecard.	1	2	3	4
25. Managers have formulated a minimum of 3 knowledge and learning objectives and related performance measures in their Personal Balanced Scorecards that are aligned to the shared organizational ambition.	1	2	3	4
26. Customer information is considered strategically valuable.	1	2	3	4
INTERNAL PROCESSES				
27. Employees do not hoard knowledge but share it spontaneously with each other. Individuals, teams, and business units systematically and intensively exchange knowledge with each other.	1	2	3	4
28. Knowledge growth is promoted through the organizational culture. This is a culture characterized by simplicity, open communication, and doing instead of talking too much.	1	2	3	4
29. Problems are tackled holistically by a systems approach. For this purpose, procedures are drafted and used routinely.	1	2	3	4
30. Knowledge gaps are systematically and continually mapped out and measures are taken to narrow and eliminate them.	1	2	3	4
31. Relevant implicit knowledge is made explicit through images and metaphors, reviewed, spread throughout the organization, and exchanged intensively.	1	2	3	4
32. User-friendly communication and information systems are used to broadly spread knowledge among all employees.	1	2	3	4
33. Obtained and developed knowledge is continually documented and made available to everyone in the organization.	1	2	3	4
34. Employees with valuable and scarce knowledge rotate among different business units and participate in a variety of improvement teams.	1	2	3	4
35. There is a learning environment characterized by positive thinking, self-esteem, mutual trust, willingness to intervene preventively, taking responsibility for business performances, openness, enjoyment, and passion. Employees are urged to continually study how they work and to adjust their work style if needed.	1	2	3	4
36. The learning processes are initiated and guided by existing or expected problems. Problems are seen as a chance to learn or change. Conflicts are seen as unresolved challenges.	1	2	3	4
37. People work and learn together harmoniously in self-guided teams. Here team members have knowledge overlaps, a balance of personalities, skills, and learning styles, and knowledge about their own favorite learning styles and those of their colleagues.	1	2	3	4
38. Knowledge is constantly being implemented and incorporated into new products, services, and processes.	1	2	3	4
39. Benchmarking is done systematically to gain knowledge. Best practices within and outside the organization are identified and propagated internally; that which is learned is generalized.	1	2	3	4
40. Knowledge and learning indicators are measured constantly and used as the starting point for process improvement.	1	2	3	4
41. Organizational knowledge is shared through informal contacts, internal lectures, conferences, problem solving and project review meetings, dialogue sessions, internal reports, memos, etc.	1	2	3	4
42. Knowledge sharing is facilitated through Internet, intranet, library, comfortable meeting rooms, auditorium, computerized archive and documentation system, and other resources.	1	2	3	4
43. Employees have varied and challenging work. There is task rotation.	1	2	3	4

Knowledge Management Quick Scan				
HUMAN RESOURCES				
44. Job appraisal and competence development are explicitly linked to the personal ambition of individuals and the shared ambition of the organization.	1	2	3	4
45. Managers and employees are judged by what they do, not by how smart they seem and how much they talk.	1	2	3	4
46. Employee knowledge is developed constantly and kept up-to-date by means of training, coaching, and talent development programs.	1	2	3	4
47. There is a proactive competence development policy, which includes internal and external training, courses, working conferences, symposia, and seminars.	1	2	3	4
48. Knowledge and learning competences are part of every employee's competence profile.	1	2	3	4
49. The knowledge of departing employees is passed on to successors.	1	2	3	4
50. Employees who deliver collective learning performances for the sake of the entire organization's well-being and constantly share their knowledge with colleagues are rewarded more them others and have more promotion opportunities.	1	2	3	4
Total Score:				
Circle the correct number: 1 = never / no / not correct; 2 = once in a while / a little / less; 3 = frequently / usually; 4 = always / yes / correct				
Remarks /Suggestions:				
Source: © H. Rampersad.				

Teamwork Evaluation Form				
We know our own team roles and learning styles as well as those of the other team members. These were accepted, appreciated, and respected.	1	2	3	4
We receive support with our personal development and help with the generation of new ideas.	1	2	3	4
Everyone listened attentively to each other until the end of the meeting. They listened to everyone's opinion, even to minority points of view.	1	2	3	4
Mostly open questions were asked.	1	2	3	4
The ideas of others were built upon.	1	2	3	4
There was constructive arguing.	1	2	3	4
The remarks of others were clarified.	1	2	3	4
Previous conversations were summarized.	1	2	3	4
People who did not participate in the meeting were asked to become involved.	1	2	3	4
Appreciation was expressed.	1	2	3	4
Constructive feedback was given.	1	2	3	4
There were no serious conflicts; there was no power struggle among team members.	1	2	3	4
We exchanged knowledge spontaneously; we did not keep it to ourselves.	1	2	3	4
The opinions of the team members were clearly expressed.	1	2	3	4
We were in agreement and spoke the same language; we understood and complemented each other.	1	2	3	4
We devoted ourselves to the shared team objective.	1	2	3	4
The team objective was clear to us; everyone found it valuable and approved of it.	1	2	3	4
We each got the chance to openly express our opinions and ideas; we could say the things we wanted (there was a frank discussion) through open communication.	1	2	3	4
There was no gossip in smaller groups.	1	2	3	4
We respected and trusted each other; we felt comfortable, equal to each other, and responsible.	1	2	3	4
Everyone had his/her own clearly defined task: timekeeper, process keeper, minute taker, data collector, etc.	1	2	3	4
We followed a clearly defined method and had the opportunity to think and act creatively.	1	2	3	4
What we were working on was transparent, and our discussions were purposeful.	1	2	3	4
We stuck to the points on the agenda.	1	2	3	4
We were clear about our responsibilities for the points of action taken; we committed ourselves to the team decisions.	1	2	3	4
The team leader/chairperson was well prepared.	1	2	3	4
We worked together harmoniously towards generating new ideas; we continuously looked for fresh points of views to tackle problems.	1	2	3	4
Total Score:				
Circle the correct number: 1 = never / no / not correct; 2 = once in a while / hardly ever; 3 = frequently / usually; 4 = always / yes / correct				
Remarks/Recommendations:				
Source: © H. Rampersad.				

Checklist of Implementation Circumstances			
Areas of Attention	**Yes**	**Somewhat**	**No**
Is there commitment in top management to implement the change?			
Have those involved formulated their personal ambition and aligned it with the shared organizational ambition?			
Do those involved consider the change crucial to the company's survival, and do they realize the usefulness of it?			
Has attention been paid to the involvement of all key-persons in the decision-making process?			
Has a competent change manager been appointed to coach and facilitate the change processes?			
Can managers handle the change?			
Has special attention been given to developing the new skills that employees will need?			
Have the most important obstacles and barriers to the use and exchange of knowledge been removed?			
Has the change been aligned to the individual and organizational values?			
Has a cultural diagnosis been conducted and the results communicated to the employees?			
Has the information regarding the introduced change been clear?			
Can the idea behind the change be made understandable to all involved?			
Can adequate information be given about the what, why, how, and consequences of the change?			
Is there sufficient necessity for the introduction of the change?			
Is the necessity for and advantage of the change been clearly communicated to all those involved?			
Have the advantages of change been carefully weighed against the disadvantages?			
Do the employees know what has to be changed?			
Does a plan exist in which the steps of the change to be implemented are clearly defined?			
Has special attention been given to those who feel they will become victims of the change?			
Have you listened effectively to the persons who resist change, and have you studied their situation?			
Have the problems that accompanied previous changes been solved?			
Has there been benchmarking regarding the change?			
Has there been fear and distrust among the employees regarding the change?			
Are there possibilities that could diminish the chances of success of the change?			
Will enough people change?			
Source: © H. Rampersad.			

References

Argyris, C., and D. Schön. *Organizational Learning*. London: Addison-Wesley, 1978.

Barton, G. M. *Communication: Manage Words Effectively*. Costa Mesa, CA: Personnel Journal 69, 1990.

Becker, B. E., M. A. Huselid, and D. Ulrich. *The HR-Scorecard: Linking People, Strategy, and Performance*. Boston: Harvard Business School Press, 2001.

Belbin, R. M. *Team Roles at Work*. London: Butterworth–Heinemann, 1995.

Bick, J. *All I Really Need to Know in Business I Learned at Microsoft*. New York: Pocket Books, 1997.

Bos, J., and E. Harting. *Projectmatig creëren*. Schiedam, The Netherlands: Scriptum Management, 1998.

Boyett, J. H., and J. T. Boyett. *The Guru Guide: The Best Ideas of the Top Management Thinkers*. New York: John Wiley & Sons, 1998.

Broek, L. van, R. van der Giessen, and A. van Oers-van Dorst. *Performance Management*. Alphen a/d Rijn, The Netherlands: Samson, 2000.

Chang, R., and M. Morgan. *Performance Scorecards: Measuring the Right Things in the Real World*. San Francisco: Jossey-Bass, 2000.

Chopra, D. *Restful Sleep: The Complete Mind/Body Program for Overcoming Insomnia*. New York: Crown Publishers, 1994.

Collins J., and J. Porras. *Het formuleren van een visie*. Amsterdam: HRM-select, no. 1, 1997.

Covey, S. R. *The Seven Habits of Highly Effective People*. New York: Simon & Schuster, 1993.

De Kluyver, C. A., and J. A. Pearce. *Strategy: A View from the Top.* Englewood Cliffs, NJ: Prentice-Hall, 2002.

Deming, W. E. *Out of the Crisis.* Cambridge: Massachusetts Institute of Technology, 1985.

Doorewaard H., and W. de Nijs. *Organisatieontwikkeling en Human Resource Management.* Utrechts, The Netherlands: Lemma BV, 1999.

Doppler, K., and C. Lauterburg. *Change Management; vormgeven aan het veranderingsproces.* Amsterdam: Addison Wesley, 1996.

Drucker, P. F. *Management Challenges for the Twenty-First Century.* Oxford: Butterworth–Heinemann, 1999.

Evans, R., and P. Russell. *De Creatieve Manager.* Cothen, The Netherlands: Servire, 1991.

Fijlstra, R., and H. Wullings. *Ondernemen met Gevoel.* Schiedam, The Netherlands: Scriptum Management, 1998.

Galpin, T. "Connecting Culture to Organizational Change." *HRMagazine,* March 1996, pp. 84–90.

Geier, J. G., and D. E. Downey. *Energetics of Personality.* Minneapolis, MN: Aristos Publishing House, 1989.

Geus, Arie De. *The Living Company.* Boston: Harvard Business School Press, 1997.

Gilbert, T. F. *Human Competence: Engineering Worthy Performance.* New York: McGraw-Hill, 1987.

Guiver-Freeman, M. *Praktisch Competentiemanagement.* Schoonhoven, The Netherlands: Academic Service, 2001.

Hamel, G., and C. K. Prahalad. *Competing for the Future: Breakthrough Strategies for Seizing Control of your Industry and Creating Markets of Tomorrow.* Boston: Harvard Business School Press, 1994.

Handy, C. *Understanding Voluntary Organizations.* Hammersworth, UK: Penguin Books, 1988.

Hargrove, R. *Masterful Coaching: Extraordinary Results by Impacting People and the Way They Think and Work Together.* San Francisco: Jossey-Bass, 1995.

Harrington, H. J. *Total Improvement Management: The Next Generation in Performance Improvement.* New York: McGraw-Hill, 1995.

Hauser, J. R., and D. Clausing. "The House of Quality." *Harvard Business Review,* vol. 66, no. 3, 1988.

Hoevenaars, A. M., J. C. M. van Jaarsveld, and J. F. den Hertog. *Naar Eenvoud in Organisaties: werken met zelfsturende eenheden.* Deventer, The Netherlands: Kluwer Bedrijfswetenschappen, 1995.

Hofstede, G. *All Think Differently: Handling Cultural Differences.* Amsterdam: Contact, 1991.

Honey, P., and A. Mumford. *Manual of Learning Styles*. Maidenhead, Berks.: Peter Honey, 1992.

Imai, M. *Kaizen*. New York: Random House, 1986.

Intermediair. *Tijdbestedingonderzoek*. Intermediair, nummer 19, Amsterdam, 2001.

Jacobs, R. F. *Real Time Strategic Change*. San Francisco: Berrett-Koehler, 1994.

Juran, J. M. *Quality Control Handbook*. New York: McGraw-Hill, 1974.

Kamp, D. *The Twenty-First Century Manager: Future-Focused Skills for the Next Millennium*. London: Kogan Page, 1999.

Kaplan, R. S., and D. P. Norton. *The Balanced Scorecard: Translating Strategy into Action*. Boston: Harvard Business School Press, 1996.

Kaplan, R. S., and D. P. Norton. *The Strategy-Focused Organization: How Balanced Scorecard Companies Thrive in the New Business Environment*. Boston: Harvard Business School Press, 2000.

Katzenbach, J. R., and D. K. Smith. *The Discipline of Teams: A Mindbook-Workbook for Delivering Small Group Performance*. New York: John Wiley & Sons, 2001.

Kolb, D. A. *Experiential Learning*. Englewood Cliffs, NJ: Prentice-Hall, 1984.

Kor, R. *Werken aan Projecten*. Deventer, The Netherlands: Kluwer Bedrijfsinformatie, 1998.

Kotter, J. P. *Leading Change*. Boston: Harvard Business School Press, 1996.

Kouzes, J. M., and B. Z. Posner. *Een hart onder de riem: hoe kan ik anderen erkenning geven en belonen?* Schiedam, The Netherlands: Scriptum Management, 1999.

Kovach, K. A. "What Motivates Employees? Workers and Supervisors Give Different Answers." *Business Horizons* 30 (1987), pp. 59–60.

Landsberg, M. *The Tao of Motivation: Inspire Yourself and Others*. London: HarperCollins, 1999.

Leifer, R. *The Happiness Project*. New York: Snow Lion Publications, 1997.

Leonard, D. *Wellsprings of Knowledge: Building and Sustaining the Source of Innovation*. Boston: Harvard Business School Press, 1998.

Leonard, D., and W. Snap. *When Sparks Fly: Igniting Creativity in Groups*. Boston: Harvard Business School Press, 1999.

Lewis, D. L. *The Public Image of Henry Ford: An American Folk Hero and His Company*. Michigan: Wayne State University Press, 1987.

Lipton, M. *De Valkuilen van het Visiestatement*. Amsterdam: HRM-select, no. 1, 1997.

Maslow, A. H. *Motivation and Personality*. New York: Harper & Row, 1970.

Mastenbroek, W. F. G. *Conflicthantering en Organisatie-ontwikkeling*. Alphen a/d Rijn: Samsom, 1996.

McCall, M. W. *High Flyers: Developing the Next Generation of Leaders*. Boston: Harvard Business School Press, 1998.

Metro. Amsterdam, August 25, 2003.

Miller, D. S., S. E. Catt, and J. R. Carlson. *Fundamentals of Management: A Framework for Excellence*. Minneapolis, MN: West Publishing Company, 1996.

Nonaka, I., and H. Takeuchi. *The Knowledge-Creating Company*. New York: Oxford University Press, 1995.

NRC Handelsblad. Amsterdam, January 22, 2003, p. 118.

Oakland, J. S. *Total Quality Management*. Oxford: Butterworth–Heinemann, 1995.

O'Tool, J. *Leading Change: The Argument for Values-Based Leadership*. New York: Ballantine Books, 1996.

PA Consulting Group. *TQM Manual*. London: PA Consulting Group, 1991.

Pareek, U., and T. V. Rao. "Performance Coaching." In T. W. Pfeifer (ed.), *Development Human Resources*. San Diego, CA: Academic Press, 1990.

Pasmore, W. *Creating Strategic Change: Designing the Flexible High-Performing Organization*. New York: John Wiley & Sons, 1994.

Peters, T. J., and R. H. Wateman. *In Search of Excellence*. New York: Harper & Row, 1982.

Pfeffer, J., and R. I. Sutton. *De Kloof tussen Weten en Doen*. Schiedam, The Netherlands: Scriptum Management, 2002.

Philips Electronics. *Customer Surveys*. Eindhoven, The Netherlands: Corporate Quality Bureau, 1994.

Porter, M. E. *Competitive Advantage*. New York: The Free Press, 1985.

Rampersad, H. K. *Integrated and Simultaneous Design for Robotic Assembly*. New York: John Wiley & Sons, 1994.

Rampersad, H. K. "Robotic Assembly System Design for Total Productivity." *International Journal of Production Research*, vol. 34, no. 1 (1996), pp. 71–94.

Rampersad, H. K. *Total Quality Management: An Executive Guide to Continuous Improvement*. New York: Springer-Verlag, February 2001A.

Rampersad, H. K. "Seventy-Five Painful Questions about Your Customer Satisfaction." *TQM Journal*, vol. 5 (September 2001B), pp. 341–347.

Rampersad, H. K. *Total Performance Scorecard: Een speurtocht naar zelf-kennis en competentie-ontwikkeling van lerende organisaties*. Schiedam, The Netherlands: Scriptum Management, October 2002.

Rampersad, H. K. "The Links between Individual Learning, Collective Learning, and Ethics." *Training and Management Development Methods*, vol. 17, no. 1 (February 2003).

Quinn, R. E. *Een Kader voor Managementvaardigheden*. Schoonhoven, The Netherlands: Academic Service, 1996.

Rees, J., and P. Rigby. "Total Quality Control: The Hewlett-Packard Way." In R. L. Chase (ed.), *Total Quality Management*. Kempston/Bedford: IFS Publications Ltd., 1988.

Remmerswaal, J. *Begeleiden van Groepen*. Houten, The Netherlands: Bohn Stafleu Van Loghum, 1992.

Schein, E. H. "Organizational Culture." *American Psychologist* (February 1990), p. 114.

Schein, E. H. *Organizational Culture and Leadership: A Dynamic View*. San Francisco: Jossey-Bass, 1992.

Schermer, K., and M. Wijn. *Vergaderen en Onderhandelen*. Houten: Bohn Stafleu Van Loghum, 1992.

Senge, P. M. *The Fifth Discipline: The Art and Practice of the Learning Organization*. New York: Doubleday, 1990.

Sharma, H., and C. Clark. *Contemporary Ayurveda: Medicine and Research in Maharishi Ayur-Veda*. London: Churchill Livingstone, 1998.

Thomas, A. *Coaching van Teamleden*. Baarn, The Netherlands: Nelissen, 1996.

Thompson, A. A., and A. J. Strickland. *Strategic Management: Concepts and Cases*. Boston: McGraw-Hill, 2002.

Togt, J. J. van der, and G. E. Kemp. *Prestatie Sturen door 360°–feedback*. Deventer, The Netherlands: Kluwer Bedrijfsinformatie, 1997.

Tuckman, B. W., and M. A. C. Jensen. *Stages of Small Group Development, Revised Edition*. Group and Organisation Studies Nr. 2, 1977, pp. 419–427.

Ulrich, D., and D. Lake. *Organizational Capability: Competing from the Inside Out*. New York: John Wiley & Sons, 1990.

Wanrooy, M. J. *Leidinggeven tussen Professionals*. Schiedam, The Netherlands: Scriptum Management, 2001.

Weggeman, M. *Kennismanagement: Inrichting en besturing van kennisintensieve organisaties*. Schiedam, The Netherlands: Scriptum Management, 1997.

Wijnen, G., M. Weggeman, and R. Kor. *Verbeteren en Vernieuwen van Organisaties: Essentiële managementtaken*. Deventer, The Netherlands: Kluwer Bedrijfswetenschappen, 1988.

Wijngaards, N. M. *Zelfmanagement*. Utrecht, The Netherlands: Het spectrum, 1988.

Yesudian, S. *Sta op en Wees Vrij: Gedachten en gesprekken over yoga*. Deventer, The Netherlands: Ankh-Hermes b.v., 1991.

Index

Page numbers followed by "t" denote tables; those followed by "f" denote figures.

About the Author

Hubert K. Rampersad, B.S., M.Sc., Ph.D., born in 1957, is an internationally respected and recognized consultant in the field of Organizational Behavior and Business Management. He is founder and CEO of Quality Management Cousulting in The Netherlands. He received his formal education in The Netherlands earning a B.S. in Mechanical Engineering from Enschede Polytechnic Institute, an M.Sc. in Mechanical Engineering from Delft University of Technology, and a Ph.D. in Management from Eindhoven University of Technology.

Dr. Rampersad is author of several books and many articles in scientific journals and conference proceedings in the field of Management and Technology. He is a member of the Editorial Advisory Board of the Emerald Journal *Training and Management Development Methods* (United Kingdom). He has been associated with:

- The Faculty Technology Science and Social Science at the Anton de Kom University of Suriname, as professor of Operations and Technology Management.

- The Rotterdam School of Management in The Netherlands, as lecturer in Operations Management.

- The Faculty of Technology Management at the Technical University Eindhoven in The Netherlands, as lecturer in Production Technology.

From 1987 on he has been successful as an international management consultant guiding, coaching, and training leading organizations in the areas of Change Management, Strategic Management, and Total Quality Management.

His mission statement is: *Sharing knowledge is my joy, especially if, by doing this, my work can mean something in the life of others.*

The development of the Total Performance Scorecard concept and the writing of this book has been a continuing learning process for him. If you would like to keep track of the latest developments in this field, please visit the website at www.Total-Performance-Scorecard.com. Dr. Rampersad can be reached at Hubert.Rampersad@Total-Performance-Scorecard.com.

Your feedback about the contents of this book is welcome at:

Quality Management Consulting
Riet Blom-Mouritsstraat 27
3066 GL Rotterdam, The Netherlands

Phone: 31-10-2096564
Fax: 31-10-2097189
Mobile: 31-6-53831159
E-mail: info@qmconsulting.nl
Website: www.Total-Performance-Scorecard.com and www.qmconsulting.nl

Quality Management Consulting is devoted to helping individuals and organizations become more successful. It provides integrated and sustainable professional services (consulting and training) based on the proven Total Performance Scorecard principles. The results are individual and organizational effectiveness and a related unique competitive advantage. Call or write us for information on our international office closest to you, or for a free catalog of TPS products and programs.

DATE			